EDUCATION FOR REFLECTIVE MINISTRY

LOUVAIN THEOLOGICAL & PASTORAL MONOGRAPHS
—————————— 24 ——————————

EDUCATION FOR
REFLECTIVE MINISTRY

Johannes A. van der Ven

PEETERS PRESS
LOUVAIN

"Hamlet: Hath this fellow no feeling of his business, that he sings at
   gravemaking?
Horatio: Custom hath made it in him a property of easiness".

(Hamlet act 5, scene 1, lines 65-66)

PREFACE

The special report of the Carnegie Foundation on the priorities
of the professoriate distinguished four functions in the work of
scholarship: the scholarship of discovery research, the scholarship of
integrative theoretical research, the scholarship of applied research,
and the scholarship of teaching.[1] This division is useful because in
practical theology and related disciplines, these four functions are often
confused, and the particular qualities of discovery research, theoretical
research, applied research and teaching become blurred. The classification provides a means of clearly differentiating between the four
different functions, in order to then look at them all together. It is
customary for scholars to give an account of their work with respect
to the first three functions, i.e., discovery research, theoretical research
and applied research, as, for example, I myself have done in, respectively, *Practical Theology, an empirical approach*[2], *Ecclesiology in
Context*[3], and *'Suffering: Why for God's Sake?'*.[4] For scholars to give
an account of their work as a teacher is less common, even though
the Carnegie Foundation rightly lays a great deal of emphasis on this
function. It is thanks to the board of the Nijmegen Divinity School that
I am able to develop in the present publication a few ideas about the
fourth function, which bears on one of the core areas of theological
education, namely education for ministry. The board granted me a free
semester to prepare this publication, and also provided the financial
resources that allowed me to seek out the personal views and advice

---

[1] E.L. Boyer, *Scholarship Reconsidered. Priorities of the Professoriate. The
Carnegie Foundation for the Advancement of Teaching* (Princeton: Princeton University
Press, 1990) 15 - 26; cf. R.E. Rice, and L. Richlin, "Broadening the Concept of the
Scholarship in the Professions," *Educating Professionals*, eds. L. Curry, J.F. Wergin,
et al., (San Francisco: Jossey-Bass Publishers, 1993) 279-315.
[2] J.A. Van der Ven, *Practical Theology: An Empirical Approach* (Kampen: Kok,
1993).
[3] J.A. Van der Ven, *Ecclesiology in Context* (Grand Rapids: Eerdmans, 1996).
[4] J.A. Van der Ven, and E. Vossen, *Suffering: Why for God's Sake? Pastoral
Research in Theodicy*, Theologie & Empirie, 23 (Kampen, Weinheim: Kok, 1994).

of Dutch, other European, American and South African colleagues. The list of names of these colleagues, to whom I am extremely grateful for the time they so generously spent discussing these issues with me, is too long to reproduce here. Moreover, to do so might create the impression that I wish to place on their shoulders some of the responsibility for this text. This is certainly not the case, particularly as there are sure to be colleagues who will raise major or minor objections to one or more of the ideas which I develop in this study. For this text presents not only an interpretative description of some models of the education for ministry in today's societal, cultural and ecclesial context in the western world, but also, as the title indicates, a proposal for a new model: the reflective ministry model. It is my hope that this proposal may elicit the discussion it needs.

TABLE OF CONTENTS

INTRODUCTION

The picture that pastors have of themselves and of their experiences in the ministry is always ambivalent. On the one hand they find the pastoral work which they perform meaningful, important and relevant. Most consider their profession in terms of a personal and religious calling. They evidently experience satisfaction in carrying out their functions such as pastoral care, worship and preaching, home visiting, pastoral groupwork, catechesis, social ministry and ecumenism.[1]

On the other hand all pastors suffer from chronic stress of some sort, caused by the following factors: the superficiality of many contacts, the dependency of core members of the parish, the impossibility of satisfying everybody's wishes and needs, the difficulty of coping adequately with criticism from parishioners, and the inadequacy of their preparation for pastoral work. Time pressure is also experienced as a source of stress, and is often considered the most pressing problem, both professionally and privately. Financial problems are another stressing factor.[2] Finally, all of this has repercussions on the pastor's family life: there is not enough time for one's partner and children, and the boundaries of the family are not seldom porous.[3]

The content of pastoral work itself has become an object of discussion, leading to many questions, doubts and uncertainties that increase the pastor's ambivalence and gnaw away at his sense of professional identity and security. Many pastors experience the secularization process — the growing disparity between the Bible and the contemporary culture as well as between the official teaching of the

[1] cf. J.A. Keizer, *Aan tijd gebonden. Over motivatie en arbeidsvreugde van predikanten* (Den haag: Boekencentrum, 1988) 114; J.B.A.M. Schilderman, C.A.M. Visscher, J.A. van der Ven, and A.J.A. Felling, *Professionalisering van het pastorale ambt* (Nijmegen: NISET, 1993) 26-27.

[2] M.L. Morris, and D. Blanton White, "Denominational Perception of Stress and the Provision of Support Services for Clergy Families," *Pastoral Psychology* 42 (1994) 345-364.

[3] C. Lee, "Toward a Social Ecology of the Minister's Family," *Pastoral Psychology* 36 (1988) 249-259.

church and the contemporary 'zeitgeist' — as a very serious problem, which negatively influences religious life within the parish. Many pastors are bowed down by uncertainty over how their work contributes to the parish mission in today's society and, even more so, by doubts over what that mission is, in particular the diaconal mission. In short, the pastor's mission and the goal of his work are under a great deal of pressure.[4]

While these experiences of ambivalence and doubt are played out at the microlevel of the concrete work that each pastor carries out from day to day, some of the factors that condition these experiences are situated at the mesolevel of the church. These factors, which are institutional in nature, give rise to some sort of ambivalence. One the one hand the position of the pastor is characterized by a great deal of freedom and autonomy, as well as a considerable degree of influence and power, inasmuch as he or she enjoys a privileged position vis-à-vis his parishioners, and is admitted into the viscissitudes and the most intimate aspects of their lives as perhaps no one else. On the other hand he or she knows himself to be bound by the written and unwritten rules of the parish, which he or she experiences as a 'total institution' and on which he or she feels himself or herself to be highly dependent. Out of these opposing tendencies emerges the picture of power ambivalence, which is not readily dealt with in an adequate manner.[5]

The pastor is caught up in the ambivalences and doubts that come to him or her from the church not only from a synchronous perspective but also from a diachronic perspective. A definitive frame of reference, a clear course, a cogent policy, an attractive set of strategies and tactics: these are no longer offered to him or her by the church. The church itself is a battlefield of clashing movements, countermovements and counter-countermovements, that follow one another over time without themselves disappearing from the scene. The pastor is confronted daily with phenomena of diachronicity ('Ungleichzeitigkeit') in his or her own church, in which modernity and the various reactions of the church or groups of churches to this modernity play a major role.

[4] J.A. Van der Ven, *Ecclesiology in Context* (Grand Rapids: Eerdmans, 1996) 485.
[5] D. Capps, "Sex in the Parish: Social-Scientific Explanations for Why It Occurs," *Journal of Pastoral Care* 47 (1993) 350-361.

An obvious and painful example is the Catholic Church in the Netherlands, which is confronted with the process of secularization like perhaps no other church in the world.[6] In the period from roughly 1850 to 1950, the Dutch Catholic Church remained firmly committed to the antimodern ideology of neo-Thomism and the strongly centralizing bureaucracy of the church apparatus. This unity of church culture and structure lent to pastoral work a remarkable unity of values, standards, aims, methods and means.[7] When, in the 1950s, modernity gradually came to be viewed more positively, neo-Thomism and the ideology of the centralized administrative apparatus were replaced by the most important documents to come out of Vatican II. In particular, the constitutions 'Lumen Gentium' and 'Gaudium et Spes' served to open up the culture and structure of the church and bring it into closer accord with society at the national, international and global level. The church was viewed as 'the people of God under way', a people moving forward through present-day society towards a hopeful future, and in which the division of power between the faithful and the clergy is preceeded by the common priesthood of all the faithful. Thus in the sixties the education for the ministry could take as its point of departure the two Vatican II constitutions and Küng's 'The Church', which was based wholly on the biblical inspiration of Vatican II.[8] In today's situation, however, these constitutions no longer correspond to the complex functions the pastor performs in his day to day work.

Modernity elicits a wide range of different reactions from groups in the church: positive and negative, adaptive and corrective, justifying and ideology-critical, quite apart from the fact that modernity as a phenomenon is itself anything but well-defined. Various conflicting movements — premodern, modern, modern-critical, late modern,

---

[6] A. Greeley, *Religion as Poetry* (New Brunswick: Transaction Publishers, 1995) 83 v.

[7] J.A. van der Ven, "Katholieke kerk en katholicisme in historisch en empirisch perspectief," *Kerk op de helling*, eds. J. Peters, J.A. van der Ven, and L. Spruit (Kampen: Kok, 1993) 62-92.

[8] J.A. van der Ven, "Evaluatie van de pastoraal tussen ideaal en werkelijkheid," *Pastoraal tussen ideaal en werkelijkheid*, ed. J.A. Van der Ven (Kampen: Kok, 1985) 12; J.A. van der Ven, "Wat is pastoraaltheologie? Een analyse van het werk van Frans Haarsma," *Toekomst voor de kerk? Studies voor Frans Haarsma*, ed. J.A. Van der Ven (Kampen: Kok, 1985) 19-20; U.T.P Stagegids (Heerlen, 1995) Foreword.

postmodern, and anti-postmodern — act, react, interact, counteract, transact with each other on the field of battle.

The premodern movements are inspired by nostalgia for the 'ancien regime', before the Enlightenment and before the ideals of freedom, equality and fraternity were brought into clear focus by the French Revolution, as well as nostalgia for the sacred canopy of the national church that encompassed, legitimized and sanctioned the whole of the life of the individual and the society.[9]

The modern tendencies seek to bring the church up to date ('aggiornamento') by opening it up to the increasing modernization of society, the growing differentiation of societal institutions, the autonomy of the developments taking place within these institutions, the tendencies towards democratization and professionalization, and the primacy of technology and science. One of the principal challenges is seen as bridging the gap between religion and 'Wissenschaft' (science); the aim is not to deny or negate the mystery of the Christian faith but merely to shed light on it.[10]

Modernity criticism emphasizes the fact that modernization leads to dehumanization, not only through the influence of capitalism in the economic sphere and bureaucratization in the political domain, but also as a consequence of the movement toward individualism in the social domain and the de-moralization in the cultural sphere. Critics of modernity believe that the all-encompassing colonialization of individual and societal life by economic capitalism should be halted.[11] The church should not adapt itself to the ethos of modernity, but instead should prophetically resist it and turn its attention to the apocalyptic interruption of modernization.[12]

From the viewpoint of late modernity, this criticism ought not to be directed at the modern society from outside, because modernity itself, in its present period, is becoming critically aware of the paradoxes and

[9] J. Auer, and J. Ratzinger, *Kleine Katholische Dogmatik*, Band I-IX (Regensburg: Pustet, 1978).

[10] H. Küng, *Existiert Gott?* Dutch translation: *Bestaat God? Antwoord op de vraag naar God in deze tijd* (Hilversum: Gooi en Sticht, 1978).

[11] J. Habermas, *Theorie des kommunikativen Handelns*, Band I-II (Frankfurt: Suhrkamp, 1982).

[12] J.-B. Metz, *Glaube in Geschichte und Gesellschaft* (Mainz: Matthias-Grünewald-Verlag, 1977).

aporias that intrinsically shape it. By virtue of its capacity for self-reflection, it is capable not only of critical self-awareness but also of critical
reconstruction.[13] The church, say the late modernists, must see itself as
a self-critical institution, which is in a permanent process of critical reconstruction in the sense of the 'Ecclesia semper purificanda', because the
'Ecclesia' is not the church, but only subsists in it (Lumen Gentium 8).
According to postmodernism, all the great stories of modernity are
over. The universal, timeless and written no longer holds any relevance. What is important is the particular, local, timely and oral.[14]
Postmodernity favours and appreciates that which differs and varies,
that which does not fit into established theories, which differentiates
and de-differentiates, which is contextualized and decontextualized. It
sees knowledge, beliefs, values and norms as contextual constructions
in a given time and space, and sees them being deconstructed from
different angles in different contexts. It also sees institutions, social
structures and political arrangements as socially and ideologically constructed, as radical historical entities that are to be approached in a
critical way. These institutions themselves are also self-reflective and
self-critical. Postmodernity sees itself as self-conscious contingency.[15]
The church must courageously face its radical contingency, just as it
must become radically aware of the contingency of the Christian faith
itself. Jesus was a Jew, and his actions and words were shaped through
and through by their context, not only in the geographic, economic
and political sense, but also in a social, moral and religious sense, yet
this contextualization does not detract from the universal character of
his message. To deny this is to strip his message of its humanity and
thus to do violence to the very paradigm of incarnation. This reduces
Jesus to Docetic quasi-humanity.[16] Just as this applies to Jesus, it

[13] A. Giddens, *Modernity and Self-Identity. Self and Society in the Late Modern
Age* (Stanford: Stanford University Press, 1991).
[14] S. Toulmin, *Cosmopolis. The Hidden Agenda of Modernity* (New York: The Free
Press, 1990) 186.
[15] Z. Bauman, "Philosophical Affinities of Postmodern Sociology," *Sociological
Review* 38 (1990) 3: 431; Z. Bauman, *Postmodern Ethics* (Oxford: Blackwell, 1994);
Z. Bauman, *Life in Fragments. Essays in Postmodern Morality* (Oxford: Blackwell,
1995).
[16] E. Schillebeeckx, *Mensen als verhaal van God* (Baarn: Nelissen, 1989) 184;
E. Schillebeeckx, "Identiteit, eigenheid en universaliteit van Gods heil in Jezus," *Tijdschrift voor Theologie* 30 (1990) 259-275.

applies also and even more so to the institutional structure and form of the church. How would the church look today if the ties to Judaism had been preserved, if the common root of the three Abrahamite religions had been respected, if the autocephalous churches of East and West had remained in dialogue, if the schism between Rome and the Reformation had been prevented, if the anti-modern council of Vatican I had not promulgated the Pope's infallibility, if the Catholic church had become a member of the World Council of Churches?[17]

Postmodernism itself is criticized by the black theologian, Cornel West, for being nothing more than the expression of the process of ideological mourning by the philosophers on the Left Bank of the Seine who are bidding farewell to the 'great narrative' of European supremacy and becoming aware of the 'little narrative' that they still have to tell in the world, but who meanwhile have no concern for the structural impoverishment and alienation of the minority groups of the first world and of whole peoples in the third world. West calls for breaking through the narcissism that characterizes postmodernism, and points out that we must open our eyes to the dehumanizing situations in the slums and favelas of the world's rapidly spreading metropolises.[18]

From this short overview it is evident that the pastor can no longer follow a straightforward and unambiguous course that has been set out for him or her by the church. There is no course, no unambiguousness. The pastor is buffeted this way and that by a polyphony of voices in the church, in the parish and even in himself: or herself premodern, modern, modern-critical, late modern, postmodern and postmodern-critical voices. He or she is influenced by a multiplicity of voices in his or her immediate environment that clamour for his or her attention, such as the team of colleagues with whom he or she collaborates, the group of pastoral volunteers with whom he or she shares his or her work, the board and parish council who oversee the management of

---

[17] J.A. van der Ven, "Kontingenz und Religion in einer säkularisierten und multi-kulturellen Gesellschaft," *Religiöser Pluralismus und interreligiöses Lernen*, eds. J.A. van der Ven and H.-G. Ziebertz (Kampen, Weinheim: Kok, 1994) 15-38.

[18] C. West, *Prophetic Thought in Postmodern Times. Beyond Eurocentrism and Multiculturalism, no. I* (Maine: Common Courage Press, 1993); C. West, *Prophetic Reflections. Notes on Race and Power in America. Beyond Eurocentrism and Multi-culturalism, no. I* (Maine: Common Courage Press, 1993).

the parish and to whom he or she is accountable, and not least the hundreds of ordinary church members — core members, modal members and marginal members — with whom he or she speaks in the course of his or her daily work, whom he or she guides and whom he or she leads in the liturgy. In addition there are the many voices that reach his or her ears from outside of his or her parish, which push him or her now this way, now that.

Not only the churches are shaped by an omnipresent theological pluralism; the theological institutions themselves are also marked by it. They not only reflect the pluralism in the church, they amplify and intensify it and in fact create it, at least in a co-creative sense, not only interinstitutionally but also intrainstitutionally. Modern, late-modern, modern-critical, postmodern, antimodern and anti-postmodern voices can be heard in all theological schools. These schools are certainly no longer islands of tranquility and harmony, if they ever were.

Moreover, the theological schools themselves are in a semi-permament state of educational crisis. There is continual criticism by the faculty and by the students that the educational orientation of the school is too orthodox or too liberal, too high church or too low church, too speculative or too positivistic, too universalistic or too contextual, too theoretical or too practical, too academic or too professional, too deductive or too inductive, too scientific or too spiritual.[19] A number of infrastructural factors also contribute to this state of affairs. In 1989, there were 202 theological schools in North America, with an average of 188 students and the equivalent of 17 full-time faculty members each. Of these schools, 29 had 50 students or fewer, the smallest had only eight students, and three had a thousand or more students, the largest having 3814. As for finances, Warren Deem, a professional consultant to the American Association of Theological Schools, remarked twenty years ago, "The average Protestant seminary today — with its 15 faculty and 170 students — has resources which are more analogous to a neighborhood primary school than to a modern graduate professional institution".[20] In addition there is, of course,

---

[19] D.H. Kelsey, *To Understand God Truly. What's Theological About A Theological School*, 22-27 (Westminster, John Knox Press, 1992).
[20] D.H. Kelsey, *To Understand God Truly. What's Theological About A Theological School*, 19.

the eternal grumbling over the lack of proper administration, management and organization, which is characteristic of all the ecclesial and theological establishments where the appeals to love and humanity have masked real problems in the exercise of power that manifest themselves when it comes to the inevitable distribution of scarce resources.

Which direction can, shall, should the pastor take if neither the church nor the theological institutions are able to provide him or her with a clear frame of reference, an attractive perspective, a convincing policy, a plausible course of action, and a meaningful set of aims, goals and objectives?

There is no alternative but to risk taking responsibility for oneself and choosing one's own course of action. To take this risk is not reckless or foolhardy, as long as the choices are always informed by a religious self-reflection that is open to tradition as well as to the future. This allows the pastor to be his or her own guide, to transgress useless customs and habits, and cross the boundaries into as yet unknown territory. The task of education must be to provide the foundation that enables the pastor to make those choices and take those risks in a well-considered, prudent and truly religious manner.

Structure of the Text

While the concept of reflective practice serves as a starting point for educational programs in many other professions in today's society, this text explains how and why it must also serve as the point of departure for education for the ministry. The reflective ministry model is therefore central to this study.

Chapter I looks at the religious developments taking place today, which confront the pastor with a complex and, moreover, constantly changing set of questions. A distinction is made between the macrolevel of the society, the mesolevel of the church, and the microlevel of the individual and the primary group of which he or she is a part.

In Chapter II, we look at two educational models which have been used since the sixties by the theological institutions to prepare their students for ministry, namely, the models of therapeuticalism and managerialism. Because these two models are no longer adequate today, a model has to be developed that transcends both of them, but which preserves and incorporates their positive elements.

In Chapter III the reflective ministry model is systematically discussed and justified. First the nature of ministry is localized within the dialectical tension between religion and church. Out of this dialectical tension the functions of the pastor are examined in detail, and then critically analyzed in terms of the model of reflective ministry. Against this background the nature of the pastor's reflective competence is examined.

Chapter IV discusses the most important educational conditions for reflective ministry. We look at the goals and contents of courses and seminars, practica, internships, supervision and coaching, and lastly theological reflection and action research.

The text concludes with a general summary and some general administrative conclusions. A list of literature is found at the end.

CHAPTER I

COMPLEXITY AND DYNAMICS OF RELIGION

Entire libraries have been written about the developments taking place today at the levels of society, the institutions and the individual. The critical evaluation of these descriptions has engendered another flood of articles and books which, on the basis of various theoretical insights and empirical data, have arrived at a wide range of different conclusions, as I mentioned in the Introduction with reference to the concepts of premodernity, modernity, modernity criticism, late modernity, postmodernity, and postmodernity criticism. In order to cope with this welter of ideas, it is absolutely essential to make and justify critical choices on the basis of a well-defined perspective, specifically formulated questions and sharply-defined objectives. Today's scholar must be a reflective researcher and today's theologian a reflective theological researcher. Without well-considered, justifiable and accountable eclecticism, a scientific description and analysis of the developments taking place today is impossible.

The perspective that I intend to adopt in this chapter is a religious-theoretical one. The religious developments taking place today, and with which we too are confronted, are divided into those taking place at the macrolevel of society, the mesolevel of the church, and the microlevel of the individual and his or her primary group. The distinction appears simpler than it actually is, because it in fact encompasses complex historical processes. First of all, the division into these three levels can be traced to the circumstance that the historical ties between church and society and between church and the state, which were (from our present point of view) characteristic of premodernity, no longer exist. This does not mean that there are no longer any ties at all between church and society or between church and state. On the contrary. Nowhere does an absolute division exist between church and state. But the functional differentiation between the two is characteristic of the development of the typical modern society and the typical

J.A. VAN DER VEN

modern state. Then, the division into three levels is based on the fact that church and religion are no longer exclusively linked together. This too is a modern phenomenon, or more precisely a modern view of a modern phenomenon. Religion also occurs outside the church, not simply as a remnant of church religion, but as a separate form of religion. This separate form of religion is expressed at the macrolevel of state and society in, for instance, the rituals surrounding national memorial days, holidays, the opening of a new session of parliament, or the inauguration of a new president. It is also expressed in speeches by politicians, debates carried out via the media over questions of life and death, in public discussions of values and norms, and in the teaching and learning processes in our educational institutions. Finally, religion occurs in yet another form in the private life of the individual person and the primary group in which he or she lives his life. To simply dismiss this form of private religiosity as the individual appropriation of one's church religion, would be to fail to do it justice. To put it in polemical terms, anyone who speaks of the gap between church and individual religiosity assumes that this gap ought not to exist, and this assumption in turn is based on the supposition that individual religiosity is or should be the internalization of church religiosity. The division between the macrolevel, mesolevel and microlevel of religion which I take here as my frame of reference makes no such assumption. Rather, the point of departure lies in the irreducible uniqueness of individual religiosity. Of course, this does not mean that the individual is an island as far as religious matters are concerned. It does mean that out of all the religious metaphors, narratives, rites and practices that exist in the broader society and culture and in the church, the individual makes his or her own choices and from them constructs his or her own religiosity.

This religious-theoretical differentiation between macrolevel, mesolevel and microlevel has a long history. It goes back at least to the beginning of this century, when the theologian and sociologist Ernst Troeltsch wrote his study of religion in modern society.[1]

---

[1] V. Drehsen, *Neuzeitliche Konstitutionsbedingungen der Praktischen Theologie. Aspekte der theologischen Wende zur sozialkulturellen Lebenswelt christlicher Religion* (Gütersloh: Gütersloher Verlagshaus Gerd Mohn, 1988) 557-576.

Troeltsch's work is significant for our own time, because he cast doubt on the one-sided secularization hypothesis according to which church attendance is equated with religiosity, and the decline in church attendance is seen as a decline in religiosity. For this reason, too, authors like Rössler[2], Drehsen[3], Heitink[4] and Dingemans[5] take this division between the macrolevel, mesolevel and microlevel as their point of departure for developing practical theology.

In the sections that follow, I intend to use this three-way division above all to describe and organize the problems having to do with religious developments with which pastors are confronted in their pastoral work. These problems are often so ambiguous as to take on the form of paradoxes, dilemmas and aporias, thereby exacerbating even further the pastor's sense of insecurity and confusion. Thus the next three sections will deal with religion at the macrolevel of society (section 1), the mesolevel of the church (section 2), and the microlevel of the individual (section 3).

1. Religion at the Macrolevel of Society

The religious developments at the macrolevel of society evoke a contradictory picture. On the one hand all signs seem to indicate that society is rapidly becoming secularized. One need only look at the societal institutions within the various systems that make up society. The institutions within the economic system are evolving according to autonomous processes over which religion no longer has any hold. The contrast between the principle of maximization of profit and the

---

[2] D. Rössler, *Grundriss der Praktischen Theologie* (Berlin: De Gruyter, 1986) 79-81; D. Rössler, "Die einheit der Praktischen Theologie," *Praktische Theologie und Kultur der Gegenwart. Ein internationaler Dialog*, eds. K.E. Nipkow, D. Rössler, and F. Schweitzer (Gütersloh: Gütersloher Verlagshaus Gerd Mohn, 1991) 43-54.

[3] V. Drehsen, "Praktische Theologie als Kunstlehre im Zeitalter bürgerlicher Kultur," *Praktische Theologie und Kultur der Gegenwart. Ein internationaler Dialog*, eds. K.E. Nipkow, D. Rössler, and F. Schweitzer (Gütersloh: Gütersloher Verlagshaus Gerd Mohn, 1991) 103-118.

[4] G. Heitink, *Praktische theologie. Geschiedenis, theorie, handelingsvelden* (Kampen: Kok, 1993) 237-241.

[5] G. Dingemans, *Manieren van doen. Inleiding tot de studie van de praktische theologie* (Kampen: Kok, 1996) 140 v.

lessons of brotherhood and sisterhood taught by the Gospel is becoming ever sharper, as Max Weber already noted at the beginning of the century. In the same way the institutions within the political system are shaped by rules that function completely independently of religion, namely the rules of democracy and bureaucracy, which themselves stand in a tense relationship to one another. Politics is aimed at the acquisition, preservation and exercise of power, which are activities which are often diametrically opposed to the principles of justice, solidarity and love that are central to the Gospel. Now, the institutions of the social system as a whole appear to have been colonized by the economic and political system, thus becoming instruments of the striving for money and power.[6] The social middle ground between the individual citizen and the state, formerly occupied by several powerful institutions such as the family, the church, ecclesial and nonecclesial associations appears to have undergone a fundamental erosion, a hollowing out from within of the profane community life that forms the infrastructure of the religious community of believers.[7] Finally, cultural institutions — most importantly the school and the university — also appear to have been severely eroded. Both are more and more coming to be viewed as businesses, while their function is increasingly seen as being aimed at supplying the needs of business. As a result, their function as institutions that initiate into the cultural tradition and contemporary culture, and thus into the religious traditions and religious culture as well, threatens to be forgotten.

On the other hand, a number of signs suggest that the so-called radical secularization theory, which is encompassed in the picture sketched above, does not accord with an accurate description of the available empirical data. The public at large, led by the mass media, frequently thinks that religion has completely disappeared from society, when in actual fact this is simply not the case. Of course, what the public at large thinks can itself tend to weaken the position of religion in the society.

In order to obtain a more nuanced picture, it may be interesting to look at the Netherlands as an example. Whether this is something that

---

[6] J. Habermas, *Theorie des kommunikativen Handelns*.

[7] D. Browning, *Practical Theology and Congregational Studies. Paper for the Empirical Sector of NOSTER in the Netherlands* (Utrecht: NOSTER, 1995).

the Dutch people should be proud of or not, the fact is that in all comparative empirical studies, the Netherlands is always found to be further advanced in the secularization process than other countries. Let me give two examples. According to the European Values Study (EVS), which also included the United States and Canada, the Netherlands, along with the Scandinavian countries, and France and Belgium, is one of the countries in which religiosity has declined most sharply in recent years.[8] The American sociologist of religion, Andrew Greeley, using data from the International Social Survey Program (ISSP), goes even further. He claims that the Netherlands is the only country — apart from a few East European countries — in which there has been a decrease in religiosity, while the other countries by and large have remained stable in that respect. Greeley[9] goes so far as to say, "'Secular man' is not alive and well, save perhaps on university campuses and possibly in the Netherlands".

What is the picture that emerges empirically from the study of religion at the macrolevel of society in the Netherlands? It is certainly a more complex one than would appear at first glance and from the ideas presented in the mass media. There is certainly no reason to speak of a radical secularization, nor even of a semi-secularization in which the role of religion has been relegated solely to the private sphere. The phenomenon of religion is too complex to be adequately covered by terms like radical secularization or semi-secularization.[10] I will elucidate this by looking at religious phenomena in the economic, political, social and cultural systems of society. In the process, it will become evident that religion is still a force that exerts direct and indirect, desirable and undesirable and often contradictory influences. The following remarks are based primarily on the data material from the SOCON program (Socio-Cultural Developments in the Netherlands) by the sociology department of the University of Nijmegen.

Let me begin with two examples from the economic system. The first example has to do with the bourgeois-capitalist ethos, which as

[8] P. Ester, L. Halman, and R. de Moor, *The Individualizing Society. Value Change in Europe and North America* (Tilburg: Tilburg University Press, 1993) 50-53.

[9] A. Greeley, *Religion as Poetry*, 91.

[10] cf. P. van Rooden, *Religieuze regimes. Overgodsdienst en maatschappij in Nederland, 1570-1990* (Amsterdam: Bakker, 1996) 17-45.

Weber demonstrated, exhibits — or at least exhibited — a certain family resemblance with the Christian ethos, or at any rate the Calvinist
variety of that ethos[11]. From empirical studies it is apparent that, today,
a number of attitudes that are representative of the bourgeois-capitalist
ethos are not influenced by the Calvinist character of faith in God, but
by the Christian faith in general. The stronger the belief in God, the
more strongly held is the belief in work as a moral duty, the focus on
systematic, continuous and career-oriented work, utilitarian and rational consumption, and thrift and honesty in financial matters.[12] In other
words, religion is not without significance, however one assesses the
influence of the Christian religion on the bourgeois-capitalist ethos.
Anyone inclined to raise critical-prophetic objections to the capitalist
economy will not be overjoyed by the results of the study, to say the
least. The second, example, however, which is taken from the same
program, points in a different direction. It concerns the relation between
Christian faith and economic conservatism. Economic conservatism
can be defined as the desire to preserve the existing economic system
in its present form. Economic conservatives are against socio-
economic leveling of the various social classes, against government
intervention aimed at promoting this leveling, and against stronger
trade union policies. The study indicates that economic conservatives
are more often to be found among those with a weak faith, and less
often among those with a strong faith.[13] These examples show that,
first, religion does appear to exert an influence in today's society, and
that, second, that influence appears to go in different and perhaps even
contradictory directions.

In the political system, too, religion functions in varying ways. From
the study of civil religion since Rousseau, we know that the common
foundation of political values in many countries, including the Netherlands, has a religious core, which is related to the nation's past tradition, its present identity and its mission for the rest of the world. In

---

[11] M. Weber, "Die Protestantische Ethik und der Geist des Kapitalismus," *Die Protestantische Ethik I* (München, Hamburg: Siebenstern Taschenbuch Verlag, 1969).

[12] M. Ter Voert, *Religie en het burgerlijk-kapitalistisch ethos*, (doctoral dissertation, Nijmegen University, 1994) 92.

[13] A. Felling, J. Peters and O. Schreuder, *Geloven en leven. Een nationaal onderzoek
naar de invloed van religieuze overtuigingen* (Zeist: Kerckebosch, 1986) 103.

the United States, the religious leaders of the previous century sought to embed American values within the Christian faith, in the process creating a civil religion.[14] Thus, the myth of origin refers to the religious convictions of the founding fathers, and the annual State of the Union address includes a religious appeal to give to the nation what the nation demands, and calls on the citizens to carry the fundamental values of freedom, justice and human rights to the rest of the world.[15] In the Netherlands, too, the myths of origin are permeated by religious motifs. Even today, the rituals and myths surrounding the annual Remembrance Day ceremonies on the 4th of May in Amsterdam, commemorating those who died in the Second World War, exude an unmistakably religious atmosphere, regardless of how secularized the Netherlands may be.[16] Every year, the Dutch nation is reborn on the Dam in Amsterdam, under the universal, all-encompassing motherhood of the queen, whose official birthday is celebrated a few days earlier, on April 30. The sacred days from April 30 to May 4 have aptly been described as a non-church Holy Week, in which the religious foundation of Dutch nation-building is celebrated. Along with its role in creating a civil religion, religious faith also has more specific effects. This function, too, may run into opposition from readers, because the influence that it exerts can once again be described as running more towards political conservatism than critical-prophetic attitudes. If one examines the effect of religious faith on people's description of their political affiliation, one finds that the stronger the religious faith, the more likely people are to express a political preference for right-wing parties.[17] This is true not only in the Netherlands. In general, findings show that religious commitment and support for leftist parties are incompatible.[18]

[14] R.N. Bellah, *The Broken Covenant* (New York: The Free Press, 1975).

[15] cf. R. Wuthnow, *Christianity in the Twenty-first Century. Reflections on the Challenges Ahead* (New York: Oxford University Press, 1993) 144-145.

[16] M. Ter Borg, "Publieke religie in Nederland," *Religie in de Nederlandse samenleving*, eds. O. Schreuder and L. van Snippenburg (Baarn: Ambo, 1990) 165-184.

[17] A. Felling, J. Peters and O. Schreuder, *Geloven en leven*, 107; R. Eisinga, A. Felling and J. Lammers, "Religious Affiliation, Income Stratification, and Political Preference in the Netherlands," *The Netherlands Journal of Social Sciences* 30 (1994) 2:107-127.

[18] R. Stark and W.S. Bainbridge, *A Theory of Religion* (New York: Peter Lang, 1987) 49.

With regards to the social system, we can again look at two examples. The first has to do with the family. The phenomenon of the deinstitutionalization or individualization of the family is common to all western countries. Important indicators of deinstitutionalization are the growing conviction that marriage is no longer a commitment for life, the declining importance attached to legal marriage, and the growing acceptance of divorce. Individualization is reflected in the circumstance that marriage is seen as a bond between two individuals that is characterized by a balance between costs and benefits. The costs are the investment in time and commitment to one another, while the benefits consist in the satisfaction of needs for emotional security, care and love. This does not mean that marriage and family values themselves are no longer important, but that their institutional importance and status has declined.[19] In most of the modernized countries in Europe, such as the Scandinavian countries and the Netherlands, marriage itself is still considered important, but it is experienced much less as an institution based on a time-honored tradition that is valued in and of itself, and is treated in a more instrumental manner. That divorce is becoming more and more accepted is not because marriage and family are valued less, but because they are in a sense valued more. Because so much importance is attached to marriage, divorce is considered acceptable if the marriage no longer meets the needs of the partners. Monogamous marriage is not in crisis, but there is an increasing tendency towards serial monogamy.[20] Religion is traditionally associated with marriage and family, and consequently is also one of the strongest brakes on their deinstitutionalization and individualization. Studies show that the stronger a person's religious commitment, the higher the value he or she places on marriage and family.[21] The same applies to church participation: as church participation increases, the importance placed on family and marriage also increases.[22] The age of respondents plays an important role in this regard. The "pre-war"

---

[19] P. Ester, L. Halman and R. de Moor, *The Individualizing Society*, 97-127.

[20] P. Van den Akker, "Modernisering en gezinswaarden in Europees perspectief. Enige resultaten van de European Values Study 1981-1990," *Gezin: onderzoek en diagnostiek*, ed. J. Gerris (Assen, 1995).

[21] A. Felling, J. Peters and O. Schreuder, *Geloven en leven*, 97.

[22] J. Peters and J. Gerris, "Familialisme: sociaal-culturele verschuivingen in de jaren tachtig en de samenhang met gezin en opvoeding," *Gezin: onderzoek en diagnostiek*, ed. J. Gerris (Assen: Van Gorcum, 1995).

generation, born between 1915 and 1929, places a significantly higher value on marriage and family than the so-called "silent generation" born between 1930 and 1940, the "protest generation" of 1940 to 1954, or the "lost generation" of 1955 to 1967.[23]

Another example of the way religion functions within the social system to preserve or promote social cohesion can be seen in attitudes towards cultural minorities. Here again the question is whether and to what extent religion affects these attitudes. And, once again, the results indicate that it does, although here, too, they fail to correlate with a critical-prophetic interpretation of the role of religion. Study shows that intensity of religious faith correlates with positive valuation of one's own group and a decline in positive valuation and indeed an increase in the negative valuation of the allochthonous group.[24] It should be added, however, that when the effects of religious faith on valuation of the ingroup and outgroup are controlled by factors like social class, education, authoritarianism, localism and subjective experience of the threat of competition, the correlation between religious belief and positive valuation of the ingroup remains unchanged, but the correlation with negative valuation of the outgroup disappears.[25] This example once again illustrates the complex and ambiguous function of religion within society.

Finally, we come to the cultural system. Let me deal first with the relationship between religious and moral values in general. From the European Values Study we know that there is a correlation between these two groups of values — as religious values rise or fall, moral values rise and fall as well — but also that this correlation is relatively loose. This means that the two groups of values represent more or less autonomous areas in the minds of many people. Moreover, quite a lot of religious people appear to be unmistakably permissive in a moral

---

[23] B. Van Dam, *Een generatie met verschillende gezichten. Culturele diversiteit onder de jonge volwassenen van de jaren tachtig* (doctoral dissertation, Nijmegen University, 1993) 73-74.

[24] R. Eisinga and P. Scheepers, *Etnocentrisme in Nederland* (doctoral dissertation, Nijmegen University, 1989) 127.

[25] R. Eisinga and P. Scheepers, *Etnocentrisme in Nederland*, 227; cf. P. Scheepers, *Maatschappelijke vooroordelen in perspectief* (inaugurale rede, Nijmegen University, 1995); P. Scheepers, "Botsende culturen in Nederland: Longitudinale trends in etnocentrische reacties onder kerkelijke mensen," *Botsende culturen in Nederland*, ed. J.A. van der Ven (Kampen: Kok, 1996) 16-43.

sense. These are indicators that religion has only a moderate influence on morality. This is true among churchgoers as well. Even there, religion and morality appear to constitute two more or less separate domains, which are only loosely correlated. This means that religion has no influence or only a slight influence on their moral ideas, judgements and actions.[26] As a consequence, many people in the countries covered by the study no longer feel that they need religious faith to 'be a good human being'. They can manage very well without God and still feel committed to fundamental values like freedom, justice and solidarity.[27] Yet this does not give the whole picture, and that brings me to a more specific example: the field of bioethics. If there is one moral sphere in which religion still exerts a strong influence, it is in the area of abortion and euthanasia. A survey of a representative sample of more than 600 students at Nijmegen University showed that as the strength of religious faith increases, the belief that abortion and euthanasia are permissible decreases.[28] As far as abortion is concerned, the result agrees with studies of the Dutch population in general. The more strongly respondents are committed to the Christian faith, the more strongly they reject abortion, even if there are particular circumstances that might justify the use of abortion for the mother's sake.[29]

From the examples drawn from the four aforementioned systems (economic, political, social and cultural), it is clear that religion at the macrolevel of society presents a complex picture. It performs several clearly discernible functions, and exerts contradictory effects, desirable as well as undesirable.

Multiculturalization

Right across the four abovementioned systems, a process is taking place today that places the Christian faith before a fundamental and

---

[26] L. Halman, F. Heunks, R. de Moor and H. Zanders, *Traditie, secularisatie en individualisering. Een studie naar de waarden van de Nederlanders in een Europese context* (Tilburg: Tilburg University Press, 1987) 15-49.

[27] J. Kerkhofs, *Waardenonderzoek. Een bijdrage tot pastoraal realisme* (Leuven, Amersfoort: Acco, 1995) 159-170.

[28] J.A. Van der Ven and B. Biemans, *Religie in fragmenten. Een onderzoek onder studenten*, Theologie & Empirie, 23 (Kampen, Weinheim: Kok, 1994) 261.

[29] L. Spruit, *Religie en abortus. Interactiemodellen ter verklaring van de houding tegenover abortus* (doctoral dissertation, Nijmegen University, 1991) 41, 201.

increasingly complex challenge: that of multiculturalization. Multiculturalization can be seen as a consequence of the increasing globalization of western society. New ethnic groups and cultures are moving into the western countries, and groups that have lived there since long before the beginning of the current globalization trend are becoming conscious of their dignity and worth, such as, for example, the Indians and Afro-Americans in North America. The policy of the governments of most western countries is neither assimilation, by which the minorities would be required to change to fit into the dominant western culture and society, nor isolation, by which the society would come to consist of a number of entirely separate cultures. The aim of official policy is integration, meaning joining themselves into the western society and culture without giving up their own identity. In the Netherlands, which is now home to the third generation of Turks and Moroccans, only about 20% of the members of these groups can be said to be integrated. It is to these 20% that the saying "eerste generatie dood, tweede generatie nood, derde generatie brood" ("first generation death, second generation poverty, third generation bread") applies. The remaining 80% are not integrated. They watch their own Turkish or Moroccan television channels, go to their own schools, shop in their own stores, visit their own cafés, play soccer in their own clubs. Multiculturalization, together with secularization, is bringing about a structural change of western society that calls for a fundamental process of reflection by the Christian religion. The influence of multiculturalization extends to all aspects of the four societal systems, and it is still far from clear how the Christian religion will respond to these changes.

In economic terms, study after study has shown that ethnic minorities are over-represented within those groups of the society that live below (in some cases far below) the poverty line. According to statistics from 1990, 15% of the allochthonous working population is unemployed and 18% are looking for work, compared with only 4% and 6% respectively of the autochthonous working population.[30] Their relatively poor living situation results in poorer health, which in turn leads to a higher level of incapacity to work.[31] The children of Turkish and Moroccan parents perform more poorly in arithmetic and

[30] *Sociaal en cultureel rapport* (Sociaal en cultureel planbureau, Rijswijk, 1992) 93.
[31] *Sociaal en cultureel rapport*, 38.

language.[32] They have at best a 50% chance of completing their primary education, and their grades tend to be poorer.[33] Areas of concentration of minority groups are characterized by a higher crime rate
and a greater risk of becoming a victim of crime. This higher crime
rate, incidentally, is not caused simply by the higher concentration of
the allochthonous groups, but by the higher numbers of unemployed,
lower levels of education and lower incomes in those areas.[34] One is
warranted in speaking of an underclass of allochthones. How does the
Christian religion respond to this situation? The correlation of religion
with the bourgeois-capitalist ethos that I described earlier stands in
contradiction to the prophetic tradition of Christianity. The tendency
to transform the existing economic relationships to the advantage of
the underprivileged underclass of allochthones, which, as I said, para-
doxically is also present in the Christian religion at the same time, should
be encouraged and strengthened.

As far as the political system is concerned, the fact that ethnic
minorities are heavily under-represented in the political elite is self-
evident. But also as clients of the political institutions, they are more
likely to encounter difficulties in their dealings with the bureaucracy
and to suffer from alienation than is the autochthonous population.
The proto-professionalism that is required in order to safeguard one's
well-conceived self-interest in dealings with the professionals in these
services, presupposes a level of schooling and linguistic competence
that is utterly beyond the reach of the ethnic minorities.[35] To remedy
this state of affairs or at least make a contribution toward doing so
ought to be a fundamental concern of all who feel bound to the Christian prophetic tradition. This imperative contrasts sharply, however,
with the empirically observed affiliation of Christians with right-wing
political parties that I described above.

The institutions of the social system that serve to maintain or
strengthen the sense of social cohesion among ethnic minorities are
under increasing pressure in today's society. The family, the church,

[32] Sociaal en cultureel rapport, 248.
[33] Sociaal en cultureel rapport, 19.
[34] *Rapportage minderheden. Concentratie en segregatie* (Sociaal en cultureel planbureau, Rijswijk, 1995).
[35] Cf. A. De Swaan, *De mens is de mens een zorg* (Amsterdam: Meulenhoff, 1982).

and the role of clubs and associations are being radically eroded, as studies of Afro-Americans in the United States, in particular, show. There, too, commodity fetishism or commodification is increasingly finding its way into the lifeworld, and threatens to colonize it in its entirety. The authentic expression of black music, that had its origin in the spirituals sung during worship, like the rhetorical strength of black preaching, are losing their significance. Black music is becoming increasingly commercialized, and black preaching lacks intellectual grounding, sophistication and self-criticism. West, for example, notes that "the influence of the black church is declining as are churches around the country".[36] In response to the growing need, the churches should be putting energy into social outreach and social ministry, especially on behalf of the ethnic minorities, but the churches themselves are part of the problem.

Finally, there is the cultural system, in which the schools occupy an extremely important place, particularly the schools in black areas. These schools, too, are part of the problem, because, in the United States as well as in other western countries, the departure of whites from these areas has made the schools increasingly into 'black' schools, if they were not so already. Dutch studies show that the level of concentration of students from ethnic minorities attending these schools has a negative effect on school achievement, future choices in schooling, future school career and finally upward social mobility and emancipation. Here, too, the churches are faced with an enormous challenge, especially where, as in the Netherlands, they have at their disposal, in the form of the state-subsidized parochial school system, an instrument that could be used to put a stop to the increasing segregation and apartheid and to reverse the trend. But here, too, the picture obtained from the empirical findings is discouraging. The majority of children of ethnic minorities attend public schools for their primary education. The Catholic schools are whiter than the public schools, and the Protestant schools are whiter still.[37] The remarkable thing is that the figures have remained constant over the years. About 47% of students from ethnic groups attend public schools in the Netherlands,

---

[36] C. West, *Prophetic Reflections. Notes on Race and Power in America*, 106.

[37] C. Hermans, M. Scherer-Rath and J.A. Van der Ven, *Ouders en de identiteit van katholieke basisscholen* (Nijmegen, 1996).

28% to 29% attend Catholic schools, 18% to 19% attend Protestant schools and 5 to 6% attend private schools.[38] The segregation that characterizes the education system is reflected in the chances of cultural encounters between ethnic minorities and the rest of the population. The chance of a member of an ethnic minority coming into contact with members of his or her own group or with people from another minority group is significantly greater than that of coming into contact with members of the population as a whole.[39] This fact calls into question the entire concept of intercultural and interreligious dialogue. Students at Catholic secondary schools say that it is important to meet members of minority groups in order to learn about their cultural and religious beliefs and views and compare them with one's own.[40] However, if they do not actually encounter members of these minority groups, these good intentions remain nothing but wishful thinking.

Let me go back to the beginning of this section. The point that I wanted to illustrate with the various examples of the role of religion in the economic, political, social and cultural systems at the macrolevel of society was twofold. First, I wanted to make it clear that neither the concept of radical secularization nor that of semi-secularization do justice to the complexities of the empirically observable function of religion in society. It is therefore better to speak of a differential secularization, to indicate that religion exerts a variety of different influences in many different areas of society, albeit not in all.[41] I also wanted to show that the picture is not only complex, but also full of contrasts and perhaps even contradictions, and that these contradictions constitute a fundamental challenge for religion, especially as far as the phenomena of globalization and multiculturalization are concerned.

[38] F. Kwakman and J. Van Oers, *Het geloof in de katholieke basisschool. Over legitimaties voor de katholieke basisschool in een multi-etnische en geseculariseerde samenleving*, Theologie & Empirie, 19 (Kampen, Weinheim: Kok, 1993) 179.

[39] *Rapportage minderheden*, 421-423.

[40] J.A. Van der Ven, "Religious Values in the Interreligious Dialogue," *Religion and Theology*, Vol. 1-3 (1994); J.A. Van der Ven and H.-G. Ziebertz, "Religionspädagogische Perspektiven zur interreligiösen Bildung," *Bilanz der Religionspädagogik*, eds. H.-G. Ziebertz and W. Simon (Düsseldorf: Patmos, 1995) 259-273; H.-G. Ziebertz, *Empirische Religionspädagogik* (Weinheim: Deutscher Studien Verlag, 1994) 105-194.

[41] Cf. O. Schreuder, "Culturele individualisering," *Individualisering en religie*, ed. J.A. van der Ven (Baarn: Ambo, 1994) 37-59.

With this description I hope to have shown that the pastor can no longer rely on a definitive interpretation of the society in which he or she carries out his ministry. Nor can he count on being provided with a definitive direction or policy with respect to his pastoral work, or with unequivocally formulated pastoral objectives and methods. The reality of society is too complex, and the function of religion too many-sided and its effects too ambivalent to allow for this.

2. Religion at the Mesolevel of the Church

Is the picture regarding the church perhaps clearer? The answer must be no. The church is not a 'heile Welt', nor does it exist as an island. The societal context in which it exists is marked by so many processes, the workings of which are complex, the direction uncertain and the outcome unknown, that the confusion that is engendered cannot help but affect the church as well. The church may then well rest in the conviction that 'God's' salvation, as manifested in the acts of Jesus, will be realized at the end of time, but for the time being this conviction does not give it any greater knowledge or insight as to the deeper processes taking place in the present and in the future than does the human intellect or, specifically, scientific research. The conviction of the church, in the classic Thomist tradition, holds the middle ground between solid science ('scientia') and pure opinion ('opinio'). It has the character of a fragile attestation that, in spite of the questions and doubts befalling it, chooses between this or that action, series of actions or strategy in an engaged, prudent and thus reflexive manner, but without final certainty, without final security.[42]

But there is more. The attestative conviction of the church is being severely tested today by dwindling church membership, shrinking participation in weekly services, and the declining importance of the rites of passage. The European Values Study found that between 1981 and 1990, the proportion of non-church members rose in all of the countries studied: in the United States from 6% to 23%, in Canada

---

[42] P. Ricoeur, *Soi-même comme un autre*, English Translation: *Oneself as Another* (Chicago: University of Chicago Press, 1992).

from 11% to 26%, in France from 26% to 39% and in the Netherlands from 37% to 49%.[43] Dutch research suggests that the figures for the Netherlands are even lower than the European Values Study indicates. The report of the Dutch Social and Cultural Planning Bureau on secularization in the Netherlands found that in 1992, 57% of the Dutch population did not belong to any church. It forecasts that that figure will grow to 62% by the year 2000, to 68% in 2010 and to 73% in 2020. Within one generation — so the estimate — 15% of the Dutch population will be members of the Catholic Church, 6% will belong to the Netherlands Reformed Church, 3% will belong to the Reformed Churches in the Netherlands, and 3% to one of the other denominations. About 20% of Catholics, says the report, will then attend church one or more times a month, which amounts to about 450,000 Catholics in all of the Netherlands. This is a high percentage compared with the percentage of Catholics that currently go to church every week. While that number was still nearly 28% in 1975, by 1995 it had decreased by more than half: 12%.[44] To get a more concrete picture of what it means if, in 2010, 20% of Catholics go to church one or more times a month: this would amount to approximately 275 Catholics per parish if spread over the present number of Catholic parishes in the Netherlands.[45] That number, of course, is too small to support the current £number of roughly 1600 parishes and the same number of churches. The bishop of Breda, for example, has already made the radical decision to shut down about half of the churches in his diocese, where the percentage of churchgoers per week is 9.7%, by the year 2000.[46] Participation in rites of passage is also on the decline. In the Catholic church, the number of baptisms as a percentage of the total number of live births fell from 31% to 25% between 1980 and 1994, and the number of church weddings as a percentage of total weddings

---

[43] P. Ester, L. Halman and R. de Moor, *The Individualizing Society*, 44.

[44] Kaski, "Kerncijfers 1994/1995. Uit de kerkelijke statistiek van het R.-K. Genootschap in Nederland," in *Kerkelijke documentatie 121*, 23, no. 23 (Utrecht: Kaski, 1995) 15; See M. Van Hemert, *Achtergronden van kerkelijk gedrag. Een onderzoek in zeven rooms-katholieke parochies* (Den Haag: Kaski, 1991) 4.

[45] J.W. Becker and R. Vink, *Secularisatie in Nederland* (Rijswijk: Sociaal en Cultureel planbureau, 1994) 69-76.

[46] M. Muskens, "Toekomst van de kerkgebouwen," *Analecta Bisdom Breda 9*, no. 9 (1995) 238-250.

declined from 31% to 18%. The percentage of church funerals remained stable at 29%. The percentage of burials, however, decreased from 82% to 67%, while the percentage of cremations rose from 18% to 33%.[47]

The decline in the number of church members, church attendance and participation in rites of passage is taking place primarily among the younger generation. As young people are staying away, the church population is greying. In 1971, 43% of Dutch youth between the ages of 17 and 24 were not members of a church; in 1991 the figure was 72%. In 1975, 29% of Dutch young people between the ages of 19 and 24 attended church at least once a month; in 1985 it was 22%. The strongest drop is observed among Dutch youth between the ages of 12 and 18. In 1975, 47% of them went to church a least once a month; in 1985 only 29% did. This represents a drop of nearly 20% in ten years. Evidently young people are giving up attending church at an ever younger age.[48] Among students at the University of Nijmegen, the figures are similar. Approximately 30% report that they are church members, nearly 20% get to church at least once a month, 26% expect to marry in the church and 28% expect to have their children baptized. Nearly 48% would like to have a church funeral.[49]

The decline in church membership, participation in weekly services and rites of passage that is taking place chiefly among the younger generation does not go unnoticed by the congregations or the pastors. One frequently reads articles or takes part in discussions in which concern is expressed about the emptying and greying of the churches, and what this trend means for the identity of the church, the course it should adopt, the goals it should pursue, and the methods and means it should use to do so. Faith in the church's mission and confidence in its leadership are being severely tested. Against this background it is easy to understand why the degree of confidence in the church has declined. The European Values Study found that on a scale of −1.00 to +1.00, confidence in the church in the United States declined from

[47] Kaski, "Kerncijfers 1994/1995. Uit de kerkelijke statistiek van het R.-K. Genootschap in Nederland," 12-14.

[48] M. Angenent-Vogt and M. Van Hemert, "Jongeren en levensbeschouwing. Een literatuuroverzicht," *Kerkelijke documentatie* 121, 8, no. 4 (Utrecht: Kaski, 1993).

[49] J.A. Van der Ven and B. Biemans, *Religie in fragmenten*, 266-273.

.71 to .61, in Canada from .43 to .24, in France from −0.1 to −.37 and
in the Netherlands from −.11 to −.21.[50]

More important than ascertaining the decline in church participation is identifying the causes of this phenomenon. This, however, is
easier said than done. Empirical studies provide no clear-cut picture
of explanatory factors. Nevertheless, there do exist a number of
hypotheses which deserve to be briefly mentioned here. They can be
classified into five groups, depending on whether one sees the causes
as being holistic, cultural, social, institutional or congregational. The
first group holds that church participation is being directly affected
by processes taking place in the societal context as a whole — hence
the term 'holistic'. The most important of these hypotheses are the
modernization or rationalization of society, leading to the disenchant-
ment of individual and societal life, the ideology of scientism which,
because of the modern importance of science and technology, is
shaping people's thoughts and behavior to an ever increasing degree.[51]
The second group of hypotheses concerns a number of cultural factors
that are, ostensibly, adversely affecting the church. These include the
pluralism of religions, ideologies, values and norms, as well as the rise
in the general level of education. The third group of hypotheses
ascribes the negative effects to certain social factors. These include
changes in marriage and family life, the rise of individualism and the
decline of group and community life, and the growth of privatism in
so-called lifestyle enclaves. The institutional hypotheses focus on institutional factors in the church at the denominational level. The decline
in church membership is seen as the result of the following processes:
the church's failure to be relevant; failure of leadership; failure of
programs; and loss of internal strength, meaning the decline of strong
religious convictions and a concomitant decline in compelling teaching concerning the ultimate purpose and destiny of humankind. The
last group of hypotheses has to do with congregational processes at
the local level. Church membership is said to be declining because the
local parish is functioning, or at least experienced as functioning, less

---

[50] P. Ester, L. Halman and R. de Moor, *The Individualizing Society.*

[51] Cf. A. Felling, J. Peters and O. Schreuder, *Geloven en leven*, 19-32; H. Peeters,
Burgers en modernisering (Deventer: Drukkerij Administratief Service Centrum,
1984).

and less as a vital community. This involves two aspects: the ritual aspect, concerning the degree to which the parish is seen as a celebrating community, and the diaconal aspect, meaning the degree to which members of the parish community support each other in times of material and spiritual need.

From the empirical data that are available, it is impossible to derive any incontestable proof — if such proof can ever be deduced from empirical data — for the rightness of one or the other of these hypotheses. This applies particularly to the holistic, cultural and social hypotheses. Several hypotheses can, however, be rejected as inadequate with some degree of certainty. This is true particularly of the institutional and congregational hypotheses. The factors put forward in these hypotheses seem to be of little or no significance from an empirical point of view. They provide little or no explanation of the decline in church membership, with one fundamental exception, which is the factor referred to as loss of internal strength. As I have noted, this factor concerns the decline of strong religious convictions and compelling teaching. This is one factor that does appear to have a real influence on the degree of church participation, according to both Dutch[52] and American studies.[53]

Realistically speaking, however, one might well ask whether the alarm and confusion that the decline in church membership occasions in church circles is justified. Secularization may well be taking its toll, but is this phenomenon not in fact merely the decline of the dominance of the church within the religious domain, and does not the religious domain itself remain quite sound? Some American sociologists take precisely this view. They reject the traditional 'sacred canopy' paradigm, so named by Peter Berger, and replace it with the emerging economic paradigm.[54] The sacred canopy paradigm is based on the assumption that religion functions as a kind of canopy over the whole of society

[52] Cf. M. Van Hemert, *Achtergronden van kerkelijke gedrag. Een onderzoek in zeven rooms-katholieke parochies*, 118-119.

[53] Hoge et al., *Vanishing Boundaries. The Religion of Mainline Protestant Baby Boomers*, 180-188 (Westminster: John Knox Press, 1994).

[54] R.S. Warner, "Work in Progress toward a New Paradigm for the Sociological Study of Religion in the United States," *American Journal of Sociology* 98, no. 5 (1993) 1044-1093.

and all the individuals, groups and organizations within it. Religion is the religion of the whole of society and of all those within the society. In this view, the churches are the institutionalization of this overarching religion. Secularization is seen as bringing about a decrease in the dominance of these churches and thus as detracting from religion itself, with the result that religion withdraws into the private domain of the citizen. Secularization and privatization of religion go hand in hand.

The emerging economic paradigm is based on entirely different premises. The main ones are as follows. First, the human person is a being that is oriented towards obtaining rewards and preventing or minimizing costs, and is continually making rational choices to that end. Next, religion is an activity directed toward obtaining a special sort of reward, known as compensators, which are obtainable not in the here and now or in the near future, but rather in the distant future or — in religious terms — the eschatological future. The ability to obtain these compensators is dependent on interaction with superhuman beings or gods, which demands an investment that is associated with certain costs. Furthermore, as long as religious organizations effect this interaction with the superhuman beings in a satisfactory manner, the costs are counterbalanced by the compensators. However, when the religious organizations become secularized, that is to say, when they adapt too strongly to the mundane environment and lose their transcendent orientation, people will move to other religious organizations in order to obtain religious quality for their money. Thus, religious pluralism and competition between religious organizations encourage religiosity in people, whereas a religious monopoly of the kind that existed in the Catholic Middle Ages and still exists in exclusively or predominantly Catholic countries, leads to religious impoverishment.[55] Finally, it is also possible that the secularization of religious organizations results in people running away from these organizations and joining new sects and cults. There they are willing to pay a higher price for the transcendent compensators which these sects and cults promise to obtain for them from the superhuman beings or gods. In other words, secularization is not something the churches are

---

[55] See I. Iannaccone, "The Consequences of Religious Market Structures," *Rationality & Society* 3, no.2 (1991) 156-177.

subjected to from the outside, but rather a process that they bring on themselves from within. And, even more importantly, this secularization does not lead to the decline but rather to the transformation of religion.[56] This theory, which incidentally was already introduced by Peter Berger[57] in his market analysis of the interaction between Christian denominations, is attractive in that it offers an explanation for religious phenomena that are not explained by the traditional secularization theory. Thus it offers an explanation for the origin and development of fundamentalism and of right-wing religious groupings, which are making their mark on public as well as political life. It also seems to explain why so many people who are marginal church members or have already left the church are attracted to new religious movements, religious sects and New Age ideas.

Nevertheless, there are also some serious objections to be made to this theory. Some are conceptual in nature, others empirical. The first objection concerns the underlying anthropology. Being human is reduced to the striving for optimization of self-interest and self-regard and, as a part of that objective, the achieving of a balance between rewards and costs. This assumption contrasts sharply with the striving that is characteristic of humanity in the most profound sense, namely the striving for a balance between self-regard and other-regard in a relation of equal regard, reciprocity, love and solidarity.[58] The second objection has to do with the concept of what religion is. To interpret faith in God, as do Durkin and Greeley, in terms of an investment one makes in order to ensure oneself the benefit of the compensators that religion provides, is to profoundly miss the fundamental gratuity that characterizes God's own being and to which the religious believer opens himself up in all his receptivity, beyond any need or activity whatsoever.[59] Anyone who claims, as Durkin and Greeley do, to have

[56] R. Stark and W.S. Bainbridge, *The Future of Religion. Secularization, Revival and Cult Formation* (Berkeley: University of California Press, 1985); R. Stark and W.S. Bainbridge, *A Theory of Religion.*

[57] P. Berger, "A Market Model for the Analysis of Ecumenecity," *Social Research* 30 (1963) 77-93.

[58] D. Browning, *Religious Thought and the Modern Psychologies* (Philadelphia: Fortress Press, 1987).

[59] J.-L. Marion, *Dieu sans l'être* (Paris: Presses Universitaires de France, 1991).

operationalized Pascal's gamble with this economic insurance theory, is missing the unequivocal, unqualified, pure love that God, in his own being, represents for humanity. Furthermore, this view utterly fails to take into account the liberty of the human being who opens himself or herself up to God on the basis of a free and personal choice. Faith is not the logical result of an economic calculation ('rational choice'), but is, rather, the vehicle of the well-considered self-surrender of the person to God.[60] The third objection is of an empirical sort. The economic theory is contradicted by phenomena occurring specifically in the Catholic church. According to the theory, religious pluralism and religious competition lead to strengthening of religiosity and religious monopolization leads to its weakening. This thesis may hold true for countries where the Protestant churches, either alone or together with the Catholic Church, predominate, such as the United States. However, in many countries where the Catholic Church possesses a de facto monopoly, there is no sign of low religiosity. The most compelling example is Ireland, which is characterized by an extremely high level of religiosity, as Greeley himself notes.[61] The last objection that I will touch on here is also an empirical one and concerns the Netherlands. The Netherlands are a religiously pluralistic country with three major churches or denominations — the Roman Catholic Church, the Netherlands Reformed Church and the Reformed Churches in the Netherlands — along with a broad spectrum of small Protestant churches from extremely orthodox to extremely liberal. And yet, the level of religiosity in the Netherlands is low. Along with East Germany, it is one of the most secularized countries, as noted previously. It is true that there is a revival of charismatic evangelical movements, but it would certainly be overstating the case to say that there is a great rush towards new religious movements, sects and cults. There is a certain interest in the New Age movements, for example, but three quarters of students in secondary schools do not feel drawn to them. The majority of those who are interested belong to the transitional category between church membership and non-membership.

[60] Bl. Pascal, *Pensées. Chronologie, Introduction etc.*, par D. Descotes (Paris, 1976) 233, 556; J.A. Van der Ven, "Religieuze individualisering," *Individualisering en religie*, 60-97.
[61] A. Greeley, *Religion as Poetry*, 19-20.

Almost half of the young people have no interest at all in religion or philosophy.[62] Although the economic theory of religion is an interesting one in itself, the situation in the Netherlands provides no support for the thesis that religion is not declining, but rather transforming. There is no evidence that would discredit the aforementioned prediction that by 2020 only 15% of Netherlanders will be members of the Roman Catholic Church, 6% will belong to the Netherlands Reformed Church and 3% to the Reformed Churches in the Netherlands. Of course, predictions can be wrong and trends can be reversed. The question is: by what? The report of the Dutch Social and Cultural Planning Bureau on secularization in the Netherlands lists possible factors: an international conflict over religious issues; growing recognition of the function of socio-cultural Christianity; the rise of invisible religion; the rise of civil religion; the spread of Islam; the further proliferation of New Age movements; increase in alienation and anomy leading to an increased demand for religion. The authors of the study, however, generally do not anticipate that one of these factors will stop the process of secularization and that a process of desecularization will then set in.[63]

Church and Culture

One factor, notably, is not mentioned by the authors of the report: a change in the church's policy in the socio-cultural domain. They assume that the policies of the church will remain unchanged in general and in this domain in particular. Admittedly, there are at the present time no signs in the churches of an imminent change in direction, and certainly not in the Catholic Church. The steadfast clinging to the sexual, bioethical and ecclesiastical doctrines which has been the hallmark of papal and episcopal leadership in the last several decades must cause any thought of a change in policy to shrivel. This state of affairs is all the more striking because, for example, the definitive ruling of the Pope that women cannot be ordained as priests, as set out in the

[62] J. De Hart, *Levensbeschouwelijke en politieke praktijken van middelbare scholieren in Nederland* (Kampen: Kok, 1990).
[63] J.W. Becker and R. Vink, *Secularisatie in Nederland*, 177-180.

Apostolic Letter "Priestly Ordination", flies in the face of socio-cultural modernization and democratization. We know that 66% of Catholics in the Netherlands believe that women should be able to become priests, and that the overwhelming majority of students at the Catholic University of Nijmegen, for example, share this view, regardless of whether they are believers, doubters or non-believers, whether they are regular or occasional church-goers or whether they never attend church at all. The ordination of women is a subject on which there is very nearly a university-wide consensus.[64]

I look at the socio-cultural factor separately here because there is no doubt that the church in the Netherlands will continue to lose ground as long as there is no critical-constructive dialogue between the church and contemporary culture.[65] This is true not only of the Catholic Church, but also, directly as well as indirectly, of the Protestant churches, since the high profile of the Catholic Church as a Christian church around the world tends to affect the societal plausibility and social reputation of the Protestant churches as well. From qualitative studies it is apparent that opposition to the leadership of the church, which is not able or willing to enter into an open, constructive and critical dialogue with the culture that forms the very context of that church, is growing not only among young people, but among older ones as well, and particularly among the core members of the church. If this opposition is not adequately heard, honored and channeled, the consequence will be a slow but steady internal emigration and then external emigration of these core members, with the result that the necessary dialogue with the culture will be suppressed even more and the decline in church membership and church participation will accelerate.[66] That this internal and external emigration are anything but hypothetical can be seen in the fact that the motivation of church members to participate in the making and implementing of policy in local churches is decreasing as the

---

[64] J.A. Van der Ven and B. Biemans, *Religie in fragmenten*, 132.

[65] E. Schillebeeckx, "Auf der Suche nach einer Kultur der Gerechtigkeit und Liebe Marginalismus und Humanismus," *Vom Rande Her? Zur Idee des Marginalismus*, ed. K.-P. Pfeiffer (Würzburg: Konigshausen und Neumann, 1996).

[66] J.A. Van der Ven, "Het religieuze bewustzijn van jongeren en de crisis van het jongerenpastoraat," *Praktische Theologie* 22, no. 3 (1995) 342-364.

emphasis on the authoritarian and hierarchical exercise of power is increasing.[67]

From a theological perspective, the motivation of the members of the church to take an active and independent role in the life and work of the church is crucial, because this is precisely what gives the church its religious identity as people of God, as movement of Jesus and as a building of the Spirit. However, it is also important for strategic reasons. The church is exhibiting more and more the characteristics of a volunteer church, meaning not only that members voluntarily join and voluntarily belong, but also that ecclesial and pastoral work is planned and carried out to an ever greater degree by nonofficial and/or nonprofessional and/or unpaid members of the church. If the motivation of these members is to be maintained, then a flat, flexible, dynamic organization and participatory and democratic lines of authority are necessary.[68] All of this requires not a hierarchical bureaucracy, but a flexible adhocracy.[69] Such a system is based not on a territorial demarcation of the power of various church officials, as is the case in the traditional, territorial parish, but on the dynamic formation of networks among the members of the church. The only way the church can exist today is as a network of individuals and groups who choose to form a community of believers on that basis.[70]

Such changes are all the more pressing when one considers that the Catholic Church in the western countries is becoming a church without priests. In 1992, there were around 45,000 parishes in Europe without their own priest, or about 33% of the total number of parishes.[71] In the Netherlands this applies to only 6% of parishes, while in Belgium it is already 27%. In response to the shortage of priests, in the Netherlands

----

[67] Kl. Sonnberger, *Die Leitung der Pfarrgemeinde. Eine empirisch-theologische Studie unter Niederländischen und Deutschen Katholieken*, Theologie & Empirie, 25 (Weinheim, Kampen: Kok, 1995).

[68] R.H. Hall, J.E. Haas and N.J. Johnson, "An Examination of the Blau-Scott and Etzionni Typologies," *Administrative Science Quarterly* 12 (1967) 118-129; H. Mintzberg, *The Structuring of Organizations. A Synthesis of the Research* (New York: Free Press, 1979) 136.

[69] H. Mintzberg, *The Structuring of Organizations. A Synthesis of the Research,* 432; H. Mintzberg, *Mintzberg on Management*, Dutch Translation (1991), *Mintzberg over management. De wereld van de organisaties* (Amsterdam: Veen, 1989) 202.

[70] J.A. Van der Ven, *Ecclesiology in Context*, 31-45, 251-260.

[71] J. Kerkhofs, *Waardenonderzoek. Een bijdrage tot pastoraal realisme*, 159-170.

there has been a growing trend since 1970 to appoint academically and professionally trained lay-theologians to serve as pastors, even though they are not ordained. In 1994 these lay-pastors represented 38% of all pastors.[72] But this does not change the fact that the church, even though it is drawing on unordained as well as ordained pastors, and in future perhaps will even make use of ordained women as well, is to a significant degree dependent on the creativity and energy of committed lay-persons who, with their input of head, heart and hand, must be seen as the real pillars of the local church. However, this demands a fundamental revision of the official structure of the Catholic Church. The longer such a revision is put off, the more internal opposition grows and eats away at the life of the church from within. Of all the scenarios that have been described in connection with the problem of "Europe without priests?", one thing is perfectly clear: without a fundamental revision of the official structure, a revision that accords to the lay-people in the local churches the full weight that is due to them, the church will become more and more deeply mired in its problems.[73]

From all of this a complex picture emerges. Religion at the meso-level of the church is being affected by a substantial decline in the number of members, in church attendance and participation in the rites of passage, while, at the same time, at least in the Netherlands, we are not witnessing any major movement towards alternative religious movements, groups, sects or cults. What is needed is a revision in the structure of the church, to establish a relationship of openness and dialogue between the church and its socio-cultural environment, but it is precisely this that the leadership of the Catholic Church refuses to do. Meanwhile, protest against the absence of such dialogue is reflected in an internal and external emigration of the members. A major issue in this dialogue should be democratically dealing with the relationship between transcendence and power in the church, that is to say, the problem of ministry. The position of the pastor thus itself becomes part of the problem.

[72] Kaski, "Kerncijfers 1994/1995. Uit de kerkelijke statistiek van het R.-K. Genootschap in Nederland," *Kerkelijke documentatie 121*, 7-9.
[73] J. Kerkhofs, *Waardenonderzoek*, 211-244.

3. Religion at the Microlevel of the Individual

The religiosity of the individual person is not solely a function of religion at either the macrolevel of the society or the mesolevel of the church. This does not mean that religion in society and in the church exert no influence on the individual at all, but that what the individual does with these influences — the choices he or she makes based on his or her own biography and the way in which he or she constructs or reconstructs these influences — is not reducible to the influences per se. For this reason we must look at the individual level separately.

That the attention focussed on the individual is determined by societal factors was demonstrated by Durkheim when he showed that individualism has its origins in the division of labour. The division of labour means that each individual or at least each group of individuals carries out a particular task and performs specific functions in the work process. Whereas Durkheim's contemporaries saw the idea of the individual as a partial producer as a source of the alienation of the individual from his/her work and thus from him/herself, Durkheim stressed the human value of individualism. This value resides, first, in the growing interdependence of individual partial producers, leading to increased necessity for cooperation. This interdependence and cooperation lay the foundation for the basic form of modern society: the contract. In the contract, the parties come to an agreement on their mutual rights and responsibilities. The contract, Durkheim argued — and this is the second point — should not be seen as amoral or immoral, as if it were aimed solely at realizing one's own self-interest at the cost of the interest of the other. Durkheim argued that "in a contract not everything is contractual".[74] The contract is to be seen as the expression of a deeper and more fundamental way of people belonging to each other. It symbolizes the respect of people for one another, since it is based on the will to honor the human dignity of the other person and the satisfaction of his or her needs. According to the law, the contract must be a bona fide contract, that is to say, it must be made in good faith. "Any act must therefore seem immoral to us

---

[74] E. Durkheim, *The Division of Labour in Society* (New York: Macmillan, 1984), 158.

that causes injury to a fellow-man who has otherwise done nothing to
alienate our ordinary human sympathies....It is because he has suffered
some unjustified injury, because in a word, such contract is unjust".[75]
Therefore, the contract has its source in respect for the other's freedom and equality. The contract is founded on justice and love.[76] In the
end, love rather than justice is the most fundamental principle, "for it
is man as a human being that we love or should love and regard, not
man as a scholar or genius or as an able man of business, and so
on...".[77] Against this background, Durkheim argues that the division
of labour correlates with the advance of the human personality. The
division of labour contributes to the 'cult of the person'[78] or the 'cult
of the individual'.[79]

From this position of the individual, which is not a result solely of
objective experiential choices, but of factors within the structure of the
society which affect the whole of society, including religion, we go
now to look at the relationship between the individual and religion. I
begin from the assumption that the actual nature of that relationship
is determined by the individual him/herself, and not by any predetermined sociological theory, as though human beings were motivated
exclusively by, for example, religious compensators[80], or by any particular theological conviction, as though the individual were an anonymous 'homo religiosus' or even an anonymous Christian.[81]

Although this assumption may seem to be self-evident, it is not
always easy to respect or accept in fact that not every individual, nor
even every individual who belongs to a church, would agree that the
Christian religion "interests him or her a great deal, has a great influence on his or her daily life, plays a part when he or she has to make
decisions, or his or her life would be different had he or she not his

[75] E. Durkheim, *Professional Ethics and Civil Morals* (London: Routledge, 1957) 207.

[76] E. Durkheim, *The Division of Labour in Society*, 338.

[77] E. Durkheim, *Professional Ethics and Civil Morals*, 219.

[78] E. Durkheim, *The Division of Labour in Society*, 333.

[79] E. Durkheim, *The Division of Labour in Society*, 338; A. Giddens, *Durkheim*
(Harvester: Harvester Press, 1978); J.A. Van der Ven, "Human Well-being and the
Cult of the Individual," *Happines, Well- Being and the Meaning of Life*, eds. V. Brüm-
mer and M. Sarot (Kampen: Kok, 1996) 99-121.

[80] R. Stark and W.S. Bainbridge, *A Theory of Religion.*

[81] K. Rahner, "Anonymer und expliziter Glaube," *Schriften zur Theologie 12*, 76-84.

or her Christian faith". Empirical studies indicate that the percentage of the Dutch people who report belonging to a church and at the same time affirm that "Christian faith interests him or her a great deal" declined from 61.3% in 1979 to 52.3% in 1990. The percentage of those who agree that "Christian faith has a great influence on their daily life" dropped from 64.9% in 1979 to 53.6% in 1990. The percentage of those who report that "Christian faith plays a part when decisions have to be made" fell from 52.8% in 1979 to 43.9% in 1990. And the percentage who replied that "life would be different had he or she not his or her Christian faith" declined from 51.2% in 1979 to 45.2% in 1990.[82] This decline in religious saliency among church members can be interpreted as a sign of secularization at the individual level.[83]

Here lies one of the main problems that pastors, Catholic as well as Protestant, have to struggle with. More than by secularization at the societal level, they are frustrated by secularization at the level of the individual. This is understandable, since the latter form of secularization directly affects their daily contacts with parishioners.[84]

Thus far we have looked at a specific form of religious saliency, namely general religious saliency, which concerns the importance of Christian religion for daily life in general. In addition, there are two other forms to be considered: comparative saliency and specific saliency. Students at the University of Nijmegen were asked about the comparative saliency of religion in relation to other sectors of daily life. The responses indicated that close friends and life partners were considered most important, followed by recreational time and family, and then studies, with politics and religion bringing up the rear as sectors of daily life considered least important.[85] The specific saliency of religion can be judged by asking to what degree religion is important in relation to the experiences or choices in various areas of people's lives. Forty percent of students reported that religion plays an important role

[82] R. Eisinga, A. Felling, J. Peters, P. Scheepers, E. Jacobs and R. Konig, *Social and Cultural Trends in the Netherlands 1979-1990. Documentation of National Surveys on Religious and Secular Attitudes in 1979, 1985 and 1990* (Amsterdam: Steinmetz Archive, 1992) 49-50.

[83] Cf. G. Dekker, *Godsdienst en samenleving. Inleiding tot de studie van de godsdienstsociologie* (Kampen: Kok, 1987) 153-157.

[84] J.A. Van der Ven, *Ecclesiology in Context*, 485.

[85] J.A. Van der Ven and B. Biemans, *Religie in fragmenten*, 224.

in the way they think about themselves and 30% said it is important in determining their attitude toward others, while 23% said it plays a role in the choice of a political party. Only for 10% or less of students does religion play a certain role in the use of time, the choice of field of study, the choice of friends and recreational activities.[86]

As these data indicate, for many people religion is a minimal or entirely insignificant factor in their personal lives. For those to whom religion is important, that importance is both differential and partial. It is differential in the sense that religion may play a role in private life, for themselves or their significant others, but play little or no role in public matters such as politics. It is partial because in the areas where religion does play a role, it is not the main factor, but simply one factor among others. In the lives of people who attribute importance to religion, religion is one issue among others.[87] Not everyone is prepared to give up his or her life for religion, to put it mildly. The ordinary believer is no potential martyr.

In relation to the foregoing, it must be borne in mind that the three forms of religious saliency which I have identified exist within the framework of the traditional Christian faith. In other words, what the studies measure is the saliency of this traditional Christian faith. The question, of course, is whether religion at the level of the individual person is not made up of patterns, contents and forms which come together to create a completely unique construction or reconstruction of elements from various religious traditions, both Christian and non-Christian, and from non-religious worldviews. These are not necessarily constructions modeled on some preconceived plan which is then systematically developed and executed. Rather, they are the accretion of practical, everyday experience, of daily life. Levi-Strauss made a distinction between the 'ingenieur', the engineer, and the 'bricoleur', the handyman. The former systematically thinks, conceives, develops and executes, while the second gathers together bits and pieces of a life, as it were, and builds something out of the disparate elements through doing and experiencing. At the microlevel of the individual, religion is the product of 'bricolage'. The constructions in question are

---

[86] J.A. Van der Ven and B. Biemans, *Religie in fragmenten*, 79.
[87] J. Pohier, *Dieu fractures* (Paris: Seuil, 1985).

self-constructions created through doing and experiencing.[88] For heuristic reasons, it is possible to distinguish several types of self-constructions.

The first kind consists of reconstructions of elements of the traditional Christian faith that do not transcend the traditional framework. Examples are the belief structure of members of the charismatic evangelical movement with their specific images of God, Jesus and the Spirit, or the charismatic Taizé movement in France.

The second type consists of reconstructions of elements drawn from the traditional Christian faith but put together in such a way that a transformation takes place, one corresponding to the process of modernization and rationalization which western culture is undergoing at present. The abstraction of the concept of God, in which the personal God is transcended in the direction of an impersonal God, is one example. From the traditional Christian perspective this is often seen as a watering down or blurring of faith, whereas studies show that people who conceive of God primarily as the impersonal power of love that lives within us and surrounds us, may indeed engage in specifically religious activities such as prayer, and also seek affiliation with critical-prophetic movements.[89]

The third type consists of reconstructions of elements of the traditional Christian faith and other religious traditions. There is nothing unusual in such reconstructions in and of themselves, for Christianity has entered into combinations with elements of surrounding cultures, religions and philosophies in all periods of its history. One need only think of the Hellenization of early Christianity, the Germanization during the early middle ages, the Aristotelization that took place in the high middle ages, and the scholasticization of the second half of the nineteenth and first half of the twentieth century, as attested to by the sermon and catechism books produced during that period. When this phenomenon takes the form of interaction with the surrounding

---

[88] J. Janssen, *Jeugdcultuur. Een actuele geschiedenis* (Utrecht: De Tijdstroom, 1994) 33-37; E. Heijmans, *Je moet er het beste van maken. Een empirisch onderzoek naar hedendaagse zingevingssystemen* (Nijmegen: ITS, 1994) 166 v.

[89] J.A. Van der Ven, "De structuur van het religieuze bewustzijn. Verkenning van de spanning tussen religiositeit en kerkelijkheid," *Tijdschrift voor Theologie* 36, no. 1 (1996) 39-60.

culture, it is called contextualization; when Christianity becomes absorbed into the surrounding culture the phenomenon is known as inculturation; and when there is a fusion or amalgamation of Christianity and the surrounding culture it is called syncretism.[90] Considering that the surrounding culture today is more and more a global one, comprising a profusion of religious and non-religious movements, there is evidently a great potential for reconstructions of this kind.

There is another, fourth type, the prevalence of which is on the rise and which represents a kind of zero-option. Contrary to the predictions of the economic theory of religion, there are a growing number of people, at least in the Netherlands, who say that in their personal opinion, religion is something to be respected inasmuch as other people derive benefit from it, but which for them no longer serves any purpose. It is not a matter of hostility towards religion, but simply of indifferent tolerance. Thus 58% of students at the Nijmegen University report that religion has no significance for their own lives, but 61% reject the view that religion no longer has much to offer to society and 77% do not agree that religion is outdated.[91]

The task thus facing the pastor is indeed a formidable one. Quite apart from the religious problems that exist at the macrolevel of society and at the mesolevel of the church, there is no doubt that at the microlevel of the individual, the pastor is confronted with tasks and challenges that are complex in nature. Insofar as the development of the religious self must be seen as a constitutive element of pastoral work, the pastor can not close his eyes to the complex nature of the responsibilities entailed by this process of development of the religious self.[92] 'The' religious person, 'the' Christian is nowhere to be found: instead there is an endless variety of individuals, each of whom, out of their own experiences and feelings, and their own, constantly changing relationship to the religious institutions, is permanently reconstructing their own religion.

---

[90] See R. Schreiter, *Constructing Local Theologies* (New York: Orbis Books, 1984) 175 v.
[91] See R. Schreiter, *Constructing Local Theologies* (New York: Orbis Books, 1984) 175 v.
[92] See H. Luther, *Religion und Alltag. Bausteine zu einer Praktischen Theologie des Subjekts* (Stuttgart: Rodius Verlag, 1992).

Summary

The developments taking place in the field of religion constitute a complex and dynamic phenomenon. At the macrolevel of society, it is misleading to speak of radical secularization or semi-secularization; instead, we are witnessing a differential secularization, in the sense that religion can be observed to exert a variety of influences within the various societal systems (economic, political, social, cultural), which sometimes reinforce and at other times contradict each other. Some of these may be considered desirable and others undesirable. At the mesolevel of the church we see a decline in the number of church members, in church attendance and in participation in the rites of passage, which does not invariably (at least in the Netherlands) lead to a corresponding increase in participation in alternative religious groups. There is a need for the church to engage in an open, critically constructive dialogue with the surrounding western culture, but such a dialogue has been impeded by the leadership of the church, at least in the Catholic Church. This refusal has created an anachronistic situation in the structure and ministry of the church, so that the pastor has become his own problem. At the microlevel of the individual, 'the' believer and 'the' Christian have been replaced by the freedom and autonomy of each individual to determine his or her own religious way through life. This demands of the pastor the flexibility and creativity to respond to the opinions and wants of each individual.

The complex nature of religion and its particular dynamic render any definitive frame of reference or any predetermined policy for the pastor an impossibility from the start. They demand of the pastor an approach based on freedom of movement, manoeuvrability and sensitivity in the face of ever new situations and contexts. They presuppose of the pastor the competence for self-direction, so that the essence of the Christian religion may be preserved and developed, and at the same time remain relevant to the values and needs of people in western society.

CHAPTER II

THE NEED FOR A NEW EDUCATIONAL
PERSPECTIVE FOR MINISTRY

The question that inevitably looms large after the preceding discussion is whether education for ministry provides the tools necessary
for addressing and coping with the complexity of the problematic religious issues that manifest themselves at the macrolevel of the society,
the mesolevel of the church and the microlevel of the individual. This
question cannot be answered with a simple yes or no. The answer is
dependent to a large extent on the particular model of education for
ministry that one has in mind.

The contemporary history of education for the ministry can be
divided roughly into the period before and the period after the 1960s.
In the period prior to the 1960s, on the Protestant side, the educational
model centered on the word of God, i.e., the proclamation of the word
of God. The most important thing the minister had to learn was to read,
understand, interpret and communicate the word of God as spoken
through the Bible in the authoritative preaching of the 'minister verbi'.
As for the Catholic side, the educational model was built around the
neo-scholastic concept of the church and the bureaucratic administrative apparatus of the church. The most fundamental thing the priest
had to learn was to maintain and expand the church as an institution
of salvation in the name of God, in order to impress upon the faithful
the teaching of the church, administer the sacraments and render assistance to them in their moral and spiritual life. That we place these two
models prior to the demarcation line of the 1960s does not mean that
they are now entirely a thing of the past. On the contrary, these models
— or certainly specific aspects thereof — are still in use to a greater
or lesser degree in various regional churches and theological schools.
Thus orthodox Protestant theological seminaries are still characterized
to a large extent by the kerygmatic model, while conservative Catholic
seminaries still proceed from an ecclesial model in which Vatican II

is interpreted on the basis of Vatican I. One can even say, in a general sense, that Protestant education models differ from the Catholic ones in that, despite the profound changes that both have undergone since the sixties, the former place greater emphasis on the use of the Bible in ministry while the latter emphasize the context of the church. However, the picture is not black and white, and nuances must be borne in mind. Over the years the two major denominations have learned much from one another, with the result that, on the Protestant side, education for ministry programs have accorded increasing importance to church and church development, while in the same programs in Catholic institutions there is a broad and deep recognition of the hermeneutically key position of the Bible.

However, since the 1960s both the kerygmatic and the ecclesial models of education for ministry have come under mounting pressure, because it is felt they no longer correspond to the requirements and needs of the time. They are being replaced or at least relativized and supplemented by two other models, which no longer correspond to a division along denominational lines but are used right across all denominations. I call them the therapeutic model and the managerial model. I have adopted these labels from the cultural diagnosis of today's society by MacIntyre[1], the religious diagnosis by Bellah[2] and the pastoral diagnosis by Hough and Cobb[3]. These authors observe the difference and even the separation between private life and public life, and between the ideal types of the therapist and the manager. The therapist watches over private life. His attention is directed towards the affective and emotional experiencing of his client. His ideal is experiential satisfaction and self-realization. His inspiration does not come from without, but from within, where the freedom to be oneself grows and comes to fruition. Not the ownership of external affairs, but the ownership of oneself is his motto. He derives his motivation from expressive individualism. His rationality is expressive rationality, in which the value of the expression is measured by its subjective and

[1] A. MacIntyre, *After Virtue* (London: Duckworth, 1981) 26-34, 70-75.
[2] R.N. Bellah, *Habits of the Heart* (Berkeley: University of California Press, 1985) 44-51.
[3] J.C. Hough and J.B. Cobb, eds., *Christian Identity and Theological Education* (Chico: Scholars Press, 1985).

intersubjective authenticity. In contrast to the therapist, who watches over the intimacy of private life, the manager stands in the public, occupational sphere as the organizer of human resources, employing these resources in such a way that the objectives of his business or institution are achieved effectively and efficiently. The manager is the model for processes of human engineering. His instruments and means are those of social technology. He draws his inspiration from the augmenting of human and cultural capital. His ideal is rooted in utilitarian individualism. His rationality is instrumental rationality, which is concerned with the relation between ends and means, the ends being predetermined and the means forming the object of a free and calculated choice.. Following from this dichotomy I would like to present a description of the therapeutic and managerial models of education for ministry. The first model is concerned above all with the pastor as professional counselor, who renders cure and care to those who belong to his client system. The second has to do primarily with the pastor as professional manager of the parish community and of all pastoral processes that take place therein. Both models aim to contribute to the professionalization of the pastor, although the professionalism of the therapist and the professionalism of the congregational manager represent two very different concepts of professionalism.

As I have said, these two models replace or relativize the two models that predominated in the pre-1960s era, that is the kerygmatic and ecclesial models, or at least are seen as complementary to them. Many theological schools in the western world have taken over various aspects of the therapeutic and/or managerial models in order to better prepare their students in the education for ministry programs for "the reading of the signs of the times from a pastoral perspective," as a number of church documents, and Vatican II, advocate. Thus, there are education for ministry programs in which, for example, aspects of the kerygmatic model are combined with those of the therapeutic model, but there are also programs in which the latter is dominant. This means that all of the functions that the pastor has to perform, not only pastoral care but also catechesis, preaching, church administration and so on, are interpreted and filled in more or less from the perspective of the therapeutic model. There are also education for ministry programs in which aspects of the ecclesial model are related to aspects of the managerial model or in which the managerial model predominates. This means that all tasks which the pastor must perform, not only church administration but also home visiting, social ministry, liturgy and so on, are viewed more or less within the frame of reference of the managerial model. Finally there are programs in which various kinds of symmetrical or asymmetrical cross-pollination occur between the kerygmatic, the ecclesial, the therapeutic, and the managerial model.

For reasons of clarity, I will not go into all of these possible combinations, and will restrict myself to describing the two models that have steadily gained in influence since the 1960s, namely the therapeutic and the managerial models. In so doing I will outline not only the principal characteristics of both, but also how they have developed over time. I will indicate the types of criticism that have been directed at these models from their own proponents, as well as the criticisms aimed at them from outside. Based on the critical evaluation of the two models, I conclude that we must seek a new model, one that is beyond therapeuticalism (section 1) and beyond managerialism (section 2).

1. Beyond Therapeuticalism

To understand the therapeutic model, it is necessary to acquaint oneself with at least the broad outlines of its history. It is here that I begin, above all because it is precisely in the twists and turns of this history that the beginnings of the later discussion and criticism are to be found.

The two names that are indissolubly linked with the history of the therapeutic model are those of Richard Cabot, a medical doctor, and pastor Anton Boisen. Cabot and Boisen had many views and ideas in common. They were the first to press for a dialogue between theology and psychology, for the education and training of pastors in pastoral counseling and therapy, and for the organizational development of Clinical Pastoral Education (CPE), as the movement has been known since 1968. Initially, however, they pursued different goals or at least emphasized different aspects of those goals. Until 1968, Cabot was the leading figure of the Institute of Pastoral Care, founded by the New

England Group in Boston, while Boisen headed the Council for Clinical Training, based in New York.[4]

The New England group sought to enhance the clinical education of pastors by establishing an institutional link with the theological training institutes, so that this clinical education would remain an integral part of theological education. Cabot also sought to develop a clinical theology and integrate it into the theological curriculum.[5] For that reason, the standards were based on those of the theological schools. The emphasis was on the description and analysis of the student/patient relationship and the development of specific clinical skills in order to further the helping quality of this relationship. The program stressed the pastoral identity of this relationship as well as the theological explicitation and development of that identity. In the view of the group, the clinical education program was not aimed solely — and perhaps not even primarily — at the training of chaplains in general hospitals, but above all at the training of parish pastors. The connection with the church followed as a matter of course. The preferred educational method was the case method, in order to train pastors to diagnose the patient's state and from that diagnosis to develop a treatment plan. Noteworthy, too, is that the majority of supervisors in this group worked toward a graduate academic degree beyond the basic theological degree. The training program itself was characterized by seven aspects: instruction and experience in hospital orderly service, training in listening, experience in observing pastoral experts, note taking, special reading assignments, seminar discussions, and personal conferences.[6] The group brought out its own journal, *The Journal of Pastoral Care*.

Initially the New York group did not differ greatly from the New England group. Boisen had taken courses with Cabot early on and Cabot in turn supported Boisen in his first efforts at clinical pastoral education. For Boisen, too, patients were central, and he, too, emphasized

---

[4] C.E. Hall, "Head and Heart. The Story of the Clinical Pastoral Education Movement," *Journal of Pastoral Care Publications* (1992) 35-45.

[5] E.E. Thornton, *Professional Education for Ministry* (Nashville: Abingdon Press, 1970) 48 v.

[6] C.E. Hall, "Head and Heart. The Story of the Clinical Pastoral Education Movement," 52-53.

the importance of listening to patients and considering them as 'living documents' that needed to be carefully deciphered in a dialogue with the 'written documents' of the religious tradition.[7] He also attached great importance to the analysis of case histories.[8] When the two groups threatened to become estranged from each other, Boisen expressed his unhappiness at this state of affairs and cautioned against it, even though the growing antagonisms had been engendered, albeit perhaps unintentionally, by Boisen's own approach.[9] Cabot sought to mediate between the two groups, but was ousted from the New York group, of which he had been a member from the beginning, in 1935.[10] The criticism which the members of this group leveled at the New England group was that the latter did not go far enough in the training of the requisite listening skills. It was felt that in order to understand and interpret the emotional processes the patient was going through, the pastor must first open himself up to his own emotional processes. The psychiatric setting in mental hospitals, which was the preferred setting for the training of the pastors, served to encourage the pastor to focus attention on his own emotional processes. For this reason, too, the 'verbatim method', in which the pastor indirectly reveals his own innermost self, was preferred over the 'case method' used by the New England group. Furthermore, student-centered learning was favored over content-centered education. Through this approach the members of the group believed they could create a new kind of theology, that would take its inspiration primarily from the 'living documents' which actual people are, rather than from the 'written documents' of the Christian or ecclesial tradition. In fact, however, the group was in imminent danger of losing contact with living theology, and a number of supervisors switched over to psychology. It is also worth noting that only few supervisors worked for graduate theological academic degrees beyond the basic theological degree. The name

[7] Cf. S. Hiltner, "The Heritage of Anton T. Boisen," *Pastoral Psychology* 1, no. 5 (1965) 5-10.

[8] R.C. Powell, *Fifty Years of Learning. Through Supervised Encounter With Living Human Documents* (1975) 19.

[9] R.C. Powell, *Fifty Years of Learning. Through Supervised Encounter With Living Human Documents*, 19.

[10] E. Brooks Holifield, "Ethical Assumptions of Clinical Pastoral Education," *Theology Today* 36, no. 1 (1979) 30-44.

of the journal published by the group, *The Journal of Clinical Pastoral Work*, also reflected this approach with its emphasis on the word 'clinical' and the use of 'work' in place of the more pastoral 'care'. Against this background it is understandable that the group sought to establish an organization that would be separate from the theological institutions. It was felt that only a separate organization could guarantee the development of the requisite pastoral competence in psychology and psychiatry, without contaminating intervention from theological schools. An effort was therefore made to have students of other disciplines take part in the training programs. One of the reasons that this was possible was that psychology, and not theology, was considered the 'reference discipline'.

The difference between the two groups is expressed in the description of the history of pastoral counseling found in the transcript of conversations that were taped during a conference in 1952: "There was a time when we talked about starting with the patient, [about]... doing things to manipulate the patient to get him where you wanted...," "the next step was where you took the listening approach, [and] instead of manipulating the patient you were listening and letting him develop," "and then you began to think much later about how do I feel, and what am I doing, ...so that the analysis of the relationship has been a progressive development," "it is a growing discovery that the relationship is really the key".[11]

The differences between the two groups led to the New England group being labelled as conservative and the New York group as radical. The former laid more emphasis on the patient and the cognitive dimension of training, while the latter focussed more on the pastor and the emotional dimension. The New England group was known as a champion of the conceptual approach, the New York group as the proponent of the experiential approach. Both drew heavily on William James, the former focusing on his psychology of the will, the latter on his psychopathology of the soul. The former derived its insights about counseling from social work, the latter from psychiatry. The New Englanders were interested in formation, the New Yorkers in

---

[11] R.C. Powell, *Fifty Years of Learning. Through Supervised Encounter With Living Human Documents*, (1975) 20.

freedom.[12] The former considered the connection with the theological school and the church indispensable, the latter established an organization separate from the theological schools and broke with the church in the 1930s and 1940s.[13]

Nevertheless, the two groups gradually came to the realization that they had more similarities than differences and that the divergent accents that characterized the two approaches need not necessarily be considered as irreconcilable.[14] This realization led to a gradual rapprochement between them during the 'era of unification' between 1947 and 1967.[15] The discussion between the two groups during this period centered on the alternatives of student or patient, training or education, the conceptual/theoretical/skill approach or the emotional/ experiential, clinical inquiry approach, objective or subjective criteria, healing or shepherding, academic theological degrees or clinical certificates, seminary or hospital, professor or supervisor, ecclesial or professional organization.[16] By 1950 the two groups had already decided to merge their separate journals into one: *The Journal of Pastoral Care*.[17] Caroll Wise and Seward Hiltner contributed greatly to ensuring that the distance between the positions was gradually bridged.[18] In hindsight it is hardly surprising then that the two groups gradually buried the hatchet and merged with two other groups, namely the Baptist CPE group and the Lutheran CPE group, to form the Association for Clinical Pastoral Education (ACPE), with the Catholics joining a few years later at their own request.[19]

Without losing sight of the different nuances, it can be said that, within the ACPE, the New York group's approach gradually won the upper hand. The alternatives listed above were roughly resolved

---

[12] E. Brooks Holifield, "Ethical Assumptions of Clinical Pastoral Education," 30-44.

[13] E.E. Thornton, *Professional Education for Ministry*, 76.

[14] C.E. Hall, "Head and Heart. The Story of the Clinical Pastoral Education Movement," 35-45.

[15] E.E. Thornton, *Professional Education for Ministry*, 111 v.

[16] E.E. Thornton, *Professional Education for Ministry*, 115-140; C.E. Hall, "Head and Heart. The Story of the Clinical Pastoral Education Movement," 203.

[17] C.E. Hall, "Head and Heart. The Story of the Clinical Pastoral Education Movement," 64.

[18] E. Brooks Holifield, "Ethical Assumptions of Clinical Pastoral Education,"44.

[19] C.E. Hall, "Head and Heart. The Story of the Clinical Pastoral Education Movement," 137-152, 171-176.

as follows: more attention on the student than on the patient, more education than training, more emphasis on the emotional/experiential approach than on the conceptual/theoretical/skill approach, more openness to clinical than to empirical inquiry, more shepherding than healing, greater emphasis on clinical certificates than on theological academic degrees, a preference for association with the hospital rather than with the seminary, focus on the role of supervisor over that of the professor, and accent on the professional rather than the ecclesial organization.

This meant that Freudian psychoanalysis, which dominated the later period of the New York group, now spread to the whole of the ACPE, much to the distress of Boisen. "The emphasis", noted Zijlstra, "was no longer on scientific investigation, but on education, and the centre of attention was no longer the patients, but the students".[20] Boisen saw the marginalization of the case method as an indication of the reduced value accorded to the scientific investigation of patients' religious processes which he had always so ardently defended. Boisen had written, for example, that, "The clinical approach is by no means the only one which provides an opportunity for the empirical study of religious experience ... But dealing with badly maladjusted or sick people ... seems especially important. ... It furnishes the nearest approach to experimental conditions with reference to the great drawing forces of human life".[21] Accordingly, he called for "controlled observation".[22] But to no avail. Even more strongly he expressed his displeasure that in the attention that was focussed on the students instead of on the patients, Freud's genetic depth psychology had pride of place. Irritated, he wrote: "There was much speculation about the oral and anal and genital stages of development. I even heard suggestions about the intra-urine and the intra-testicular stages".[23] Be that as it may, the developmental theories of Freud clearly occupied a very prominent place. Especially his vision of the working through of the processes

---

[20] W. Zijlstra, *Klinisch pastorale vorming. Een voorlopige analyse van het leer- en groepsproces van zeven cursussen* (Assen: van Gorcum, 1969) 22.

[21] A. Boisen, "Cooperative Inquiry in Religion," *Religious Education* 40, no. 5 (1945) 290-297.

[22] A. Boisen, *Religion in Crisis and Custom* (New York: Harper, 1973)

[23] A. Boisen, *Out of the Depths* (New York, 1960) 186.

entailed by the Oedipus complex and dependence on authority as well as the defence mechanisms which these engender, long shaped the practical thinking and acting of many supervisors and still does so today. Later on, thanks primarily to the pastor, Rollo May, Freudian psychoanalysis was supplemented by the approaches of other depth psychologists such as Jung, Rank, Adler and Horney, each of whom brought their own unique points of view. It is worth noting that May sought to combine the eros of Freud with the will of James in order to achieve full spiritual maturity.[24]

Nevertheless, the limits of depth psychology gradually became apparent. Thus the question was asked more and more frequently, whether, in place of the sick patient, who occupied the central place in Freud's thinking, it was not the relatively healthy person who ought to constitute the point of departure in pastoral counseling. Doubts were also expressed about whether the complicated methods of psychoanalysis were really necessary in order to accomplish the tasks with which the pastor is confronted. Added to that was the problem that psychoanalysis was so time-consuming that there was little room left for the religious dimension of pastoral assistance, let alone for theology.

When, in the 1940s and 1950s, Carl Rogers published his well-known books on counseling and client-centered therapy, a desire gradually arose within the ACPE to incorporate the non-directive approach, because it provided an answer to the increasingly persistent questions and doubts with regard to psychoanalysis. Attention, empathy, nearness, authenticity, acceptance and self-realization were the key words in this approach.[25] It did much to liberate both the pastor and the client from the conventional culture and legalistic morality that were experienced as unhealthy.[26] Many people contributed to rendering Rogers' ideas fruitful in terms of pastoral work, such as C. Wise, S. Anderson and above all S. Hiltner. The latter, in particular, dedicated a great deal of effort to expounding and legitimating, both psychologically and

---

[24] R. May, *Love and Will* (New York: Norton, 1969).

[25] C. Rogers, *Counseling and Psychotherapy* (Boston: Houghton, 1942); *Clientcentered Therapy* (Boston: Houghton, 1951); *On Becoming a Person* (Boston: Houghton, 1961).

[26] E. Brooks Holifield, *A History of Pastoral Care in America. From Salvation to Self-Realization* (Nashville: Abingdon Press, 1983) 259-306.

theologically, the importance of Rogers' counseling method for pastoral work.[27] He also tried to bridge the differences that still existed, below the surface at any rate, between the New England group and the New York group. For example, he overcame the opposition between healing and shperding in which the two groups were still caught up, by defining shepherding as the generic theological concept, and establishing healing ('binding up wounds'), sustaining ('standing by') and guiding ('eductive counseling') as three co-ordinative and specific concepts.[28]

To this day, the two giants, Freud and Rogers, still dominate the CPE scene, supplemented, of course, by other representatives of depth psychology and humanistic psychology as well as by the insights of other more forward-looking schools and movements, such as the object relations psychology of the self.[29] Despite the nuances that have been added and the corrections that have been made to their theories, these two great authorities on the human soul continue to act as the dominant reference figures in the practical thought and action of supervisors.

From these beginnings, the clinical pastoral movement spread around the world. In the sixties, the movement took off internationally. Pastors and theologians from Canada, the Netherlands, Australia and New Zealand came to the United States, even before the ACPE was formally established, to take the supervisor education program. The ACPE on its side encouraged its own members to take their sabbatical year in Europe, Africa, Asia and Latin America in order to give courses and educate supervisors.

In the early sixties, a few Dutch pastors/theologians came to the United States to acquire first-hand knowledge of the clinical pastoral movement. They included Faber[30] in 1960, Zijlstra[31] in 1962 and

---

[27] S. Hiltner, *Pastoral Counseling* (New York: Abingdon Press, 1949); *Preface to Pastoral Theology* (New York: Abingdon Press, 1958); *Theological Dynamics* (New York: Abingdon Press, 1972); S. Hiltner and L. Colston, *The Context of Pastoral Counseling* (Nashville: Abingdon Press, 1961).

[28] S. Hiltner, *Preface to Pastoral Theology*, 68 v.

[29] H. Kohut, *The Analysis of the Self* (New York: International Universities Press, 1971); *The Restoration of the Self* (Madison: International Universities Press, 1977).

[30] H. Faber, *Pastoral Care and Clinical Training in America* (Arnhem: Van Loghum Slaterus, 1961).

[31] W. Zijlstra, *Klinisch pastorale vorming. Een voorlopige analyse van het leer- en groepsproces van zeven cursussen.*

Berger[32] in 1964. From then on the influence of the movement spread all over the Netherlands. Pastors were sent to the United States to be trained as supervisors, among them Alting van Geusau and Van der Klei. Several twelve-week training sessions were organized in the Netherlands, a supervisor training program was established, and a national council for clinical pastoral education was founded, based entirely on the American model and independent of the universities and of the churches. All this was greatly appreciated by the Americans and held up as an example to other countries, especially because the Dutch supervisors had a reputation for bridging the historical differences between the New Englanders and the New York group and bringing about a true synthesis between head and heart. That at least is how the Dutch efforts were seen by Charles E. Hall, former executive director of ACPE: "Dutch CPE was of both the head and the heart and an attempt to integrate the two".[33]

Meanwhile, CPE in America continued to evolve. Particularly during the late sixties and early seventies, American society was shaken by the protest movements of social critics who pressed for the restructuring of national and international relations, by human rights movements, women's movements, and the social movements of ethnic minorities. The churches were also changing in complex ways. On the one hand, America was taken unawares by the decline in church participation. On the other hand, a wind of change and renewal was blowing through the churches, bringing both 'resourcement' and aggiornamento. And, at the same time, charismatic and fundamentalist groups were flourishing as never before.

These developments confronted the ACPE with questions about its legitimacy, relevance, authenticity, ethical quality and theological identity. The question of legitimacy was implied in the objection brought against the ACPE to the effect that it was training pastors to be chaplains, that is, religious functionaries who, as in the feudal Middle Ages, helped to maintain and reinforce the status quo in the institutions in

---

[32] W. Berger, *Op weg naar empirische zielzorg. Notities over een reis langs enige pastorale vormingscentra in de Verenigde Staten* (Nijmegen: Dekker en van der Vegt, 1965).

[33] C.E. Hall, "Head and Heart. The Story of the Clinical Pastoral Education Movement," 200.

which they served. The question of relevance originated in doubts about whether clinical pastoral counseling, which the ACPE stood for, really contributed to the healing of people whose troubles were caused not (only) by individual-psychic but (also and above all) by social and societal factors. The question of authenticity had to do with whether the clinical pastoral movement was merely aimed at satisfying the narcissistic needs of the pastors instead of being motivated by an objective concern for and healing of the patients. The question of ethical quality was expressed in the suggestion that the clinical pastoral movement de facto was inspired by an anthropology based on so-called moral egoism, in which self-realization of the individual is seen as the highest criterion and in which costs are always weighed against benefits. From moral egoism to complete moral relativism is only a small step.[34] It is "the ethics of 'do your own thing'".[35] The question of theological identity, finally, was not a new one. From the beginning the New York group had been criticized for ostensibly sacrificing theology to other disciplines, such as Freud's depth psychology, Rogers' humanistic psychology or Kohut's object relations psychology of the self.[36] Now, however, the question was not merely whether theology had been marginalized or even eliminated, but whether the clinical pastoral movement was setting in motion processes which were contrary to and in conflict with the prophetic tradition of Christianity, as expressed in political theology and liberation theology.

How did the ACPE respond? It cannot be said that the clinical pastoral movement ignored these questions. On the contrary. Thus, in 1969 a conference was held on the theme of "Training a Ministry in the Seventies for a World of the Seventies and Beyond". The idea was to focus the attention of participants on the interaction between the individual, on the one hand, and the economic, political, social and cultural systems in which he or she exists, on the other. This led to the

---

[34] Cf. D. Browning, *Religious Thought and the Modern Psychologies* (Philadelphia: Fortress Press, 1987) 71v.; *A Fundamental Practical Theology. Descriptive and Strategic proposals* (Minneapolis: Fortress Press, 1991) 245-246.

[35] D. Browning, *The Moral Context of Pastoral Care* (Philadelphia: Fortress Press, 1976) 129.

[36] Cf. Wilson and P. Robinson, "Something Within Reaches Out: Multicultural Dialogues," *Journal of Supervision and Training in Ministry* 16 (1995) 170-195.

establishment of both the Pastoral Care Network for Social Responsibility and the Task Force on Public Issues.[37]

At the same time, however, one senses in the literature and in personal conversations a certain reserve when it comes to the question of whether the clinical pastoral movement took sufficiently seriously the aforementioned doubts about its legitimacy, relevance, authenticity, ethical quality and theological identity. This is true not only of those whose attitude toward this movement is fundamentally critical, but also of those who take a generally loyal view. The only thing that the movement did integrate is a systems theory approach which makes possible an understanding of the functioning of individuals and dyads within the system of the family. A striking example is Friedman's systems analysis of the family, which he expressly presents as beyond pastoral counseling and as a critique of the world of psychotherapy that has become specialized ad absurdum. This systems model not only gives the pastor tools to help families in his parish who need him, but also to function adequately in the family of which he himself is a part. Above all, it enables him to look at and deal with the parish as a network of families and, even more so, as a family in its own right.[38] But besides this application of the systems model to the family and the parish, the clinical pastoral movement has done little or nothing to give a scientifically founded accounting of the societal context in which it finds itself, let alone attempted to intervene in this context in a critical-prophetic manner. This is not to disregard the efforts of pioneers like Boisen and Clinebell. Boisen was clearly sociologically oriented, as is evident from his *Religion in Crisis and Custom*.[39] Boisen, however, came off worse in the debate over Freud's and Rogers' influence in the New York group, as described above. Clinebell made an attempt to transcend what he himself called the hyperindividualism of the clinical pastoral approach by seeking to

---

[37] C.E. Hall, "Head and Heart. The Story of the Clinical Pastoral Education Movement," 165.

[38] E.H. Friedman, *Generation to Generation. Family Process in Church and Synagoge* (New York: Harper, 1985); cf L.K. Graham, *Care of Persons, Care of Worlds. A Psychosystems Approach to Pastoral Care and Counseling* (Nashville: Abingdon Press, 1992).

[39] A. Boisen, *Religion in Crisis and Custom*.

place pastoral counseling in the context of the social institutions of the society and to orient it toward emancipation from racism, sexism, ageism, speciesism, nationalism, militarism, economic exploitation and political oppression.[40] But this list of societal wrongs is too long and Clinebell's treatment thereof too short to enable us truly to speak of a societal re-orientation. The foregoing is not to suggest that pastoral counseling is context-independent or context-free. On the contrary, pastoral counseling, as it de facto takes place in America and Europe, is influenced by the societal context of America and Europe, just as pastoral counseling in Africa is shaped by the societal context of Africa.[41] It is quite another matter, however, to ask whether and to what extent pastoral counseling can and will contribute in a purposive, effective and appropriate manner to emancipation from oppressive structures in these societal contexts. We must agree with Rodney Hunter, who notes that "only lip service [has been] paid to cultural, economic, and political aspects of human problems and the practical actions appropriate to addressing them".[42]

More interesting than the conclusion that the clinical pastoral movement has remained primarily individual-oriented is the attempt to explain that orientation. Explanations can provide a broader and deeper insight and clarify the conditions under which the phenomena in question occur. I see three possible explanations, which are mutually reinforcing.

The first explanation is a professional one. Because of the nature of the healing activity of which pastoral counseling consists and the rules that constitute it, such as attention, empathy, unconditional positive regard and acceptance, such counseling is aimed at restoring to health the individual person or at least the relationships in which individuals are caught up. Of course it can — and often is — the case that psychic and spiritual pain and suffering is caused at least partly by external factors that are part of the institutional context of the individual's life.

---

[40] H. Clinebell, *Basic Types of Pastoral Care and Counseling* (Nashville: Abingdon Press, 1966) 33.

[41] Cf. J. Masamba ma Mpolo and D. Nwachuku, *Pastoral Care and Counselling in Africa Today* (New York: Harper, 1991).

[42] R. Hunter, "The Therapeutic Tradition of Pastoral Care and Counseling," *Pastoral Care and Social Conflict*, eds. P. Couture and R. Hunter (Nashville: Abingdon Press, 1995) 17-31.

These, however, are not directly addressed in and through pastoral counseling. Nor can they be, since to do so requires other professional activities, methods and resources, such as those of social ministry, community building or church development. To seek to stretch the work of pastoral counseling to include critical-prophetic activities aimed at bringing about certain societal transformations is quite simply to miss the limited scope of pastoral counseling. Pastoral work is made up of more than pastoral counseling alone. It also includes for example the aforementioned tasks of social ministry, community building and church development, but also religious education, worship and preaching, mission, and spiritual direction.

The second explanation is an institutional one. It is possible that the clinical pastoral movement has been so strongly marked by the attempt to legitimate the work of the pastor in mental and general hospitals, relative to work of the (other) helpers in that setting, that the orientation toward parish and church were neglected. This orientation was not overly strong to begin with, and thus the critical regard from the parish and the church onto the rest of society and the societal institutions (including the hospital itself), was disregarded. This is the opinion of Rodney Hunter, who says, "It was perhaps inevitable that heavy pressure to legitimate themselves professionally vis-à-vis physicians and other health care professionals should build under such circumstances".[43] This strikes me as a plausible explanation, even though Hunter rightly adds that hospital chaplains simultaneously fulfilled and still fulfil a critical function by pursuing a personalistic and humanistic vision of the human being that stands in contrast to the objectifying and technocratic view of medical science.

The third explanation is theological. Hunter and Patton point out that the theology on which the clinical pastoral movement is based originates from two different sources, namely, Protestant liberalism and pietism. The first source, Protestant liberalism, emphasizes God's immanence in the world by virtue of his creation, humankind's capacity to make a substantial contribution to the liberation of the world, and the hope that the history of humanity and culture will be completed by God. This means that what is considered to be good and valuable

---

[43] R. Hunter, "The Therapeutic Tradition of Pastoral Care and Counseling," 17-31.

in the life of the individual and of society is regarded as the direct vehicle of God's grace, and there is not overly much concern about the flaws and fissures of evil and sin. Therefore, therapeutic methods that bring out the good in human beings and perform an eductive function, such as counseling methods, are sure to be positively received. Rogers' optimism about the potentiality of human flourishing is of a piece with this theological optimism. The second source, Protestant pietism, stresses the individual experience of God's grace, both in the feeling of God's personal presence and in the intimate sharing with and mutual support of fellow-believers through common prayer. Rogers' emphasis on the unconditional positive regard corresponds to this desire for experienced and emotionally felt intimate acceptance by God.[44]

These three factors together offer an explanation for the one-sidedness of the clinical pastoral movement. Because of the theological background (third factor) and the hospital setting in which it developed (second factor), it is directed principally toward professionally alleviating the pain and suffering of individual people (first factor), and thus does not and cannot be concerned primarily with emancipation from oppressive societal structures. Against this background, Mette's criticism that the clinical pastoral movement, by neglecting the societal context, threatens to lead to the establishment of a new sort of Salvation Army, must be seen as an unwarranted attack.[45]

In fact, two other phenomena show that there were indeed developments in the clinical pastoral movement that moved beyond the setting of the hospital, particularly the mental hospital, and were explicitly directed at the larger context of church and society.

The first of these is that, in the sixties, programs were already being developed in parish-based centers for clinical pastoral education, for example, in Houston, Texas; Greenville, Pennsylvania; St. Paul,

---

[44] R. Hunter and J. Patton, "The Therapeutic Tradition's Theological and Ethical Commitments Viewed Through Its Pedagogical Practices: A Tradition in Transition," *Pastoral Care and Social Conflict*, eds. P. Couture and R. Hunter (Nashville: Abingdon Press, 1995) 32-43.

[45] N. Mette, *Theorie der Praxis. Wissenschaftliche und methodologische Untersuchungen zur Theorie- Praxis-Problematik innerhalb der Praktischen Theologie* (Düsseldorf: Patmos Verlag, 1978), 233; Cf. G. Heitink, "Pastoraat in Nederland. Een overzicht," *Praktische Theologie* 13, no. 5 (1986) 535-550.

Minnesota; Littleton, Colorado, and Atlanta, Georgia. As Hall notes, "Those who supervised parish programs claimed that such a setting provided some experiences to theological students and pastors that the programs in health care institutions could not provide".[46] Ten years later, Browning[47] also argued for the establishment of links between the clinical pastoral education movement, on the one hand, and the churches and congregations, on the other. Hunter and Patton are currently calling for a further extension of the clinical method into congregations, and the establishment of more 'teaching parishes' in which pastoral volunteers can also receive training. They note that certain methods ought to be further developed, such as the analysis of parochial and ecclesial systems in multicultural contexts, while the use of other methods should be reduced, such as the "intense and continuous exposure to crisis of hospital-based CPE programs".[48]

The second phenomenon that needs to be noted is that some CPE centers have developed programs that are centered not on the problems of patients in hospitals nor on those of parishioners in congregations, but rather on the members of the society's underclass and social outcasts. Thus, there are so-called urban CPE centers that offer programs in the setting of shelters for drug addicts and alcoholics, prostitutes, victims of rape and assault, juvenile delinquents and the homeless.[49] For example, six theological schools in Chicago established an urban CPE whose mission is "theological and pastoral formation and competence in the path of public ministry." One of the aims is "to participate and to learn about ministry both to the marginalized and to those who hold power." To this end the students are required to "discern and maintain a balance between ministry to individuals and ministry to structures." In 1995 two groups of six students took part in the program.[50]

---

[46] C.E. Hall, "Head and Heart. The Story of the Clinical Pastoral Education Movement," 164.

[47] D. Browning, *The moral Context of Pastoral Care*.

[48] R. Hunter and J. Patton, "The Therapeutic Tradition's Theological and Ethical Commitments Viewed Through Its Pedagogical Practices: A Tradition in Transition," 42.

[49] C.E. Hall, "Head and Heart. The Story of the Clinical Pastoral Education Movement," 163-164.

[50] ACTS URBAN CPE, Association of Chicago Theological Schools Urban Clinical Pastoral Education. *Papers: Mission Statement; Composition and Functional Roles; Historal Outline* (Chicago: Chicago University Press, 1989-1996).

This raises the question of what the word clinical means in this context. The question is not a new one. It was already at the root of a discussion between the New England group and the New York group in the fifties. During a discussion between members of the two groups, Paul Johnson of the New England group asked whether clinical training could only take place in the hospital or whether it could also be held in a prison or a parish. Ernie Bruder of the New York group replied that he disagreed with Boisen that the hospital was the only suitable setting for clinical training, and that he himself would be amenable to judicial and church settings. Fred Kuether, also of the New York group, commented: "There are outpatient clinics. In that sense the definition of the term clinical doesn't have to stand...I think the thing that is important, as I find it, is not whether or not it is in institutions or in the community, but again it goes back to the quality of supervision." Carl Plack of the Lutheran Advisory Council noted at the time that "then the social-work orientation kind of thing could be a pattern".[51] In that case, the term, clinical pastoral education, comes to mean nothing more than supervised ministry, as will be discussed in more detail further on (chapter IV, section 4), and one wonders whether it is not better to avoid misunderstandings and call things by their proper names.

2. Beyond Managerialism

As pointed out earlier, MacIntyre, Hough and Cobb, as well as Bellah and others, distinguish between the therapist, who functions primarily in the private domain, and the manager, who operates in the public domain. This division, i.e., between the therapeutic and the managerial model, is also encountered in the education for ministry programs, as I noted above, albeit always in combination with aspects of other models, i.e., the kerygmatic and ecclesial models.

In this section I confine myself to the description of the managerial model that has influenced curriculum development within theological schools since the 1960s. From a material perspective, this model is

---

[51] C.E. Hall, "Head and Heart. The Story of the Clinical Pastoral Education Movement," 82.

concerned with guiding, leading and sustaining, in a scientifically and technically warranted manner, processes that take place in the congregation, and with achieving the goals that this congregation has set for itself in as efficient and effective a manner as possible. The pastor is seen as a congregational manager and the education for ministry program is seen as the system of learning experiences that adequately prepares the pastor for this managerial task. From a formal perspective, this managerial model is based on a vision of professionalism that is in turn founded in what can be called science-based technical rationality.

In the following I will seek to describe how this model of the science-based professional has been and continues to be applied to the work of the pastor. For the purpose of the present discussion, I will look first of all at two major professions, namely that, of medical top specialist and business top specialist, because, consciously or unconsciously, these function as a sort of ideal for the professionalization movements of all other professions, including that of the pastor. After that I turn my attention to the 'minor professions' of other medical doctors and teachers. Finally I come to speak of the profession of the pastor and pastoral professionalization. All of this will lead to the conclusion that, even when the model of the science-based profession is stringently applied to the work of the pastor, the fit between the managerial model and the work of the pastor is really only moderate. Nevertheless, the application of this model raises so many problems and questions that we need to look for a model that is beyond managerialism, as the title of this subsection indicates.

The approach of science-based technical rationality that forms the foundation for managerialism contains a number of assumptions. The first is that there exists a body of knowledge that is relevant to the solution of societal problems. The knowledge making up this body is valid knowledge because it has been scientifically verified or at least corroborated by empirical and experimental research. This knowledge is also specialized knowledge, specifically directed at carefully documented classes of cases. Moreover, it is also standardized knowledge. The specialized knowledge can be adequately applied with the help of standards that have been established for this purpose on the basis of scientific research. Therefore, a great deal of energy is invested in the solid codification and clear presentation of this scientific, specialized and standardized knowledge. Another assumption is that from the fundamental knowledge obtained through fundamental scientific research, applied knowledge can also be derived by way of applied scientific research. Fundamental knowledge is relevant to fundamental, long-term problems, while applied knowledge is important for short and medium-term problems. Still another assumption is that, from this body of knowledge, it is possible to derive scientifically-based skills with the help of which societal problems can be tackled. To that end, lists of skills are matched to lists of problems that need to be solved by professionals. Yet another assumption is that these skills need to be taught and appropriated in the various professional training programs in laboratory situations specially designed for this purpose and, after that, in carefully controlled practice situations. It is also assumed that the true professional has learned to select the right skill or group of skills for the particular problems with which he is confronted, to apply these in a standardized manner and, thereby, to solve the problems. The last assumption, finally, is that the true professional possesses the right motivational attitude toward service to deal in a standardized fashion with the problems brought to him by his clients. All of these assumptions together can be called the epistemology of technical rationality. This epistemology is emphatically present in the major professions of the medical top specialist and business top specialist.[52]

The source of this technical rationality is twofold. First, it arises from a particular scientific theory, that of positivism, which can be said to have originated with Auguste Comte. Drawing on the ideas of Condorcet and Saint-Simon, Comte holds that the history of humanity can be divided into three stages: the theological, the metaphysical and, finally, the scientific. And, inspired by the English empiricism of Locke, Hume, James Mill and John Stuart Mill, he believes that this scientific stage is purely positive. The word positive here refers to various contrasting pairs, of which only the first element is always seen as positive: factual versus imaginary, certain versus indeterminate,

---

[52] Cf. D. Schön, *The Reflective Practicioner. How Professionals Think in Action* (New York: Harper Collins, 1983), 21-30.

precise versus vague, useful versus vain, relative versus absolute.[53] This (limited) concept of science also implies a kind of faith, namely, faith in the evolution of history and of society. Science gives persons the tools not only to master nature, but also to master society. And this mastery is important because it can be used to systematically and methodically improve individual and collective life. Therefore, the encyclopedia of the sciences includes not only mathematics and astronomy, physics and chemistry, but also biology and, especially, sociology. This last science which, like all science, is concerned with the relation between observation and prediction, can be used to systematically better social, political and moral life.

An important instrument for influencing individual and societal life in a progressive manner through science, in the view of the representatives of positivism, is education and, above all, formal schooling. This brings us to the second source of technical rationality, which has to do with the changes undergone by the universities in the second half of the nineteenth and the first half of the twentieth century. The way for those changes was paved by the establishment of the university of Berlin in 1810 by Wilhelm von Humboldt who, incidentally, took only sixteen months to complete this process. This marked the end of the medieval university which, in Germany, did not survive the Napoleonic era and was now replaced by a university in which the ideals of the Enlightenment were put into practice. The difference consists in that, in the Humboldtian university, research is central, and the instruction which the students receive is research-based and research-oriented. By contrast, in the *gymnasium*, or academically-oriented secondary school, only the results of the research are passed on to the students, even though this should nevertheless be done in a critical spirit.[54] It is important to emphasize the word 're-search', because the very essence of the Enlightenment, after all, was that it broke with the notion that knowledge is based on 'auctoritas', that is, the authority of the author and his/her text. Regardless of what assertions are made, what positions are taken and how they are expressed, they must always

[53] J. Habermas, *Erkenntnis und Interesse. Mit einem neuen Nachwort* (Frankfurt: Suhrkamp, 1975) 95-96.
[54] Cf. Th. Wilhelm, *Theorie der Schule* (Stuttgart: Metzler, 1969) 233-237.

be re-searched and, in such a way that the research procedures can be re-peated publicly, e.g., by any researcher, and the results re-confirmed. With that the university emancipated itself from the influence of the church and other tradition-bound institutions. Moreover, that academic freedom, consisting of the freedom to learn as well as the freedom to teach, was guaranteed by the state. While the English university system with its colleges, and the French system with its academies remained intact, the universities in Germany and in a number of surrounding countries, including the Netherlands and, above all, some time later, in America, came to be structured on the Berlin model. This was already true of the University of Michigan, but above all of Johns Hopkins University which, along with the English system of colleges, would have a profound influence on university life in America. The view of science that predominated at the new universities, as in Berlin, was that of positivism, in which the only true knowledge was considered to be knowledge based on the two 'positive' criteria of empiricism and rationality.[55] And the price that the professional schools had to pay in order to be incorporated into these universities and not be considered as second-class, tertiary education institutions, was the acceptance of the 'positive' criteria of empiricism and rationality. The professional schools, consequently, developed in the direction of technical rationality-based professionalism. As I said earlier, this form of professionalism was founded on the assumption of a hierarchically descending chain from fundamental empirical science, through applied science, skills and practicum, to the concrete professional practice.[56]

To what extent does the epistemology of technical rationality, of which we have described a number of characteristics, accord in fact with the actual work of the managerial professional, and to what extent does it form an ideology that legitimates the position of power of the managerial professional but obscures the actual reality of his or her work?[57] To what extent does the descending hierarchy from fundamental research

[55] D.H. Kelsey, *To Understand God Truly. What's Theological About A Theological School*, 78-85.

[56] D. Schön, *The Reflective Practicioner. How Professionals Think in Action*, 36.

[57] H. Kunneman, *Van theemutscultuur naar walkman-ego. Contouren van postmoderne individualiteit* (Amsterdam, Meppel: Boom, 1996) 229-233.

through applied research and skills analysis to the application of skills in concrete situations actually occur? Does it apply to the same degree in all of the major professions? Perhaps this question can be answered primarily in the affirmative for the top medical specialist and the top business specialist, but this is not true for the physician in general practice and even less so for minor professions such as town planning, education, therapeutic work, social work and pastoral work. Inasmuch as the term ideology has to do with the legitimation of power, the difference between 'major' and 'minor' professions is in itself revealing. The major professions are said to have greater societal power and prestige not only because they satisfy needs that are rated as more important by society than are the needs that are met by the minor professions, but also because they are a more perfect embodiment of the epistemology of technical rationality.[58]

The epistemology of technical rationality does not generally apply to the 'minor professions', including that of the pastor, at least not in the sense of the hierarchically descending chain from fundamental empirical research to concrete professional practice. The 'minor' professions simply do not possess a codified body of fundamental-scientific knowledge from which, by way of applied knowledge, the necessary skills are derived, which are then applied to concrete cases in a standardized manner. Moreover, the skills that the minor professions need to master are not determined on the basis of a body of knowledge that is stored, or is supposed to be stored, in the universities, but rather by analyzing the functions that these professionals fulfil in society and the tasks they carry out as part of this function, and deriving from this information the requisite skills. The overriding factor here is not science, but society. This does not mean, however, that science has no role to play. Insofar as the model of managerialism is applied to the aforementioned minor professions, what happens is that the analysis of the societal functions and tasks, as well as the skills derived from this analysis, are scientifically legitimated, as much as possible, after the fact. The epistemology of technical rationality is used as a facade, as it were; science does not act primarily as a source before the fact but chiefly as a justification and legitimation after the fact. In other

---

[58] D. Schön, *The Reflective Practicioner. How Professionals Think in Action*, 23.

words, the managerial model performs a different function in the 'major' professions of medical top specialist and business top specialist than in the 'minor' professions. In these 'major' professions, the epistemology of technical rationality plays primarily a deductive role, in the 'minor' professions primarily a reconstructive role.

I will demonstrate this using the example of three 'minor' professions, i.e., those of the general medical doctor, the primary school teacher and, last but not least, the pastor. In these three professions science plays a reconstructive rather than a deductive role, as I will show.

My picture of the profession of the general medical doctor is based on the situation in the Netherlands. There, the Landelijke Huisartsenvereniging (National Association of General Practitioners) began in the 1970s to draw up a 'job description' for the general practitioner. The question was, how does one come up with such a job description? From what is it derived? The Association did not go directly to the university practitioners of medical science, but decided to observe closely what general practitioners actually did in the course of their work, to describe their actions and then to organize these into categories. The result was a description of the function of the general practitioner in terms of the helping process, in which the physician assists people in making choices in order to promote or maintain their physical, mental and social well-being from the medical perspective. The main steps in this helping process are: admission, problem clarification, hypotheses, medical examination, treatment and referral. Once the function was described, the tasks that the general practitioner performs in the framework of this function could be brought into the picture. The draft of the report in which these tasks were specifically described was submitted to seven groups of general practitioners, and was modified and completed on the basis of their experiences and findings. Finally, the report, which lists a total of 210 tasks, was unanimously approved.[59]

Since then the Association has been busy converting these tasks into a list of skills that can be used in the training of general practitioners. The prospective general practitioner is given a test that measures his

---

[59] Landelijke Huisartsenvereniging, *Basistakenpakket van de huisarts* (Vademecum Juni 1987).

or her knowledge of these skills. Interviews with people posing as patients are recorded on video in order to determine to what extent the future physician is able to apply these skills. And, finally, the application of the skills is tested in interviews with real patients.[60]

Notably, neither the job description nor the tasks or skills of the general practitioner were taken directly from medical science, but rather were arrived at through the description and analysis of the professional helping process as it actually takes place. Furthermore, the authority to make a final decision on the list of tasks did not rest with the representatives of science, although they were frequently consulted and although the reports in question were furnished with a scientific justification, but rather with the association of the general practitioners themselves.

My example of the primary school teacher is also drawn from the Netherlands. In response to the policy of the Dutch Ministry of Education and Science as laid down in the report 'Vitaal leraarschap' (The Vital Teaching Profession)[61], two umbrella organizations for primary instruction at Catholic schools published a report on the function and tasks of the teachers at these schools.[62] The work of the teacher was described in terms of three domains: the domain of the teacher as a professional generally, the domain of education, and the domain of the school for primary education. Within these three domains 40 tasks were identified, consisting of a total of 210 subtasks. In a later report these 40 tasks are combined with 38 general skills and 234 subject-specific skills, for a total of 272 skills.[63]

Here again one notes that the description of the teacher's function, tasks and skills was not produced by the respective scientific disciplines,

[60] *De begeleiding in de praktijk. Bijlage 4. Landelijk evaluatieformulier voor huisartsopleiders.* Nijmeegs Universitair Huisartseninstituut (NUHI), Nijmegen.

[61] *Vitaal Leraarschap, Beleidreactie naar aanleiding van het rapport 'Een beroep met een perspectief' van de Commissie Toekomst Leraarschap* (Ministerie van Onderwijs en Wetenschappen, Den Haag, 1993).

[62] *Beroepsprofiel leraar primair onderwijs op katholieke scholen.* Rapport in opdracht van de Bond van Besturen van Katholieke Scholen voor Basisonderwijs en de Katholieke Onderwijsvakorganisatie (Uitgave Vereniging Samenwerkende Landelijke Pedagogische Centra, Den Haag, Rijswijk, 1994).

[63] *Startbekwaamheden leraar primair onderwijs.* Concept-rapport in opdracht van het Ministerie van Onderwijs, Cultuur en Wetenschappen. (Uitgave Vereniging Samenwerkende Landelijke Pedagogische Centra, 1995).

although they were frequently consulted, but rather by the professionals in the field and their organizations. My thesis is that science here does not function primarily in a deductive sense as a sort of reservoir filled with a fundamental body of knowledge, from which functions, functional aspects, tasks, subtasks, general skills and specialized skills are derived, but rather in a primarily reconstructive sense to legitimate after the fact the results of the description and analysis of the actual work of the 'minor' professionals in question.

The same holds true for the profession of pastor. Here, too, the function or functions that the pastor performs, the tasks he or she carries out and the competencies, including skills, that he or she must possess, are determined on the basis of the description and analysis of the pastor's actual activities and operations, and not derived from scientific premises. To this we need to add the element of 'valuation'. The actual activities and operations are not only recorded, but sometimes also rated according to their importance. Finally, a last element is that not only the pastors themselves are asked about their experiences and findings with regard to the functions and tasks they perform; in some cases the observations and evaluations of the people entrusted to the pastor's care, that is the lay people, are directly incorporated into the study.

In the following I give a general account of the results of some research projects that sought to give an empirical reconstruction of the function or functions, tasks and competencies, including skills, of the pastor. The purpose is to make it clear that science, insofar as it is involved in the study of the function or functions, tasks and competencies of the pastor, plays a reconstructive and not a deductive role. But that is not all. At the same time I wish to show that this scientific-reconstructive approach, as indispensable as it may be, fundamentally fails to provide an adequate description and understanding of the actual work of the pastor.

The first research project that I report on here dates from the 1960s and was designed to map out the functions of Catholic and Reformed pastors in the Netherlands. The researchers asked a number of pastors to keep notes on what they did every day for several months. After classifying the results, a list of 38 activities was produced. These included, for example, visiting old people, visiting sick people, visiting widows, visiting people living alone, visiting people who no longer come to church, helping the dying, preparing sermons, organizing discussion groups, taking part in interchurch activities, seeking to resolve problems between members of the parish. These activities were logically grouped into nine more or less classic areas of work: individual pastoral care, liturgy and worship, study and meditation, catechesis, evangelization, congregational meetings, regional meetings, non-pastoral visits, organizational and administrative work. In this way the functions and tasks of the pastor were empirically described; in this case, as noted, the pastors themselves were the informants. Afterwards these lists were submitted to about 150 Reformed and 150 Catholic pastors and to about 300 Reformed and 300 Catholic church members. The following activities were consistently rated as the top three in terms of their importance: liturgy, preaching, and individual pastoral care.[64]

The second research project concerns the functions and tasks of pastors from the Netherlands Reformed Church and the Reformed Churches in the Netherlands. The researchers began with a list of 20 activities that had been obtained from a previous study. This list comprised the following activities. Under the heading, liturgy: presiding at the liturgy, preparing liturgy, working together with volunteers in preparing liturgy; under the heading, individual pastoral care: home visits and visits to the sick, visits to the aged, other pastoral contacts, working together with volunteers on pastoral work; under the heading, instruction and education: catechesis, discussion groups, religious education, working with volunteers in instruction and education; under the heading, reflection: spirituality, study; under the heading, organization and administration: inside the parish, outside the parish; under the heading, other activities: diaconate, church and society, ecumenism, collegial contacts, publicity. The pastors were asked to indicate how much time they spent on each of these activities in an average week in the winter. The top three activities that emerged from this study, in terms of the percentage of time accorded to them, were: liturgy (approximately 25%), individual pastoral care (approximately 25%), and instruction and education (approximately 20%). The other groups

[64] J. Fabery de Jonge, W. Berger, C. Boekestijn and J. van der Lans, *Zielzorger in Nederland. Een onderzoek naar positie, taak en ambt van de pastor* (Meppel: Boom, 1968).

of activities scored significantly lower (10% or less). The researchers carried out several factor analyses on the pastors' data in an attempt to discover a structure in their activities and thus to contribute to the job description of the pastor. In these analyses the statistical criteria could not be met in such a way as to be able to show clear factoral structures. The researchers were unable to go beyond a simple enumeration of tasks.[65]

The third research project in which pastoral functions, tasks and competencies (expressly consisting of more than just skills) were studied, was commissioned by the Association of Theological Schools in the United States and Canada. It is entitled the Readiness for Ministry Project, and was started in 1973. The objective of the study was to identify the tasks and competencies that are considered important for the work of the pastor. To this end, questionnaires were given to five groups of respondents, namely, theologians, pastors, senior seminarians, denominational officers and lay constituents. The study consisted of three phases. In the first phase, approximately 1200 people were asked the 'critical incident' question. The respondents were asked to recall a specific moment when an ordained pastor was either clearly effective or clearly ineffective. At the same time they were asked to express a judgement about the incident and to give the reasons for that judgement. From the analysis of both the results of the study and the literature on the practice of ministry and the related helping professions, a list of thousands of activities was drawn up. Based on that list, in the second phase of the study a questionnaire containing about 850 specific selected activities was sent to approximately 2000 people, about half of whom were pastors and the other half laity. These people were asked to rate the 850 items according to their importance, and then to correct and complete the list with other items. The analysis of the results of the second phase resulted in a list of 444 activities. These were incorporated into the questionnaire for the third phase, in which 5131 randomly selected persons participated, and of which 4895 completed questionnaires could be used. Conducting cluster analysis, the 444 activities were grouped into 64 clusters. It is interesting to see

---

[65] J.A. Keizer, *Aan tijd gebonden. Over motivatie en arbeidsvreugde van predikanten* (Den Haag: Boekencentrum, 1988) 59-62.

what the top nine clusters were, that is, the clusters with the highest rating: "service without regard for acclaim," "personal integrity," "Christian example," "responsible, skillful functioning," "community building," "perceptive counselling," "theological intelligence demonstrated in communication," "handling stressful situations" and "acknowledgment of limitations." Next, a second-order factor analysis was performed on these clusters, resulting in 11 factors.[66] In a ranking order from more to less important, these factors are: "Open, Affirmative Style," "Caring for Persons under Stress," "Congregational Leadership," "Theologian in Life and Thought," "Ministry from Personal Commitment of Faith," "Development of Koinonia and Worship," "Denominational Awareness and Collegiality," "Ministry to Community and World," "Priestly-Sacramental Ministry," as well as two negative factors: "Privatistic, Legalistic Style" and "Disqualifying Personal and Behavioral Characteristics".[67] On the basis of further analyses, four different models of ministry, with four different emphases, were identified: spiritual, sacramental-liturgical, social action, and combined (spiritual/sacramental, spiritual/social, sacramental/social). These four models appeared to cut across the divisions between the 47 denominations from which the respondents came.[68]

In the eighties, the Association of Theological Schools in the United States and Canada updated the Readiness for Ministry Project as part of the Profiles for Ministry project by administering a shorter version of the Readiness for Ministry survey along with a few new items. The

[66] D. Schuller, M. Brekke and M. Strommen, *Readiness for Ministry. Volume 1. Criteria.* (Vandalia: The Association of Theological Schools in the United States and Canada, 1975); M. Brekke, "How Criteria for Assessing Readiness for Ministry Were Identified and Analyzed," *Ministry in America. A Report and Analysis, based on an In-Depth Survey of 47 Denominations in the United States and Canada, with Interpretation bij 18 Experts*, eds. D. Schuller, P. Strommen and M. Brekke (San Francisco: Harper and Row, 1980) 525-563.

[67] D. Aleshire, "Eleven Major Areas of Ministry," *Ministry in America. A Report and Analysis, based on an In-Depth Survey of 47 Denominations in the United States and Canada, With Interpretation by 18 Experts*, eds. D. Schuller, P. Strommen and M. Brekke (San Francisco: Harper and Row, 1980) 23-53.

[68] P. Strommen, "Models of Ministry," *Ministry in America. A Report and Analysis, based on an In-Depth Survey of 47 Denominations in the United States and Canada, With Interpretation by 18 Experts*, eds. D. Schuller, P. Strommen and M. Brekke (San Francisco: Harper and Row, 1980) 54-89.

result was surprising in a certain sense, because the clusters and factors identified differed only in minor respects from those of the previous survey. Moreover, the ratings on the scales based on the clusters and factors also differed from those of the previous survey only in details. In other words, there was no sign of time-related trends or fashions; the patterns were stable. On the basis of these findings, two groups of assessment instruments and interpretative resources were developed: one for entering seminary students and one for graduating seminarians or pastors. For the first group, a casebook containing 24 cases, followed by a total of 484 statements, was put together, along with a design for an oral interview with a series of questions. For the second group, in addition to a casebook and an interview design, a field observation form with 116 statements was developed, to be completed by persons who have had the opportunity to observe the candidate while functioning as a pastor.[69]

How did the clinical pastoral movement respond to the inductive-empirical investigation of the functions, tasks and competencies of the pastor? Did the project fit into the movement's vision of the pastor, or did the clinical pastoral educators dismiss the study as a form of technical-rationality-based managerialism? It appears that, initially, the Association of Clinical Pastoral Education (ACPE) took a positive view of the study. In 1982 the chairman of the Association's research committee reported on a joint initiative undertaken with the director of the Readiness for Ministry Project to set up an Expectations of Ministry Project, designed to determine empirically which tasks, in the view of the members of the ACPE, the pastor must perform and which competencies he or she must possess. About 400 items from the Readiness for Ministry Project were supplemented with statements from the ACPE for a total of 476 items. These were incorporated into a questionnaire that was completed by approximately 350 members of the ACPE, representing nearly 30 church/denominational groups. The analysis of the data was performed using the analysis structure of the 64 clusters in the Readiness Project. The responses were further

---

[69] D. Aleshire, "ATS Profiles of Ministry Project," in *Clergy Assessment and career development*, eds. R. Hunt, J. Hinkle and H.N. Malony (Nashville: Abingdon Press, 1990) 97-103.

analyzed by means of T-tests for differences based on age, sex and
CPE-status. The differences were also compared with the results of
the Readiness Project. To give one example, which should no longer
come as any surprise, it was found that the clinical pastoral educators
appeared to be more focussed on the needs of individuals than of
communities. For this reason, the interpretation portion asked whether
the individualistic focus was blinding ACPE members to social justice.[70]

The Expectations project led in 1983 to the establishment of an
instrument developed especially for the clinical centers: the Clinical
Ministry Assessment Profile (CMAP). From the 64 clusters of the
Readiness Project, those clusters that were found to be the most important (rated 6.0 or higher on a seven-point scale) were selected. The
result was an instrument with 26 clusters, comprising a total of 80
items. These 26 clusters were classified into eight major areas: ministry to the religious community, ministry to the community and world,
ministry to persons under stress, the pastor as theologian and thinker,
the pastor's personal commitment of faith, the pastor as leader, positive characteristics of the pastor as a person, negative characteristics
of the pastor as a person.[71]

What tentative conclusions can we draw from all this? From the
research projects discussed here, the point that I raised earlier is clearly
apparent. The description of the functions, tasks and competencies of
the pastor is not derived from the premises of the scientific knowledge
that is acquired at the universities, as demanded by the epistemology
of technical rationality that forms the basis of the model of managerial professionalism. Science plays not a deductive but rather a reconstructive role, which is to say that the researchers closely observed and
analyzed the activities the pastor actually performs and introduced a
structure into what they observed. In several projects they also asked
respondents to rate these activities, so that insight was obtained into
the importance attached to them. Some projects also explicitly took
into account the judgement of the people entrusted to the pastor's care,

[70] G. Rowatt, "What does ACPE expect of ministry," *Journal of Pastoral Care*,
36, no. 2 (1982) 147-159.

[71] G. Fitchett and G. Gray, "Evaluating the Outcome of Clinical Pastoral Education:
A Test of the Clinical Ministry Assessment Profile," *Journal of Supervision and Training in Ministry* 15 (1994) 3-22.

the lay people in the parishes. Finally — and this is important to show that the therapeutic model and the managerial model are not mutually exclusive — there also appears to be an interest on the part of the Association of Clinical Pastoral Education in this approach to pastoral professionalization.

The next step is the use of this kind of scientific study for educational goals, in particular with a view to educational evaluation within the education for ministry program. Some examples do exist of this type of use, though they are still infrequent. At the same time this gives me an opportunity to describe the criticism that gradually came to be made against this kind of study and certainly against this sort of educational evaluation study. It is precisely this criticism that indicates that we need to find another model of education for the ministry, one that is beyond managerialism, but that does not throw overboard the positive aspects of the managerial model.

Despite the fact that the CMAP instrument gave the ACPE a research vehicle developed especially for clinical pastoral education, there are only three published studies in which this instrument was actually used.[72] One of these three studies had to do with the administering of a pre- test and post-test with respect to trainings in the context of clinical pastoral education. A so-called quasi-experimental design was chosen for this purpose which did provide for a pre-test/post-test set-up, but — regrettably enough, as the researchers themselves report — did not include a control group, making it impossible

---

[72] This is not to say that no other empirical studies have been carried out in the context of clinical pastoral education. Thus, Derrickson found 136 articles that give an account of measurements of changes in the framework of clinical trainings. In 39 studies, which are described in these 136 articles, 51 different standardized tests or instruments are used, especially the Minnesota Multiphase Personality Inventory. However, these tests are oriented toward general personality changes in the intrapersonal and interpersonal domain, and inasmuch as they are concerned with competencies and skills, the focus is on general skills of communication and listening, rather than on the specifically pastoral context, objectives and content of the pastor's competencies and skills (Derrickson 1990). Since then several other studies have been published. Two of these focus on self-actualization and professional confidence, one in conjunction with depression (VandeCreek/Valentino 1991a), and the other with death (VandeCreek/Valentino 1991b). Another study looked at five subjects: maternal and paternal bonding, self-esteem, death anxiety, depression, and working alliance with the supervisor (VandeCreek/Glockner 1993). None of these studies, however, made use of the CAMP instrument.

to determine to what extent the differences between the pre-test and
post-test are attributable to the influence of the CPE training: the one-
group pre-test — post-test design.[73] The CMAP instrument was used
in this study, in which 33 participants took part, for two different pur-
poses. The first was to determine differences between the pastoral
skills and attitudes of the participants at the beginning and after the
completion of training, using the CMAP instrument. In addition, the
participant's supervisor as well as two peers, selected by the participant, were asked to fill out the instrument for the participant in question after the end of the training. The differences on 16 of the 26 pre-
test and post-test scales were significant (p œ .05). It is interesting that
the supervisors were generally positive about the participants at the
end of CPE, but roughly saw them at the level at which the participants saw themselves at the beginning, whereas the peers were more
positive than the supervisors, but less positive than the participants
themselves. The second objective of the study was to establish some
statistical properties of the CMAP instrument through the use of
item measure analysis and item fit analysis. Both analyses led to relatively positive but tentative conclusions with regard to the statistical
quality of the instrument, with the comment that research would have
to be conducted on a larger population in order to come to definitive
conclusions.[74]

The fact that the CMAP instrument is based on solid empirical
survey research on pastoral tasks and competencies in the Readiness
Project does not, of course, render the use of other instruments redundant. I therefore refer here to another study that concerns the measurement of increasing pastoral competence as a result of participation
in clinical pastoral education programs. This study used the Personal
Information Form, consisting of a list of 20 items, which Presbyterian
ministers complete when looking for a new church. These items have
to do with worship leadership, preaching, sermon preparation, administration of the sacraments, special services, spiritual development of

---

[73] Th. Cook and D. Campbell, *Quasi-Experimenation. Design & Analysis Issues
for Field Settings* (Boston: Houghton, 1979) 99-103.

[74] G. Fitchett and G. Gray, "Evaluating the Outcome of Clinical Pastoral Education:
A Test of the Clinical Ministry Assessment Profile," *Journal of Supervision and Training in Ministry*, 15 (1994) 3-22.

members, congregational visitation, congregational fellowship, counseling, planning local mission programs, mission beyond the local
community, development of educational programs, support of education, teaching responsibilities, involvement in community social problems, ecumenical and interfaith activities, communication, administrative planning and leadership, evaluation of programs, and pastor's
self-evaluation. To this the researchers added an additional, concerning
"the ability to reflect theologically on everyday pastoral experiences
and life events." The participants' responses were statistically analyzed
and, from the results, the director of the CPE centre concluded that
the CPE programs should be modified so as to offer students more
opportunities to lead worship, participate in administration and study
community issues. Although — as the researchers themselves pointed
out — objections can be made to the retrospective character of the
study (the participants were asked to recall after the training to what
degree they possessed the competencies in question before the training), the only point that I wish to emphasize here is that assessment
measures have been found to be relevant and that the results have been
used to improve programs.[75]

Within the frame of reference of ACPE, studies of this sort are
exceptions. When the CMAP instrument became available in 1983,
there was at first a great deal of interest in it. In 1983, over one thousand test booklets were processed, in 1984, half that number, in 1988,
only twenty-five booklets, and, in 1990, the test was no longer available.
In addition to various technical and practical circumstances, there was
a growing resistance to this sort of educational evaluation research in
the context of education for ministry, and certainly in clinical pastoral
education.[76] Of what did and does this criticism consist, and how ought
it to be assessed?

The criticism is expressed most clearly in the contrast between quantitative educational evaluation research, as seen in the above-mentioned
studies, and qualitative evaluation procedures, which are used by many

[75] P. Derrickson, "What does CPE Contribute tot Pastoral Competence?" *Journal
of Supervision and Training in Ministry*, 16 (1995) 137-143.
[76] G. Fitchett and G. Gray, "Evaluating the Outcome of Clinical Pastoral Education:
A Test of the Clinical Ministry Assessment Profile," *Journal of Supervision and
Training in Ministry*, 15 (1994) 17.

centers for clinical pastoral education. Patton, for example, expressly refers to a Clinical Pastoral Education Perspective on the issue of clergy assessment. And, from this point of view, clergy assessment equals clergy self-evaluation based on relational experience. The structures that are available for this self-evaluation are the admission interview, the contract of learning, and the midterm and final evaluations. The relational experiences on which the self-evaluation is based appear to be strongly authority-oriented. They are: experiences with authorities, with peers, and with those for whom the pastor is an authority. These experiences are discussed and clarified in an open and narratively structured interview. The distance between the CPE perspective and the quantitative-empirical approach is clearly expressed in this following statement: "In emphasizing the importance of the candidate's self-evaluation, this interview model attempts to deemphasize the subject-object dichotomy and to emphasize peership — or at least potential peership — between the candidate and the evaluator".[77]

The criticism of the quantitative educational evaluation research, in my view, is not merely a matter of educational misgivings, but is, consciously or unconsciously, the product of experiences and insights that go much deeper. To elucidate this I return to the *leitmotiv* that I tried to bring out in Chapter I. There I stated that pastoral practice is increasingly characterized by ambivalence and uncertainty, owing to the complexity and multidimensionality of the questions, problems and challenges with which the pastor is confronted. This ambivalence and uncertainty are further reinforced by the dynamic of the many religious changes taking place at the macrolevel of the society, the mesolevel of the church and the microlevel of the individual. However, this complexity and this dynamic are not characteristic only of the practice of the pastor today, but also of the practices of the two other professions we examined earlier: the general practitioner and the teacher. Generally speaking, the professions which consist at their core of social interaction and communication with other people, are

---

[77] J. Patton, "Self-Evaluation Through Relational Experience," *Clergy Assessment and Career Development*, eds. R. Hunt, J. Hinkle and H. Malony (Nashville: Abingdon Press, 1990) 123-128.

marked by increasing levels of complexity and an increasingly complex dynamic.[78]

The difference is that both the general practitioner and the teacher perform rather strictly formulatable functions under rather strictly formulatable conditions of professional domain, space and time. The function of the general practitioner is that of the general medical helper, and the function of the teacher is that of the facilitator of learning processes. The function of the pastor, however, cannot be captured in a formula, as we have seen. He or she performs a number of functions in a number of pastoral sectors: that of helper in individual pastoral counseling, that of teacher in catechesis, that of congregational leader in church development, that of ritual presider in liturgy and preaching, that of community worker in social ministry, that of missionary worker in evangelization and mission, and that of guide in spiritual direction. Further, the professional domain of the general practitioner is medicine, and that of the teacher is education, while the professional domain of the pastor is as broad as religion itself. It encompasses the macrolevel of the society, the mesolevel of the societal institutions, and the microlevel of the individual. Next, the work of the general practitioner is limited in space mainly to the consulting room and that of the teacher is limited mainly to the classroom, whereas the work of the pastor may in principle be performed anywhere and everywhere: from the church building to the market place, from the hospital room to the city square where the gay movement 'Dignity' holds its protest meetings, from the elegant drawing-room in an exclusive residential area in the suburbs to a hovel in the slums. As far as time is concerned, too, the work of the pastor differs from that of his or her counterparts. Both the general practitioner and the teacher work from breakfast to dinner time. The pastor's work, however, stretches into the evening, because he or she is there, or should be there, where the people are.

When the pastor is now confronted with quantitative assessment instruments that measure his or her readiness for ministry, he or she cannot help but perceive these instruments as contrasting sharply with

---

[78] F. Siegers, Instellingssupervisie. *Leren over werk in de context van leiden – begeleiden – (samen)werken* (Houten, Diegem: Bohn Stafleu Van Loghum, 1995) 101-105.

the complexity and dynamism that characterize his or her work. What irritates and offends the pastor is the lack of fit between these instruments and the intricacy and ambiguity of the many, pluriform concrete situations in which he or she carries out his or her ministry. The measuring instruments appear to measure skills in order to provide standardized solutions to standardized problems, whereas the pastor is not confronted with problems, let alone standardized problems, but with problematic situations which as such are characterized by obscurity and indeterminacy, fortuity and ambivalence, infinite variety and ultimate uniqueness. In pastoral practice, as in every professional practice outside the laboratory, there are no problems, only problematic situations: "The situations of practice are not problems to be solved but problematic situations characterized by uncertainty, disorder and indeterminacy".[79] Standardization of ministry is a contradiction in terms, although the process of professionalization in general might almost autonomously require standardization.[80] But it is precisely here that pastoral professionalization reaches its limits. The contrast between standardized assessment procedures and complex pastoral practice causes pastors to shake their head and exclaim: the researchers do not know what pastoral practice is!

Summary

At the end of this chapter, is is not difficult to come to a conclusion. The two models for education for ministry, which up until the 1960s and even long afterward characterized the theological schools, i.e., the kerygmatic model and the ecclesial model, no longer appeared to meet the needs of the time. They were replaced or at least supplemented by two other models, based on insights derived from developments in the social sciences and empirical research, i.e. the therapeutic model and the managerial model.

In general, the advantages of the therapeutic model can be described as: sensitivity for the emotional situation of both the patient and pastor,

---

[79] D. Schön, *The Reflective Practicioner. How Professionals Think in Action,* 15-16.
[80] Cf. R. Brouwer, *Pastor tussen macht en onmacht. Een studie naar de professionalisering van het Hervormde predikantschap. Pastores en profiel. Supplement bij Pastor tussen macht en onmacht* (Dissertation Utrecht University, Zoetermeer: Boekencentrum, 1995) 259 v.

emphasis on communicative quality of the patient/pastor relationship; concern for free and authentic self-actualization on the part of both the patient and the pastor. The disadvantages, however, are no less definite: insufficient integration between the experiential/emotional sides of human life and functioning and the cognitive/conceptual/volitive sides; insufficient concern for the societal context of which both patient and pastor are part, and insufficient contribution to the liberation from alienation and oppression. Therefore, the conclusion of this part can only be that we need to go in search of a model that is beyond therapeuticalism, albeit without rejecting the achievements of the therapeutic model.

The advantages of the managerial model are also evident: in contrast to the epistemology of technical rationality that forms the foundation for the 'major' professions of medical top specialist and business top specialist, the managerial model that has been developed in the course of pastoral professionalization possesses a sensitivity for the actual practice and actual functioning of the pastor; this practice is carefully observed, recorded, described and analyzed with the aim of improving it. The focus is not just on a single area of the pastor's work; all sectors which his or her work covers are taken into account, from the microlevel of the individual to the mesolevel of the societal institutions to the macrolevel of the society as a whole. The research instruments that are employed for this purpose can also be useful in the framework of education for ministry programs. But this is also where the most important drawback of this model lies, namely that it does not do justice to the complexity and the dynamism that characterize day-to-day pastoral practice. As a result the real problems that pastors face in their concrete practice day in and day out remain out of reach. Once again, the conclusion can be no other than that we must go in search of a model that is beyond managerialism, but yet without discarding the positive aspects of this model.

CHAPTER III

REFLECTIVE MINISTRY IN CONTEXT

In this and the following chapter I attempt to descibe the model of reflective ministry that in my view fulfils the conditions that must be met by the education for ministry program, if it is to adequately prepare the future pastor for his or her function or functions in the increasingly complex and dynamic religious context of today's western society, and that makes optimal use of the advantages of the foregoing models (kerygmatic, ecclesial, therapeutic, managerial). In chapter III I will emphasize the concept of reflective ministry, and in chapter IV I will elaborate on its educational conditions.

Briefly put, the epistemology of technical rationality is not central to the reflective ministry model, as it is to the managerial model, in either a deductive or a reconstructive sense. Rather, the central focus is on the idea of practical, rationality-based self-responsibility and self-direction. For, as we have seen, pastors who performs their pastoral work at the macrolevel of society, the mesolevel of the church and the microlevel of the individual, all of which are undergoing constant change and becoming increasingly complex, can no longer set their course by aims and goals that are held up and transmitted as being valid once and for all time. Neither the churches nor the theological schools, as stated in chapter I, possess such fixed points of reference. What the pastor must learn, and what the education for ministry program must lay the foundation for, is to develop the professional competence to deal adequately with problematic situations, to discover, formulate and analyze the religious problems contained therein, to use the basic tools to consider and weigh alternative solutions, to arrive at judgements while experimenting, and to reach decisions while acting, and to realize that in the ongoing dynamic of problematic situations, new religious problems will arise time and again which may have their origin in solutions resolved on previously, and to do all of this in full participation and cooperation with fellow professionals and lay people.

In other words, reflective ministry is not accomplished solely within what can be called a pastoral circle but rather in a pastoral cycle, in which, because of the complexity and inherent dynamic of the situation in which the pastor is involved, every solution generates its own problem or even problems. Ministry is a reflective, iterative, cyclical process.[1]

In order to delineate the characteristic nature of the work of the pastor as clearly as possible in relation to other professions in society and societal institutions, I begin by examining the significance of the term, religion, so as to define the professional domain that is unique to the pastor, namely, the religious domain. To avoid any misunderstanding that the term, domain, is meant to be understood in a restrictive sense, let me say at the outset that the concept of domain expressly includes interdependence with other domains, such as the economic, political, social and cultural (section 1). After that I look at the church, the institutional base from which the pastor carries out his or her pastoral work. In order to preclude a narrowly ecclesiological approach, I situate the church in the field of dialectical tension generated by processes taking place at the macrolevel of the society and the microlevel of the individual (section 2). Against this background I analyze the pastor's general and special functions (section 3). All of this then forms the basis for a closer analysis of the reflective ministry model which I advocate here. I take as my point of departure the — to European (and American!) ears — still foreign-sounding pragmatism of the Golden Age of American philosophy at the beginning of this century, particularly as developed by Peirce and Dewey (section 4). Finally, I consider the nature of the reflective competence that the pastor must possess in order to be capable of reflective ministry (section 5).

1. The Religious Domain of Ministry

In the clinical pastoral education movement, the lament was sometimes heard that the identity of the pastor is far less well defined than that of members of the other helping professions. What distinguishes

---

[1] Cf. J. Holland and P. Henriot, *Social Analysis: Linking Faith and Justice* (New York: Orbis Books, 1983); H. Janssen et al., *Zeichen der Zeit. Pastoraler Zirkel, Gesellschaftsanalyse, Bibel-Teilen.* Missio-Reihe 13 (Aachen: MISSIO, 1996).

the pastoral counselor from the therapeutic counselor? How is the work of the pastoral therapist different from that of the psychotherapist? That these questions were asked, sometimes provoking acrimonious debate, can be blamed on the split between the clinical movement, on the one hand, and the theological schools and churches, on the other.[2] These questions are not only relevant to the past, for today, too, one frequently observes the embarrassment of pastoral counselors who avoid having to answer even the explicitly religious questions and doubts that are brought to them by their patients by turning them into issues of psychic health: "In the 1990's religion has replaced sex as the major taboo among pastoral caregivers".[3] This is not surprising, perhaps, in view of the psychic dysfunctions that religion often brings about. In this sense, then, clinical pastoral education is right in emphasizing a modern 'distinctio spirituum', thereby contributing to a partial 'de-religionization' of pastoral counseling, as I have elaborated elsewhere.[4] An extreme case, of course, is that of the trainee who, as one clergyman revealed, was "not accepted for CPE until he promised not to mention God".[5]

However, the questions that I have indicated above do not apply only to individual pastoral counseling, but equally to the other functions that the pastor performs, such as religious education or social ministry. What distinguishes the religious educator from teachers in other fields, for example, cultural or social studies? What does the pastor in social ministry do differently from the social or community worker? These questions must be translated into questions about the progessional domain in which the pastor carries out his work. Interestingly enough, a rather large number of practitioners of other professions also appear not always to have a very precise idea of the goals and aims of their profession, but they are well aware of the professional domain in which they exercise it. And the pastor? Sometimes he or she is

---

[2] W. Zijlstra, *Klinisch pastorale vorming. Een voorlopige analyse van het leer- en groepsproces van zeven cursussen*, 27-31.

[3] H. W. Stone, "Religious Beliefs in Pastoral Caregiving," *Journal of Supervision and Training in Ministry,* 15 (1994) 63-69.

[4] J. A. van der Ven, "De identiteit van pastorale counseling," *Praktische Theologie*, 18, no. 2 (1991) 230-256.

[5] J. Fichter, *A Sociologist Looks at Religion. Michael Glazier* (Wilmington, Delaware, 1988) 82-83.

claiming that in the hospital, the prison, the army, where he or she carries out his or her work, the pastor is — and must be — a *Randseiter*, a marginal figure, even an *Aussenseiter*, an outsider, in order that he or she can fulfil his or her scripturally based sanctuary function. Now I do not mean to discount in any way the dialectical tension between the institutions in which the pastor works and the critical-prophetic function which he or she is called on to perform, but terms like 'marginal figure' and 'outsider' do not tell us the domain in which the pastor fulfils his task.[6]

The point, of course, is not to put the pastor on the defensive because he or she is often unable to answer the most essential question, namely in which domain he or she performs his or her functions. It is much more useful to look for an explanation, and that explanation is not hard to find. The embarassment and speechlessness of the pastor can be seen as the result of the deep-reaching societal process of modernization that characterizes the western world, and of the accompanying process of secularization.

Without going into the whole phenomenon of modernization, and certainly not into the differences between "premodern" and modern society, a few remarks are nonetheless called for. There are historians who hold that in the second half of the nineteenth century and first half of the 20th, some Christian churches, or at least the Catholic Church, responded to the growing trend of modernization and resultant secularization by resorting to a combined defensive and offensive strategy.The defensive part of the strategy consisted in throwing up institutional barricades behind which the Christian communities could hide in order to be protected from the 'heathen' influences of liberalism and socialism as well as the anticlericalism, agnosticism and atheism that went hand in hand with them. The offensive part of the strategy consisted of an attempt to systematically and methodically influence, evangelize and rechristianize the surrounding society from the vantage point of these institutions. This led to a 'churchification' of the Christian religion and a further bureaucratization of the church.[7] The

---

[6] Cf. P. Christian-Widmaier, *Krankenhausseelsorge und todkranker Patient* (Berlin: De Gruyter, 1988).

[7] K. Gabriel and F.-X. Kaufmann, *Zur Soziologie des Katholizismus* (Mainz: Matthias-Grünewald-Verlag, 1980).

Catholic Church was not alone in adopting such a strategy[8], the Reformed Churches in the Netherlands mounted a similar campaign.[9] The attitude of the Old Catholic Church during this period, on the other hand, can be seen as the antithesis of this strategy. It sought to remain always open to modern society and culture and, by way of the "Catholic Enlightenment," to enter into a dialogue with them.[10] Within the Catholic Church in particular, an idealized picture of the Middle Ages — the "premodern" period par excellence — was constructed that served as a legitimation for the aforementioned defensive and offensive strategy. In that picture, the Christian religion occupied the central place in the life of the individual and society, and ensured individual and societal integration. All of life — or so the church claimed — was played out under the sacred canopy of the church, from which it also drew its inspiration and orientation. Just as the Middle Ages had undertaken the crusades against the threat of Islam, so the church now embarked upon a holy war against modern heathendom: a counterrevolution that sought to restore the theocracy of the Middle Ages.[11] Since then historians have put some rather large question marks beside this picture, pointing out that it is more a nineteenth-century ideological construction of the Middle Ages than a factual description.[12] Cultural-anthropological studies have been very helpful in correcting this depiction. "Anthropologists have also helped to 'de-churchify' the history of the Middle Ages, by pointing out that in the Middle Ages the church was not an institution that regulated the life of the faithful down to the smallest detail, as the churches in the nineteenth century sought to do — with notable success, one might add — but that many forms of religiosity and religious commitment existed side by side and that if [the church as] a whole can be said

---

[8] A. Van Harskamp, *Theologie: tekst in context* (dissertation Nijmegen University, 1986).

[9] J. Hendriks, "De stille revolutie in de Gereformeerde kerken?" *Ouderlingenblad*, 70 (1993) 815. "Veranderingen in de Gereformeerde Kerken sinds 1960. Wat steekt daarachter?" *Ouderlingenblad*, 70 (1993) 817.

[10] J. Visser, "Kirchenstruktur und Glaubensvermittlung," *Internationale Kirchliche Zeitschrift*, 79, no. 3 (1989) 174-191.

[11] D. Menozzi, "Het belang van de katholieke reactie op de revolutie," *Concilium* 1 (1989) 59-67.

[12] P. Raedts, "De christelijke middeleeuwen als mythe," *Tijdschrift voor Theologie*, 30, no. 2 (1990) 146- 158.

to have existed, it was at the least chaotic and full of contradictions. This has even raised the question of whether one can properly speak of a 'Christian Middle Ages' at all".[13] Some historians therefore prefer to speak of the 'heathen Middle Ages".[14] Some sociologists react to the complaint implicit in the expression 'the faith we have lost' by noting that 'we haven't lost anything, we are at the same level again'.[15]

Now there is no doubt that the present-day picture of secularization — in the sense of the declining importance of institutionalized, church religion — is shaped by the position of institutionalized religion in the 19th century and, concommitantly, by the ideological picture of the Christian Middle Ages constructed by the church in the 19th century. And this, of course, puts the pastor in an awkward situation, leaving him perplexed and at a loss for words, as I said earlier. The position of institutionalized religion is indeed marginalized relative to what it was during the second half of the nineteenth and first half of the twentieth century. In historical terms, however, that period must be considered a modern anomaly. Institutionalized religion is currently gearing down from a 'war economy' to a 'domestic economy'. From a fever pitch, it has returned to a more normal state.[16] And the same applies, naturally, to the pastor. The position and the reputation of the pastor rise and fall with the fortunes of institutionalized religion.

As far as institutionalized religion and the pastor are concerned, the process of institutional differerentiation that is rooted in the division of labour and which affects the whole of modern society leaves no alternative: their domain is the religious domain. Alongside the economic domain with its code of 'money', the political domain with its code of 'power', the medical domain with its code of 'health', the scientific domain with its code of 'truth', and the educational domain

[13] P. Raedts, *Toerisme in de tijd? Over het nut van middeleeuwse geschiedenis* (inaugurele rede Nijmegen University, 1995) 10-11.

[14] Cf. L. Milis, *De Heidense Middeleeuwen*, bibliotheek 32 (Brussel, Rome: Belgisch historisch instituut te Rome, 1991); *De Heidense Middeleeuwen*. Wetenschappelijke nascholing (University of Gent, 1994, 1995).

[15] A. Greeley, *Religion as Poetry*, 57-82.

[16] J. A. Van der Ven, "Katholieke kerk en katholicisme in historisch en empirisch perspectief," 69.

with its code of 'learning', the religious domain has developed with its code of 'transcendence'.[17]

This does not mean that religion develops entirely apart from and independent of the other domains, or they apart from and independent of it. The various domains form their mutual boundaries, but this certainly does not mean that there is no interdependence among them. On the contrary, interdependence is intrinsic to the concept of domain, since every person plays the role of professional in one or several domains, and the complementary role of 'layperson' in all the others, as consumer, voter, patient, student and so on. Two aspects of this interdependence must be distinguished: influence and relevance. The term 'influence' means, for example, that a colonializing effect can be and is exerted by the economic domain on the other domains[18], especially the political, medical, scientific, educational and religious domains, just as a guiding or at least mediating force emanates from the institutions of the cultural domain toward the economic domain.[19] Hence one can speak of the economic colonialization of the social-cultural sphere and the culturalization of the economy.[20] The term 'relevance' can be understood within the context of culturalization, with respect to the positive, desirable and legitimate influence of religion on the other domains. It has to do with the circumstance that professionals and 'laity' in the religious domain are in a position to explicitate and clarify the needs and desires that remain unfulfilled in the other domains, to inspire people and spur them to protest critically against injustice and oppression and initiate emancipation and liberation processes.[21] In other words, when we say that the domain of the pastor is the religious domain, this does not mean that religion exerts no influence and holds no relevance for

---

[17] N. Luhmann, *Funktion der Religion* (Frankfurt: Suhrkamp, 1992).

[18] J. Habermas, *Theorie des kommunikativen Handelns*, Band II, 489 v.

[19] M. Weber, *Gesammelte Aufsätze zur Religionssoziologie* (Tübingen: Mohr, 1978) 252.

[20] H. Kunneman, *Van Theemutscultuur naar walkman-ego*, 261 v.

[21] P. Beyer, *Religion and Globalization* (London: Sage, 1994); *Religious Traditions and the Global Religious System. Theoretical Prolegomena to an Empirical Investigation*. Paper presentend at the Meeting of the Association for the Sociology of Religion (Los Angeles, August 3-6, 1994); *The Religious System of Global Society*. Paper presented at the Congress of the International Society for the Sociology of Religion (Quebec City, June 26-30, 1995).

the other domains. What it does mean, though, is that when the pastor enters the other domains, he or she does so or, at least from a social theory viewpoint, ought to do so, from the religious domain, and that his or her attitude and actions within those other domains draw their inspiration and orientation, and thus their legitimacy, from the religious domain.

Although I have just said that in modern social theory the central code within the religious domain is that of transcendence, I have given only a summary indication of the richness that is contained within that domain. In order to reveal this richness, a theory of religion is needed. Such a theory is furnished by the cultural anthropologist, Clifford Geertz, who describes religion thus:

> "Religion is a system of symbols, which act to establish powerful, pervasive and longlasting moods and motivations in men and women by formulating conceptions of a general order of existence and clothing these conceptions with such an aura of factuality that the moods and motivations seem uniquely realistic".[22]

Based on Geertz's interpretation of that description, a number of elements can be focussed on. First of all, there are convictions active in religion, which formulate a general order of human existence. These convictions function as order (nomos) as opposed to the increasing threat of disorder (chaos). This disorder is of a varied nature: cognitive, emotional and normative. One can talk of cognitive chaos if one is inundated by contradictory data, messages, opinions and interpretations about reality. This easily leads to an emotional chaos, as a result of which the person is incapable of structuring the confusion of experiences and emotions, especially when confronted by suffering and death. This can in turn lead to a normative chaos, in which one can no longer distinguish good from evil, or be sure why good is good and evil is evil, or why one should do good and not evil. Now it is religion that brings order to chaos. The religious convictions structure the cognitive, emotional and normative household.

Next, these convictions activate certain symbols. These symbols describe how reality works (descriptive). They provide a model of

---

[22] C. Geertz, "Religion as a Cultural System," *The Interpretation of Cultures* (New York: Basic Books, 1973).

reality. They also indicate whether and how we should act (norma-tive). They provide a model for reality.

Furthermore, these convictions induce certain moods. These moods correspond to the content of the symbols, in so far as these contain a model of reality. These moods have a complex structure because they have to do with the depth of existence. They are composed of both positive and negative emotions, such as sad joy and glad sorrow, pro-ducing a sense of highmindedness, of the sublime.

These convictions and moods produce motivations, which are an orientation towards the actual realization of the model for reality through action. In this way religion becomes the 'applied religion' of everyday life.

There is another aspect of this description of religion that strikes us. It is that the convictions become clothed with an aura of factuality. Because of this, Geertz says, the moods and motivations become uniquely realistic. What Geertz means here can only be gleaned from the whole of his theory of religion, in which the ritual aspect of religion holds a central position. The sublimity of the ritual play allows the convictions which are expressed in the ritual to make a pertinent impression. In this they refer the participants to the true reality. They are not involved with ordinary reality with its daily routines and worries. The convictions which are raised to consciousness by the pen-etrative power of the ritual are precisely what breaches the structure of daily life. What is thoughtlessly taken for granted to be true, good and beautiful in daily life, is broken through in the ritual. The rituals represent the convictions about the true reality in such a powerful way, that the moods and motivations which stem from them confirm the impression of actual reality. Some cultural anthropologists indeed hold the ritual aspect to be the essential core of religion.[23]

I want to refer to one last aspect of Geertz's description of religion: the social context. Religion is intrinsically communitarian, owing to two other aspects just mentioned, namely the symbolic and ritual aspects. The symbols that are activated by the convictions create, so it is said, definitions of reality: both the descriptive model of reality

---

[23] E. Lawson and R. McCauley, *Rethinking Religion. Connecting Cognition and Culture* (Cambridge: Cambridge University Press, 1993).

and the normative model for reality. These definitions are social definitions. They are not invented by solitary monads, but in and through
the interaction and communication processes that occur among people
who together form a group or community and thus appeal to the symbols and interpretations of these symbols that are contained in the religious traditions.[24] The ritual aspect, too, is inconceivable without a
community. People perform rituals together and it is precisely in and
through this being together that the typical ritual atmosphere, the typical ritual climate of 'effervescence', as Durkheim calls it, is created
that clothes the convictions and symbols with 'the aura of factuality'.

All in all this leads to the following six aspects that are at the core
of religion and cannot be excised without crippling religion itself: the
experiential aspect (symbols), the cognitive aspect (convictions), the
emotional aspect (moods), the moral aspect (motivations), the ritual
aspect, and the communitarian aspect.[25]

Looking at this description of religion, one may wonder whether the
central code of transcendence, which constitutes that which is unique
to the religious domain compared with other domains, is not being left
out of consideration. The answer is that the aforementioned aspects are
all aspects of how human beings approach transcendence. The experiential aspect concerns the contexts in which, the manner in which, and
the degree to which people experience transcendence in their lives.
Sometimes transcendence is experienced in positive or negative contingency experiences such a birth, suffering or death, in breaks in the
routine of daily life such as divorce or intense conflict, in the course of
reflection about oneself and one's life, or during liturgical ceremonies.
The cognitive aspect concerns people's convictions with regard to transcendence and how these are linked with ideas about individual and
societal life, nature and the cosmos. The emotional aspect lies in
people's feelings about transcendence, positive as well as negative
(gladness, sorrow), the feelings they have about themselves and others
(pride, caring), feelings related to their autobiographical or collective
past (gratitude, disappointment) or future (hope, fear). The moral aspect

[24] Cf. P. Berger and Th. Luckmann, *The Social Construction of Reality. A Treatise in the Sociology of Knowledge* (New York: Penguin Books, 1967).
[25] Cf. Ch. Glock and R. Stark, *Religion and Society in Tension* (Chicago: Rand McNally, 1965); U. Boos- Nünning, *Dimensionen der Religiosität* (München: Kaiser, 1972).

relates to action tendencies, to that to which one is inspired by the prospect of transcendence, in terms of good and bad, just and unjust, wise and unwise. The ritual aspect has to do with the direct approaching of transcendence in individual and collective prayer that takes place according to free or fixed patterns. The communitarian aspect points to the sense of belonging to smaller or larger groups, the richness of which people experience and interpret in the light of trancendence.

With this description of religion in terms of transcendence, I have tacitly taken a particular standpoint in the debate concerning the so-called substantial and functional approaches to religion. According to the functional definition, anything that operates or functions as religion is religion. Anything that has importance to a person as an 'ultimate concern' is, by this definition, a religion. For real devotees, the Chicago Bulls or the Dutch Orange baseball club are a religion. According to Luckmann, who advocates the functional definition, every person in every society is religious, because every person in every society needs some kind of picture of humankind and the world that goes beyond his or her own self, even if that picture works in an invisible way, in terms of what is called 'an invisible religion'.[26] Peter Berger, on the other hand, rejects a functional definition because the term 'religion' becomes redundant if it can mean anything and everything. In Berger's view, religion essentially consists of humanity's relation to transcendence, which implies not only a self-transcendent image of humanity or of the world, but a suprahuman, supraworldly reality.[27] Geertz adopts a rather ambivalent position in this discussion. He says, "A man can indeed be said to be 'religious' about golf, but not merely if he pursues it with passion and plays it on Sundays: he must also see it as symbolic of some transcendent truths".[28] The question is what transcendent means here. There are modern cultural anthropologists — self-declared agnostics! — who on empirical and conceptual grounds take the view that the the word 'transcendence' refers to 'culturally postulated suprahuman beings'.[29]

[26] Th. Luckmann, *The Invisible Religion* (New York: MacMillan, 1967).
[27] P. Berger, "Some Second Thoughts on Substantive versus Functional Definitions of Religion," *Journal for the Scientific Study of Religion*, 13, no. 2 (1974) 125-133.
[28] C. Geertz, "Religion as a Cultural System," 98.
[29] E. Lawson and R. McCauley, *Rethinking Religion*, 89.

Whether personal or impersonal traits are ascribed to these 'culturally postulated suprahuman beings' — or in monotheistic terms,
'suprahuman being' — is something we can set aside for the time
being. The anthropomorphic images of God clearly have the upper
hand in the monotheistic religions. In the literature by mystics such as
(Pseudo-) Dionysius the Areopagite and Meister Eckhart, however,
references to 'the Godhead' predominate, and Catherine of Sienna
describes God in images borrowed from nature, such as sea, ocean,
abyss, desert, fire, light, sun. Feminist theology has brought a renewed
awareness of the impersonal metaphors of God, such as source, aim,
ground, depth, the ultimate, totality, force, plan, and principle.[30]
Through discussion with non-Christian religions, some theologians
arrive at a description of God as 'Great Depth' or 'Compassion'.[31] At
the beginning of this century, the founding father of psychology,
William James, had already suggested that God be called 'the divine
more'[32], and the no less influential philosopher and psychologist, John
Dewey, described God as "something beyond the self, that imaginative totality we call the Universe".[33]

To avoid the reification of this 'culturally postulated suprahuman
being', I will follow Tillich in emphasizing that God is 'no thing',
'no-thing'.[34] Transcendence means that God is never quite pinned
down by our ideas of God. The texts and images that refer to God are
diverse and polyphonic, and out of the network of meanings of these
texts and images, out of their 'intersignificance', emerges a premonition
of a God that coordinates these polyphonic meanings, for they refer
to God, but at the same time the insight arises that God evades these
meanings, because they can never do God justice. God initiates and
coordinates these images and thoughts as a receding horizon.[35]

---

[30] E. Johnson, *She Who Is. The Mystery of God in Feminist Theological Discourse*
(New York: Crossroad, 1995).

[31] J. Krüger, *Metatheism* (Pretoria: University of South Africa Press, 1989).

[32] W. James, *Varieties of Religious Experience* (New York: Crowell-Collier,
1961).

[33] J. Dewey, *A Common Faith* (New Haven: Yale University Press, 1962).

[34] P. Tillich, *Systematic Theology* (Chicago: University of Chicago Press, 1966).

[35] P. Ricoeur, "Naming God," *Union Seminary Quarterly*, 34 (1978) 215-227;
J. Fodor, *Christian Hermeneutics. Paul Ricoeur and the Refiguring of Theology*
(Oxford, 1995) 239-257.

To conclude this section, let me summarize what the specific domain of ministry is and what tasks the pastor must fulfil in this domain. What distinguishes the work of the pastor from all other professions is that it takes place specifically in the domain of religion. Because religion is relevant to the other domains such as economics, politics, health and culture, the pastor moves from his or her specific domain into these other domains as well, but his or her appearance there is always legitimated, or at least legitimatable, by religion. The religious domain is a complex domain in itself, that requires a careful balancing of the six aspects: experiential, cognitive, emotional, moral, ritual and communitarian. The pastor's work specifically consists in the reflective and iterative processes of raising and solving religious problems in highly complex situations arising within the religious domain and extending from there to the other domains, and vice versa.

2. The Ecclesial Context of Ministry

At the beginning of chapter II, I indicated that the relation of the clinical pastoral education movement to the church constituted a problem, or rather a challenge, that challenge being to bring about emancipation from the slavery of conventionalism, moralism and legalism. However, it is not only the pastoral supervisors, counselors and therapists in hospital settings who experience the church as a problem, but also pastors who work in other institutional settings, such as prisons, schools, the army or the mass media. It is no less true, however, of pastors who work within the church itself, albeit at the margins of the church, like pastors for youth and adolescents or pastors who are responsible for social ministry at the interface between church and society. Studies consistently show how negatively the church is seen among many of those with whom these pastors come into contact. Thus a survey of students at Nijmegen University shows that 82% see a sharp discrepancy between the way in which they actually experience the church and their ideal of the church. What they dislike the most is that the church consistently, and without any real rational argument, invokes traditions, rules and laws which it seeks to impose on its members. What they wish for most strongly is a church that takes action on behalf of humanity and in the process relativizes its own importance.[36] It is evident from the European Values Research that confidence in the church has decreased since 1981 in all countries, not only in Europe but also in the United States and Canada. It does not make much difference whether the respondents are core members or modal members. Marginal members and non-church members have always had far less confidence in the church. And in all countries, including the United States, confidence is lower among the youth.[37] Findings of this kind do not make exercising the function of ministry which operates from the perspective of the church any easier.

What exactly do we mean by the phrase 'context of the church'? In order to answer this question I once again refer to the different levels of religion which I outlined in chapter I. I described how religion operates at the macrolevel of the society, the mesolevel of the church and the microlevel of the individual, and what problems are associated with this. In speaking in this chapter of the church context of ministry, I take as my starting point the complex relationship between the church and society, on the one hand, and between the church and the individual, on the other. The relationship, I have said, is complex, because there is a dialectical tension between direct and indirect, passive and active, desirable and undesirable functions. The church is influenced directly and indirectly by the religious processes in society, just as it also exerts direct and indirect influences on that society. The same is true of religious processes taking place at the level of the individual. How individuals and groups handle religion directly and indirectly influences the church, just as the church directly and indirectly, influences the religiosity of individuals.[38]

Bearing in mind these complex relationships, it becomes obvious that there can be no ministry within the church that is not influenced by or does itself exert influence on religion at the level of society and of the individual person. The reverse is also true: ministry in institutional settings outside the church, like hospitals, prisons, schools or mass media, is not conceivable which is not affected by the church. Ministerial practice is not only church or congregational practice but

---

[36] J. A. Van der Ven and B. Biemans, *Religie in Fragmenten,* 279-280.

[37] P. Ester, L. Halman and R. de Moor, *The Individualizing Society,* 53-54.

[38] Cf. R. Merton, *Social Theory and Social Structure* (New York: Free Press, 1968).

always also societal practice and the other way around[39], and the same is true of individual-oriented pastoral practice, like pastoral counseling or pastoral therapy. By this I do not mean that these practices occur or should occur within the institution of the church per se, although they often do take place within the church, for example in parish-based centers for pastoral counseling. I mean that pastoral counseling that takes place outside the church is also influenced by developments in the church and in turn exerts an influence on the church.[40]

The tension between the church, on the one hand, and the individual and society, on the other, presents an even more complex picture if one takes into account that the church constituency is pluriform in nature. The classic distinction is between three categories: the marginal members, who for example visit the church once a year; the modal or conventional members, who attend church at least two times a month; and the core members, who attend regularly and moreover engage in various kinds of church and pastoral work during the week. Among non-church members, three groups can also be distinguished: the former church members, the first generation unchurched, and the second generation unchurched.[41]

If one combines these categories with various categories of belief in God, one comes to realize that the simple dichotomy between believing church members and non-believing non-church members can not adequately reflect the far more complex reality. According to Dutch studies, the two-way distinction does apply to 75% of the population, but not to the remaining 25%. Thus 16% of the Dutch population are non-believing, but go to church, while 9% are believing but do not go to church.[42]

In a recent American research study, these classical distinctions are broadened and relativized by asking the question of church constituency not in terms of church-going behavior, but in terms of

---

[39] Cf. D. Browning, *Practical Theology and Congregational Studies.*
[40] Cf. D. Browning, *The moral Context of Pastoral Care.*
[41] R. Eisinga, A. Felling, J. Peters, P. Scheepers, E. Jacobs and R. Konig, *Social and Cultural Trends in the Netherlands 1979-1990. Documentation of National Surveys on Religious and Secular Attitudes in 1979, 1985 and 1990*, 74.
[42] A. Felling, J. Peters and O. Schreuder, *Geloven en leven*, 70.

church-relatedness. The first distinction that is made is between churched and unchurched. The two criteria for being categorized as churched are: being a member of a religious body and having attended a religious service at least six times during the past year. Persons who do not meet both criteria are categorized as unchurched. They fall into four groups: the unchurched attenders, who meet the attendance criterion but not the membership criterion; the unchurched members, who meet the membership criterion but not the attendance criterion; the uninvolved but religious persons, who meet neither criterion but who identify themselves as religious liberal, religious conservative or somewhere between the two; and the non-religious. These four groups have given rise to the concept of vanishing boundaries.

In other words, church and faith, church and religion form a complex and dynamic phenomenon. They no longer follow sharp, clearly defined lines. The boundaries between ecclesial and non-ecclesial, religious and non-religious are not fixed, but are flowing and permeable. Each dichotomy in this domain has to be replaced by a variety of categories, which are only a pale reflection of the complex richness that is church and religion.

The question that emerges is on what ecclesiological basis the pastor is to carry out his or her ministerial work within the church or within the other societal institutions. Without seeking to derive an entire ministerial ecclesiology from the Trinity, I call attention here to three aspects of the church, namely its vision, mission and imagination, which I will describe in terms of three fundamental images of the church: the people of God, the movement of Jesus, and the community of the Spirit.[43]

Vision: The Church as the People of God

The vision of the church concerns its identity: how does the church see itself, how does it deal with itself and how does it deal with the communities and institutions of which it is made up? To answer this question, I will go to one of the most significant — perhaps the most significant — images of the church: the people of God.[44]

---

[43] Cf. J. A. Van der Ven, *Ecclesiology in Context*; E. Henau, *De kerk: instrument en teken van heil* (Leuven, Amersfoort: Acco, 1989).

[44] H. Küng, *Die Kirche* (München: Piper, 1967) 139.

The image of the people of God is indissolubly linked with the origin and history of the Jewish people. It is rooted in the economic and political uprisings against the monarchy and the towns by the peasant families and clans who formed an alliance among themselves, an alliance that was later to grow into the people of Israel, in order to liberate themselves from the hands of the Egyptians, Philistines and other mighty neighboring peoples. The processes that led to this alliance were economic and political, but the social cement was religious. It was religion that gave the people of Israel the strength to assert themselves against their powerful neighbors. Over time, these processes resulted in a religious self-attribution and legitimation, in that the groups concerned conferred a religious significance on their identity and on their existence as a collectivity. They saw this identity as deriving from the tension between the activity of JHWH and that of the collectivity itself. The choices they had made for the JHWH religion were linked to their notion that JHWH for his part had chosen them as the people of Israel. The alliance among tribes was therefore experienced as a covenant between JHWH and Israel. Historically, then, the people of Israel came first and only subsequently became the people of God; theologically speaking, from God's perspective the people of God come first.[45]

In the definition of Israel as the people of God we gradually begin to see two different lines of thought. The first is imperialistic. Since Israel sees only itself and no other people as the people of God, it imagines itself to be superior. The expansion that takes place under David and Solomon is viewed as the extension of the power of God over other peoples. The people of Israel take the view that the God who joins in the fight on Israel's side will rule over all peoples.

The second line of thought is universal. Israel becomes aware that God is the God of all the peoples and that Israel is only one people among many. This entails a certain relativization of Israel's importance. However, at the same time, Israel becomes aware of its vocation towards the peoples: the vocation of universalism.[46]

[45] L. Boff, *Und die Kirche ist Volk geworden* (Düsseldorf: Patmos, 1987) 58-59.

[46] G. Pixley, "Het volk Gods in de bijbelse traditie," *Concilium*, 17, no. 6 (1984) 23-30.

What shape does this vocation take? One can discern three aspects. The first is centripetal. It involves the idea that the peoples will, or should, advance towards Jerusalem on a pilgrimage (Is 2: 2-4; Ps 87; Jer 3: 17). The second is decentral, and is expressed in texts in which it is said that the peoples can participate in the revelation of God's kingdom in their own towns and cities (Is 45: 18-25). The third, and least obvious, is centrifugal. One can discern it in the texts concerning the mission of the suffering servant of the peoples (Is 42: 1-9), the mission of Jonah, and a number of psalms (Ps 117). In this the universal subservience of Israel to the peoples is expressed.[47]

The image of the 'people of God' does not occur in the gospels, but it is present in the rest of the New Testament literature. It played an important, implicit role in the actions of Jesus. His proclamation was determined by the message of the kingdom of God. This message took up an old tradition which went back to the peasants' revolts, in which the rights of the poor were central. The monarchy was rejected because it was the cause of exploitation and oppression. The attempts that were later made to establish a monarchy for Israel were also opposed on the basis of this tradition, as appears from the stories about Gideon (Judg 8: 22-23) and Samuel (1 Sam 8: 4-18). Jesus preached the kingdom of God without earthly kingship, because the poor were closest to his heart. In this kingdom according to Jesus' message, there will be no titles or badges, no places of honor, no power and esteem. He shall be the great power, who is most subservient to the poor (Mk 10: 41-45). The gospel is for the poor (Lk 4: 18; 7: 22). This is its essential meaning.[48]

It remains to clarify the relationship between the first Christian communities and the old Israel. How was it that both the people of Israel and now these Christian communities could define themselves as the 'people of God'?

Initially, the communities understood themselves as the true, faithful people of God and not as the new people of God. They believed that through their belief in Jesus they had been taken up into a covenant with God, so that the promises of the Old Testament were

[47] W. Vogels, *God's Universal Covenant* (Ottawa: Novalis, 1986).
[48] G. Pixley, *"Het volk Gods en de bijbelse traditie"*.

realized in them. Because they took the twelve to refer to the twelve tribes, they viewed themselves as forming a continuity with Israel. They experienced themselves as being in continuity with Israel as the people of God.

A change came over these communities as a result of the missionary work done by Paul among the Gentiles. Initially, Paul did his work of proclamation among his fellow Jews. He appeared in synagogues (Acts 13: 5; 13:14; 17: 1-2). He did not restrict himself to Jews in this, because he knew he was called upon to proclaim to both Jews and Gentiles (Acts 9: 15). Later, however, resistance to Paul among the Jews grew, gradually pushing him exclusively towards the Gentiles (Acts 22: 18-21). Thus, he became the apostle of the Gentiles (Acts 26: 17). Paul's breaking away from the Jewish community and his mission as an apostle of the Gentiles are outlined in the three stories of Paul's Damascus experience in Acts 9: 22 and 26.[49]

All this had far-reaching consequences for the relationship between the Christian communities and Judaism. The relation become more and more strained. On the one hand, Paul remained faithful to the tenet of God's promise to, and election of, the Jewish people. He continued to refer to the Jewish people as the people of God, and he made use of the traditions that were alive within Judaism at the time. One of these was that being a child of Abraham in the flesh offers no guarantee of God's salvation, as only being a child of the promise counts in the eyes of God (Rom 9: 8). Another was that salvation would fall only to a remnant of Israel, owing to the unfaithfulness, callousness and obduracy of many (Rom 9: 27; 11: 5.7). Finally, there was the tradition that Israel had as its duty to be a light to other peoples and to lead them in the service of God. In the latter lies a call to Israel for universalism. On the other hand, Paul reversed the perspective of election and universalism. He did not propose that when Israel was collected around Mount Zion, the people would flock to it for the sake of their own salvation, as Jewish tradition would have it. He proclaimed that Israel would only gain salvation when the peoples had entered into salvation (Rom 11: 15-16). In this dialectical manner Paul

---

[49] E. Schillebeeckx, *Jezus, Het verhaal van een levende* (Bloemendaal: Nelissen, 1974) 295-310.

found a way to reconcile the Jewish people and the Christian church, at least in his letter to the Romans.[50]

When the church now sees itself as the 'people of God', it must of necessity see itself as forming a continuity with Israel, at least if it wants to remain true to Jesus' evangelical message. Consequently, it has to appreciate the vocation to which Israel was and is called. Earlier, this vocation was described in terms of three aspects: centripetal, decentral and centrifugal.

The centripetal orientation consists in the church's consciousness of its own identity as well as of the richness that is contained in its traditions. The preservation and defence of this heritage is one of its essential tasks, in the knowledge that, as the people of God, it persists despite temptations and tribulations (Lumen Gentium 9), while being aware of the defects and shortcomings to which it is subject.[51] It is important to underscore that the heritage in question is the heritage of the church as the people of God, and not of a particular, privileged group within the church. The image of the 'people of God' serves as a reminder that the church must be understood first and foremost as a unit, before any divisions between certain groups, such as higher and lower-ranking groups, are made. The 'people of God' stands in stark contrast to the ideas promulgated by certain theologians in the Middle Ages, to the effect that the church consists not of one people, but of two, the clergy and the laity, of which the former is concerned with liturgy and sacraments while the latter should occupy itself only with worldly things.[52] The first group gives orders and the second group carries them out.[53] Vatican II finally rehabilitated the image of the 'people of God' and reaffirmed the church as one people (Lumen Gentium 9-17). It declared that all differences are preceded by a fundamental collectivity and equality.[54] With this the council performed an act that was revolutionary for the history of the Catholic

---

[50] E. Schillebeeckx, *Gerechtigheid en liefde, genade en bevrijding* (bloemendaal: Nelissen, 1977) 552-555.

[51] Y. Congar, "De kerk als volk Gods," Concilium, 1, no. 1 (1965) 11-34; *Vraie et fausse réforme dans l'église* (Paris: Cerf, 1968).

[52] Y. Congar, *Jalos pour une théologie du laïcat* (Paris: Cerf, 1964) 32.

[53] L. Boff, *Und die Kirche ist Volk geworden*, 62.

[54] O. Semmelroth, "De kerk, het nieuwe Godsvolk," *De kerk van Vaticanum II*, ed. G. Barauna (Bilthoven: Nelissen, 1966) 451-465.

Church.[55] It implies that the identity of the church belongs to the church as a collective that, as a collective, is conscious of its own richness. For ministry in the church this means that, regardless of what kind of leadership the pastor exercises, in the most fundamental sense he or she shares this leadership with the other members of the church, predicated on the identity and richness that they all possess only in community with one another.

The decentral and centrifugal aspects of the church as the people of God contain the call to inculturation and interreligious dialogue. The call to inculturation means that the church takes seriously the need for peoples and population groups to express their own socio-cultural identity in all of those aspects that make the Christian religion a religion: experiential, cognitive, emotional, ritual, moral and communitarian. This is not simply a matter of clothing the religion in a new cultural costume. Out of their own concept of their own identity, the peoples and population groups must be able to say unconditionally: "The church is us"![56] This inculturation prevents the establishment of alienating dual systems, in which the dominant culture, the western one, sets the tone, but remains without any connection to the cultural aspirations and expressions of the groups in question.[57] The problems and challenges that inculturation implies for ministry will become more numerous and more difficult, as more and more members of the church come from cultures other than the western culture. Multicultural ministry is one of the most important signs of the times for ministry.

The call to interreligious dialogue means that the church, out of its deep respect for its own traditions, opens itself up to an even deeper respect for the richness contained in other religious traditions. In the process it must leave behind a number of overt or covert forms of exclusivism and inclusivism that are predicated on the absoluteness of the Christian religion, but without renouncing its own identity and universalism.[58]

---

[55] G. Alberigo, "Het volk Gods in de gelovige ervaring," *Concilium* 20, no. 6 (1984) 31-43.

[56] Cf. D. Bosch, *Transforming Mission* (New York: Orbis Books, 1991).

[57] R. Schreiter, *Constructing Local Theologies* (New York: Orbis Books, 1984).

[58] P. Knitter, *No Other Name? A Critical Survey of Christian Attitudes Towards the World Religions* (London, SCM Press, 1985); "Wohin der Dialog führt," *Evangelische Kommentare 10*, (1990) 606-610; E. Schillebeeckx, "Identiteit, eigenheid en universaliteit van Gods heil in Jezus," *Tijdschrift voor Theologie* 30 (1990) 259-275.

However, if this dialogue is to be truly open and free, the church must be prepared to open up for discussion itself and everything it encompasses, and to explore, in a process of mutual exchange of perspectives, what should remain and what should be considered for improvement or correction. The readiness for self-correction is perhaps the most difficult, but also the most important criterion for a free and open interreligious dialogue.[59] In the area of interreligious dialogue, too, the pastor will increasingly be confronted with questions and problems, if only because, due to the phenomenon of multiculturalization, he will increasingly come into contact with individuals and groups belonging to other religious traditions. The concrete challenge for pastoral practice is to translate this interreligious dialogue into practical pastoral action, for example, religious education, social ministry, community building and ritual development.

Mission: The Church as the Movement of Jesus

The description of the church as the people of God contains yet another aspect that has not yet been spelled out. As has been pointed out by liberation theology, the term, 'people', does not refer only, or primarily, to 'populus', but to 'plebs'. The word, 'plebs', is associated with the lower classes or even outcasts in contrast to the higher classes, the masses versus the elite. The church as the 'people of God' is the church of the poor, the church of the peasants who rose up against the monarchy and the cities in ancient Palestine.[60]

This orientation towards the poor is central to the second symbol that we discuss here: the church as the movement of Jesus. The primary picture in this respect is that of Jesus, whose life and work were played out mainly in the countryside. Jesus traveled from place to place, surrounding himself with a group of followers and drawing crowds, sometimes large and sometimes small. He was one of what can be called 'wandering charismatics', who gave voice to people without property, without a roof over their heads, without family ties. Their discontent was often directed against those in power in

[59] H. Häring, "Religieuze integratie en desintegratie," *Botsende culturen in Nederland?*, ed. J. A. Van der Ven (Kampen: Kok, 1996) 58-90.
[60] L. Boff, *Und die Kirche ist Volk geworden*, 66-71.

Jerusalem. Not only the caste of the high priests of the temple and all the other groups who made a living from the temple felt their anger, but also the property-owning class of the Sadducees who were, moreover, seen as collaborators of the Romans.[61]

Jesus was affiliated with the Pharisaic movement, although his radicalism and transcendence precluded his totally identifying with it. Jesus accepted those people who were marginalized both socially and religiously and were considered outcasts. Jesus' message was that the kingdom of God could only be realized when salvation was given to all people, without consideration, even religious consideration, of the person. Therefore he traveled around doing good without prejudice, granting boons to all, healing anybody, joining at the table of those who were shunned, speaking to those who had been found guilty or even sinful, and granting forgiveness to those who had been cast out in a religious sense. The most profound base of Jesus' message was religious. It lay in the notion that not the person, but God is the one who brings about the reconciliation of all people in his kingdom of justice and love. Jesus embodied in his person, his life and works the unconditional acceptance and becoming whole of all humanity through God. The parables of the lost sheep, the lost coin, the lost son, the Pharisee and the publican, and the workers of the eleventh hour, all bore witness to this acceptance. Jesus took away the self-contempt of people he met. He healed the leper. He made people laugh. He brought people together in the brotherly and sisterly sharing of the loaves and fishes. In short, Jesus' actions pioneered the universal reconciliation of the kingdom of God. Jesus was the promised Messiah.[62]

In Jesus' actions everything revolved around God. In the language of his time it was the kingdom of God. In Jesus' time it was not customary to define God directly as 'God'. This God who allows the sun to shine on both the good and the evil and who excludes no one was a dissident God for the official Judaism of the time. His dissidence was contingent on His absolute freedom, which broke through all rules and procedures. Proceeding from this absolute freedom He was a continual surprise as a dissident God. The Jesus movement was borne

---

[61] G. Theissen, *Soziologie der Jesusbewegung* (München: Kaiser, 1977); *Studien zur Soziologie des Urchristentums* (Tübingen: Mohr, 1979).

[62] E. Schillebeeckx, *Jezus, het verhaal van een levende*.

by this surprise of divine gratuity. The first communities were characterized by the belief in this dissident God of Jesus.[63]

The movement of Jesus developed in several waves, which led to different kinds of communities. The first wave took place mainly among Hebrew- (Aramaic)-speaking Jews. They felt drawn to the Jesus movement by their experience of the historical Jesus, who preached a radical religion and a radical ethic. They formed what are aptly termed messianic communities.

The second wave occurred mainly among the Greek-speaking Jews of the diaspora. The power that drew them to Jesus did not have its source in a personal encounter — they had, after all, had no contact with him — but lay in the experience of the presence of the Spirit of Jesus. In the awareness of these followers God had not left Jesus at his death, but turned him into a life-creating and life-giving Spirit (1 Cor 15: 45). Jesus was present to this group of followers in his Spirit. One can define these groups as pneumatic communities.

The religious union that Jesus himself had founded continued to exist in these communities in an anamnestic-pneumatic sense. In the memory handed down (anamnesis) Jesus was present in his Spirit (pneuma) for his followers. This anamnestic-pneumatic experience was the basis for fundamental freedom, equality and solidarity in these communities. Thus it is written in the charter of freedom in the letter to the Galatians: "As many of you as were baptized into Christ have clothed yourselves with Christ. There is no longer Jew or Greek, there is no longer slave or free, there is no longer male and female; for all of you are one in Christ Jesus" (Gal 3: 27-28). An egalitarian view of the community as brotherhood and sisterhood is evident in this. For every kind of discrimination is removed: of Jew against Gentile, of man against woman, of the free against the slaves. These communities form a prophetic-pneumatic community, founded in the baptism of the Spirit.

This baptism in the Spirit could lead to the notion that the fullness of the promised salvation had already been realized. To some extent the communities were already fully alive to an actualized eschatology.

[63] S. Sandmel, *The First Christian Century in Judaism and Christianity* (New York: Oxford University Press, 1969); D. Rhoads, *Israel in Revolution* (Philadelphia: Fortress Press, 1976) 6-74; E. Schillebeeckx, *Mensen als verhaal van God*, 130-141.

The future aspect of salvation in the kingdom of God therefore disappeared completely into the background. This sometimes led to an abundance of ecstatic processes such as healings and glossolalia. Paul was later to intervene correctively.[64]

The charter of freedom in the letter to the Galatians sets out the orientation of the Jesus movement towards the poor. From thence the church must be seen as the church of the poor. Yet this definition of the church cannot be accepted without qualification. To clarify the problem contained in this definition, the critical question can be asked: how does the church relate to the poor? The relationship can take three forms: the church for the poor, the church with the poor and the church of the poor.[65] The church for the poor goes to the poor. It organizes aid to combat the poverty of those who fall outside of it, as it were. The poor are the object of the church's care. The church of the poor stands in contrast to this. It is formed by the poor themselves, who are the subject of their own project to liberate themselves from their poverty, in the perspective of the kingdom of God. In this project the poor become a people, to the extent that they are less a 'mass' and bid farewell to the accompanying mass spirit. In other words, they become a people to the extent that they take on the historic task of their own freedom and equality as a people[66], and to the extent that they express their own historic credo. The church stems from this people of the poor. The church of the poor is the church from within the poor. The people of the poor form the people of God.[67] The church for the poor is an ethical task of the church; the church of the poor implies an ecclesiological approach on the part of the church itself.[68]

And what about the church with the poor? Those who come from the higher classes and who wish to belong to this people identify with the cause of the poor and stand in solidarity with them. They are on

[64] E. Schillebeeckx, *Pleidooi voor mensen in de kerk* (Baarn: Nelissen, 1985) 42-47.

[65] L. Boff, *Kirche: Charisma und Macht* (Düsseldorf: Patmos, 1985) 19; "Leergezag en bevrijdingstheologen onder het oordeel van de armen," *Concilium*, 23, no. 4 (1987) 5-6.

[66] L. Boff, *Kirche: Charisma und Macht*, 209.

[67] G. Gutiérrez, "De armen in de kerk," *Concilium*, 13, no. 4 (1977) 82-88.

[68] J. Sobrino, *The True Church and the Poor* (New York: Orbis Books, 1989) 92, 135.

the side of the poor and involved with them.[69] Ultimately, the concept
of the church with the poor is an appeal to the existing church in western society to reform itself to meet the needs of the poor and to engage
with them.[70] This assumes that the western church must learn to read
its own history, which is part of the history of western society itself,
in a new way: with the eyes of the poor. This demands a fundamental reinterpretation, touching upon the very structure and culture of
western society and of the church. Only after such a rereading will it
become clear that Jesus' kingdom of God is shaped in solidarity with
'the least of mine', 'the least of those who are members of my family'. For the rereading is not a purely intellectual act; it assumes the
praxis of evangelical 'diakonia' and 'koinonia'.[71]

We can do no better than refer to the image of the last judgement.[72]
The gospel paints us the following picture: "When the Son of Man
comes in his glory, and all the angels with him, then he will sit on the
throne of his glory. All the nations will be gathered before him, and
he will separate people one from another as a shepherd separates the
sheep from the goats, and he will put the sheep at his right hand and
the goats at his left" (Mt 25: 31-33). Which criterion will be used at
the last judgement? What shall we be judged on? The touchstone will
be what we have done for individual people.[73] What really matters is
feeding the hungry, giving drink to the thirsty, taking in the stranger,
clothing the naked, visiting the sick and those in prison. Whether we
are conscious of having done this does not play a role, according to
the gospel. The gospel goes on to state that: "Then the righteous will
answer him, 'Lord, when was it that we saw you hungry and gave you
food, or thirsty and gave you something to drink?'" (Mt. 25: 37). The
fact that we reached individuals will be decisive, and this may well be
by way of abstract institutions rather than in brief relations of face-to-
face contact. The 'Last Judgement' means that we will be judged on
that which has remained hidden to us, because we do not always know

[69] L. Boff, *Und die Kirche ist Volk geworden*, 68.

[70] Cf. J. van Nieuwenhove, *Bronnen van bevrijding. Varianten in de theologie van
Gustavo Gutierrez* (Kampen: Kok, 1991) 176-177.

[71] G. Guttierez, "De armen in de kerk," *Concilium*, 13, no. 4 (1977) 82-88.

[72] Cf. M. Terpstra, "*Zo spreken de schuldigen*," *Schuld en gemeenschap. Hoofdstukken uit een genealogie van de schuld,* ed. M. Terpstra (Baarn: Nelissen, 1991) 113.

[73] P. Ricoeur, *Politiek en geloof* (Utrecht: Ambo, 1968).

whether or when we have reached other individuals. We can be wrong about the significance of brief relations, and not see through our own autocentric wants. The meaning of long relations can not be assessed by us. We often think we have not reached anyone through the abstract systems of economics, politics and our own profession. Here, too, we can be wrong. All will be revealed to us. Whether or not we fed the hungry, gave drink to the thirsty, clothed the naked and visited the sick and imprisoned: in the end the judgement is not ours to make. We have neither the right nor the power. And the standard by which we will be measured is beyond our reach.

What this means for the pastor is clear enough: he must give priority to social ministry. And his engagement with the poor in this social ministry should not be restricted to the poor at the mesolevel of his own congregation, but include the poor outside of his own parish at the microlevel of the individual as well as the poor as a collective outside of the church at the macrolevel of the society.

Imagination: The Church as a Community of the Spirit

The messianic and pneumatic communities to which I alluded in the preceding section were characterized by the enthusiasm of the Jesus movement. As the years passed, however, a certain structuring and regulation began to impose itself in these communities. In this respect the so-called pre-Pauline and (post-)Pauline communities differ. The Jesus movement begins to display some features of what is called a movement organization.

The relationship between the pre-Pauline communities, on the one hand, and the Pauline and post-Pauline communities, on the other, must be approached subtly. Some pre-Pauline communities displayed almost no or very little organization. Others were relatively highly organized. This immediately strikes us when we look at matters like social relations, authority structures, and processes of admittance and expulsion. Some communities were more hardline and more radical in a social and ethical sense, others more flexible. Smaller communities tended to put the reins in their members' hands, larger ones tended to impose regulatory measures. Communities which were strongly influenced by wandering Christian charismatics emphasized the baptism in the Spirit, while more sedentary communities emphasized baptism with water as a (verifiable) sign of the baptism in the Spirit.[74]

This range of variation needs to be borne in mind so as to prevent the setting up of any facile opposition between pre-Pauline and Pauline communities. Nevertheless, a certain trend towards movement organization in the Pauline and post-Pauline communities is undeniable.

An important thing that strikes us in the Pauline literature is that the communities in the cities were made up of representatives of the broad middle class. The upper class appears to be absent, as is the lowest one. One can not speak of a typical rural deprivation, which characterized the first wave of the Jesus movement.[75] In general, one can say that social and religious movements in the first century exert an attraction on the middle class, which tends to prefer a certain order and regularity.[76]

First, it appears that life in these communities was characterized by a certain amount of discipline. One sees Paul slowing down the pneumatic movement of the first generations to a certain extent. He corrected the actualized eschatology, proceeding from his own parousia eschatology: he shifted the emphasis from 'already' to 'not yet' with respect to the coming of Jesus.[77] With this he restored the irrational ecstasy found in pneumatic communities to manageable proportions, fearing that it would lead to chaos.[78] That is why he wanted to restrict and restrain glossolalia.[79]

Not only disciplining but also structuring of the organization characterized these communities. Doctrinal teaching was given, disciplinary instructions were issued, conflicts were dealt with and solved in an orderly fashion, leaders performed their duties of proclamation, admonition and guidance. This did not involve a hierarchical organization structure of the kind that was later established in the church. The ministry in the Pauline and post-Pauline communities in the New Testament was not an 'ordo' in the sense of the Roman ranking, as the

---

[74] G. Theissen, *Soziologie der Jesusbewegung*, 21-26.

[75] E. Schillebeeckx, *Pleidooi voor mensen in de kerk*, 44.

[76] G. Theissen, *Soziologie der Jesusbewegung*, 34-36.

[77] E. Schillebeeckx, *Jezus, Het verhaal van een levende*, 328-358.

[78] E. Schillebeeckx, *Pleidooi voor mensen in de kerk*, 44.

[79] G. Theissen, *Psychologische Aspekte paulinischer Theologie* (Göttingen: Vandenhoeck und Ruprecht, 1983) 269-340.

church was later to use this term. It was functional leadership for the development of the community.[80]

In the disciplining and structuring we can trace features of a movement organization. In such an organization a certain ambivalence, a certain tension, is recognizable. One may ask, on the one hand, to what extent the Pauline and post-Pauline organization provided the necessary conditions for the continuity of the spiritual dynamics which determined the movement of Jesus, and, on the other, to what extent it fixed them and stripped them of the character of a movement.

It is here that the image of the church as a community of the spirit comes in. This symbol has its origin in the messianic and pneumatic communities of the first generation of Jewish and Gentile Christians who were under the spell of the Jesus movement. They perceived the spiritual excitement they experienced within their communities as Jesus' excitement within them, their spiritual strength as Jesus' strength, and their own spiritual inspiration as the inspiration of Jesus' Spirit. This Spirit was not primarily experienced as a kind of personified being that assails humanity like a demon, takes possession of persons and drives them to all sorts of activities in speech or action. The Spirit was seen rather as an impersonal force ('dunamis') which is present in human beings, and which pulls and pushes them. This dunamis was tangible in wisdom, hope, courage, endurance, joy and charisma.

The latter is significant: charisma was felt to be the power of the Spirit ('dunamis pneumatos') (Rom 15: 13). In charisma the power of the Spirit is given expression.[81] This charismatic power is given to believers of any rank, as Vatican II affirms (Lumen Gentium 12), and is bestowed directly, without any mediation by priests or clergy. The Spirit is received directly.[82]

These communities were convinced that everyone who believed and who had been baptized had received the Spirit. The focus was, therefore, not on the individual, as though the person in question had

[80] E. Schillebeeckx, *Pleidooi voor mensen in de kerk*, 50-72.

[81] R. Bultmann, *Theologie des Neuen Testaments* (Tübingen: Mohr, 1965) 158-159.

[82] F. Haarsma, *Kandelaar en korenmaat. Pastoraaltheologische studies over kerk en pastoraat* (Kampen: Kok, 1991).

undergone a special pneumatic experience. Rather, the community of which one was becoming a part was seen as the bearer of the Spirit. Those who participated in the community participated in the strength of the Spirit. The Spirit was felt to be present in the community and active in the community. That is why the author of the following passage, concerning circumcision, part of the letter addressed to the communities in Antioch, Syria and Cilicia by which the council of Jerusalem was closed, could write: "For it has seemed good to the Holy Spirit and to us to impose on you no further burden than these essentials: that you abstain from what has been sacrificed to idols..." (Acts 15: 28-29). To the Holy Spirit and to us!

However much the presence of the Spirit in the community was emphasized, it did not mean that the Spirit and the community were one and the same. The Spirit was not the church. The Spirit was not of the church, but of God and Jesus. There was a radical distance between the Spirit and the church, however great the connection was. There could be no other way, since the church was a 'communio mixta', a community of people that was just and sinful at the same time ('simul justus et peccator'), as was already pointed out by the Church Fathers.[83] The church was not only a church of sinners, but was also a sinner itself.[84] The symbolum says, "I believe in the Holy Spirit" ("credo in Spiritum sanctum"), and then, "I believe the holy church" ("credo sanctam ecclesiam"). We believe in the Spirit, but not in the church; we believe the church.[85] The Spirit is free from the shortcomings and guilt of the sinful church. As Haarsma has said very trenchantly, "Holy is the last and definitive word about the church, sinful is the first that one has to say of the church. We may believe in (sic!) the holy church, but we experience it as the sinful church".[86]

The fact that the Spirit is not identical with the community means that the Spirit is earlier, further, broader and deeper than the community. The Spirit is earlier in the sense that the Spirit is the origin and

---

[83] Y. Congar, *L'eglise. De Saint Augustin à lépoque moderne* (Paris, 1970) 14-15.

[84] K. Rahner, "De zonde in de kerk," *De kerk van Vaticanum II*, ed. G. Barauna (Bilthoven: Nelissen, 1966) 431-447; Y. Congar, *Vraie et fausse réforme dans l'eglise*, 83-84; 108-119.

[85] H. Küng, *Die Kirche*, 203.

[86] F. Haarsma, *Geest en kerk* (Dissertation Nijmegen University, Utrecht: Ambo, 1967) 333.

source of the community. The community can not exist without the working of the Spirit. The Spirit calls upon the church to be the church. This does not cancel out the coming together and joining of believers in the community, because it is the Spirit that gives the believers the task of coming together.

The Spirit is further than the community, because the Spirit is ahead of it and inspires, summons, admonishes and corrects the community. The Spirit draws the community into intercourse and connectedness, including across denominational boundaries, in the direction of the ecumenism of God ('oikoumene tou Theou'). Thus, in the texts of Vatican II, the Spirit is regarded as the principle creating unity among the churches (Unitatis Redintegratio 3). In the constitution on the church this is dealt with as follows: "And so the Spirit stirs up desires and actions in all of Christ's disciples in order that all may be peaceably united, as Christ ordained, in one flock under one shepherd" (Lumen Gentium 15). The Spirit carries the church beyond the boundaries that separate the churches from each other: papalism, episcopalism, presbyterianism, synodalism, conciliarism, congregationalism, independentism.[87]

The Spirit is broader than the community, and broader than the Christian churches, as it blows where it will, outside of the churches, in other religions and other philosophies of life. The Spirit reconciles Jews and Christians, believers and non-believers, as the letter to the Ephesians (2: 17-22; 4: 3-6) indicates. Here the prospect of a universal ecumenism is offered.[88] Those who deny this close their eyes to the 'ecclesial fugitiveness' of God. God is always ahead of any religious institution; God's being ahead is God's Spirit.

Finally, the Spirit is deeper than the community. The Spirit knows how to penetrate into layers of human existence that come into little or no contact with the surface of the church: layers of spirituality and mysticism, reflection and prayer, contemplation and meditation. These are the deeper layers of awe and wonder at the secret of human existence, in which people participate without words in a passive-active

---

[87] J. Moltmann, *Kirche in der Kraft des Geistes* (München: Kaiser, 1975) 318.

[88] E. Schillebeeckx, *Gerechtigheid en liefde, genade en bevrijding* (Bloemendaal: Nelissen, 1977) 175-195.

presence.[89] Through this the Spirit opens up the community to God's presence in Islamic Sufi mysticism, the Hindu Veda and the Buddhist Bhagavadgita.[90]

What conclusion can be drawn from this for the pastor? The description of the Pauline and post-Pauline communities suggests that a certain discipline and structure is necessary. However, the pastor must ensure — in a negative sense — that the Spirit of inspiration and enthusiasm is not extinguished, and — in a positive sense — that the boundaries of the church are continuously and systematically explored in order to determine where they can be transcended so as to seek out the wind of the Spirit outside the church. The image of the church as the community of the Spirit encourages a permanent process of creative imagination. It calls on the faithful to explore boundaries and work always at the frontiers.

Summary

From the preceding overview, it becomes clear that the church context of ministry is a much more complex and dynamic matter than it might appear to be at first glance. The images of the 'people of God', 'movement of Jesus' and 'community of the Spirit' continually push the pastor to the boundaries of the church, and encourage him to transcend those boundaries in the direction of the society and the individual members of the society. If the church is to be a true church, its hub will always be its faith in God, Jesus and the Spirit, but its centre of gravity will lie in the people all around, be they inside or outside the church.

3. The Functions of Ministry

In this section we turn our attention to the function, or rather functions, that the pastor fulfils in the domain of religion (section 1) from

---

[89] J. Krüger, *Metatheism.*

[90] J. Walgrave, "Standpunten en stromingen in de huidige moraaltheologie," *Tijdschrift voor Theologie*, 1, no. 1 (1961) 48-70; P. Schoonenberg, *De Geest, het Woord en de Zoon* (Kampen: Kok, 1991).

the perspective of the church (section 2). I speak of functions in the plural, because what is true of the 'major' and 'minor' professions, such as those of top medical specialist, general practitioner and teacher, namely, that they can be defined in terms of one primary function, does not apply to the pastor (chapter II, section 2). The question that we will look at here is: what are the functions of the pastor and how do they relate to one another? We will focus first on the general function of the pastor, which consists of hermeneutic communication (section 3.1), and then on the functions, which consist of liturgy/ preaching, catechesis, church development, social ministry, mission, pastoral counseling and spiritual direction (section 3.2). Finally we will discuss the 'second-order' function, which is the recruitment, training and guidance of pastoral volunteers (section 3.3).

3.1. The General Function

Despite the steps we have taken so far, the function or functions of the pastor are still far from clearly defined. This lack of a clear-cut definition is not unusual, however. At the present time, the practitioners of a great many professions are permanently in search of their professional identity and function. In a time when the term 'professionalism' still denoted the static, well-established nature of the professions, the notion of this sort of constant quest was unheard of. Now, however, that the term 'professionalism' has been replaced by 'professionalization', which reflects the dynamic nature of the ongoing discussion and change to which the modern professions are subject, one can no longer speak of stable, fixed, solid and clear-cut criteria which serve to define any particular profession. This dynamic is a result of the growing criticism of professionalism since the 1960s, and the efforts of the professions to continually improve their ability to respond to the wants, needs and expectations of society.[91] Pastors are not the only ones who disagree among themselves on what their most important function is; teachers, general practitioners, pharmacists and architects seem to be permanently seeking to clarify their vision, mission and imagination. It almost seems that lack of clarity,

---

[91] Cf. C. Houle, *Continuing Learning in the Professions* (San Francisco: Jossey-Bass Publishers, 1980) 19-33.

or at least the continuous search for clarity, is a characteristic of the modern profession.[92]

The search for clarity leads us back to the question of what the pastor's functions are. In the process we will distinguish between general and special functions. The special functions have to do with the work the pastor performs in various sectors, that is, liturgy, catechesis, church development, social ministry, mission, pastoral counseling, and spiritual direction. In the next section of this chapter we will examine the problems associated with this division into seven functions and seek to arrive at a certain justification of them. For now, however, we will take these seven functions for granted and look for the common denominator among them in order to arrive at an understanding of the pastor's general function.

Some authors believe that the common denominator lies in the concept of 'practice'. What links the special functions is said to be the fact that in them the pastor gives form to a 'practice' sustained by an Aristotelian 'phronesis' or 'practical reason'.[93] These authors are inspired by the definition of 'practice' given by the moral philosopher, MacIntyre, who, following in the footsteps of Aristotle, defines practice as "any coherent and complex form of socially established cooperative human activity through which goods internal to that form of activity are realized in the course of trying to achieve those standards of excellence which are appropriate to, and particularly definitive of, that form of activity, with the result that human powers to achieve excellence, and human conceptions of the end and goods involved, are systematically extended".[94] From this description, the difference between 'practice' and the technical rationality discussed in Chapter II becomes evident. The pastor's practice does not consist of a series of acts aimed in an instrumental manner at achieving certain goals, which in turn are instrumentally aimed at the realizing of certain goods. Rather, the practice consists of activities seen as worthwhile in

---

[92] Cf. C. Houle, *Continuing Learning in the Professions*, 35-40.
[93] Cf. C. Dykstra, "Reconceiving Practice," *Shifting Boundaries. Contextual Aproaches to the Structure of Theological Education*, eds. B. Wheeler and E. Farley (Westminster: Abingdon Press, 1991) 35-66; cf. Kelsey, *To Understand God Truly. What's Theological About A Theological School*, 118 v.
[94] A. MacIntyre, *After Virtue*, 175.

and of themselves. The value that lies in these activities is not external to people's happiness, which consists in acting in accordance with standards of excellence, but the activities themselves bring happiness nearer. Through this practice, human potentials are fostered, thereby contributing to self-realization.

Although this Aristotelian approach to 'practice' is indeed fundamental, it does not answer the question about the common denominator of pastoral work in the various functions, because immediately the question arises which 'practices' (in the plural) the pastor is performing. Does one limit oneself to the practice of the congregation, to which the pastor gives guidance and leadership[95], or does one take a broader perspective of the practice of Christian life, which takes place both inside and outside the congregation[96], or a still broader perspective of religious and religiously informed practices in society in general?[97] The conclusion must be that the term 'practice' only serves as an adequate starting point if it is more precisely qualified.

I believe that a suitable qualification can be found by focussing on the practice of hermeneutic communication[98] or, as Firet would say, the practice of hermeneutic agogics.[99] Before announcing that the practice of hermeneutic communication can rightly be seen as the common denominator of the seven special functions, we must have a closer look at the two parts of this concept, 'hermeneutics' and 'communication'.

Hermeneutics

It is not necessary to provide here a comprehensive exposition of the presuppositions, principles and methods of hermeneutics.

---

[95] Cf. Kelsey, *To Understand God Truly. What's Theological About A Theological School*, 131 v.

[96] M. Miles, *Practicing Christianity. Critical Perspectives for an Embodied Spirituality* (New York, 1992).

[97] D. Browning, *Practical Theology and Congregational Studies*. Paper for the Emperical Sector of NOSTER in the Netherlands.

[98] Cf. J. A. van der Ven, *Practical Theology: An Empirical Approach*, 41-59; E. Henau, *Pastorale vorming in een postmoderne context*. Lezing gehouden op het symposium 'Pastorale vorming van de toekomst — Toekomst van de pastorale vorming te Heerlen' (Nijmegen University, May 31, 1996)

[99] J. Firet, *Het agogisch moment in het pastoraal optreden* (Kampen: Kok, 1988), English Translation: *Dynamics in Pastoring* (Grand Rapids: Eerdmans, 1987).

Instead, I shall present only those aspects that are essential to an under-standing of how hermeneutic communication functions as a common denominator of the pastor's functions.

The most important consideration is that pastoral work is always concerned with the verbal and non-verbal understanding of texts from the past, because therein lies the real source of the Christian religious tradition. The primary source consists of the texts of the Old and New Testament. The secondary sources, which can be considered as inter-pretations of these texts, conditioned by the time and space in which they were created, are just as much part of the legacy that serves as a collective memory for the work that the pastor performs. As a collec-tive memory, all of these sources exert their influence in the present through the medium of their 'Wirkungsgeschichte', the history of their influence over time.

To further clarify the significance of these texts for the present, the pastor — like every believer who approaches these texts in order to arrive at an understanding of them — builds a bridge to connect the shores of past and present. On either shore it is necessary to take into account the differences in context which determine the meaning of the text then and the meaning of the text now.

Without understanding the context of the past, which is determined by a number of economic, political, social and cultural factors, it is impossible to understand the text from the past. A simple text exegesis, which still all too often underlies pastoral work, does not suffice. The meaning of the text from the past can only be grasped by asking what this text meant in the past for different people and groups of people from different social backgrounds, in different societal contexts, in different times. Therefore, the simple text exegesis must be replaced by text/con-text hermeneutics, as contemporary theologians, inspired to no small degree by the cultural anthropology of Levi-Strauss, rightly assert.[100] This context, of course, also includes the conflicts and struggles that played a role in the genesis of the text. The text must be seen as an expression of opposition between individuals, groups and generations.[101]

---

[100] C. Boff, *Theologie und Praxis* (München: Kaiser, 1983); E. Schillebeeckx, *Theolo-gisch geloofsverstaan anno 1983* (Baarn: Nelissen, 1983); *Mensen als verhaal van God.*
[101] Cf. B. Shore, *Culture in Mind. Cognition, Culture, and the Problem of Meaning* (New York: Oxford University Press, 1996) 176-177; R. Bernstein, *Beyond Objectivism*

Without an awareness of the context of the present from which the text is now being approached, one can not be aware of the prejudices — legitimate as well as illegitimate — that one may harbor with respect to the text.[102] However, the process of becoming aware of one's own (legitimate and illegitimate) prejudices can not take place until one meets the text. The process occurs in and through that meeting. Precisely in the confrontation between one's own prejudices and the 'otherness' of the text, hermeneutic understanding takes place. No understanding of the 'otherness' of the text is possible except through the confrontation between one's own prejudices and of the 'otherness' of the text: that is the paradox of human understanding.[103]

In order to guard against the danger of 'inegesis' that always slips into a hermeneutic understanding, no matter how strictly it is focussed on 'exegesis', Ricoeur's three-phase model can be used as an ideology-critical measure. In the first phase the interpreter understands the text by participating in its unproblematized meaning, the spontaneous, common, conventional meaning in which he or she has been socialized. He or she considers the text and its meaning as the house in which he unproblematically lives his or her life. In the second phase the interpreter distances himself or herself from the text and its conventional meaning in order to investigate it as objectively as possible with the help of all kinds of historic, semiotic and empirical studies. Having passed the text through this sieve of critical description and explanation, in the third phase the interpreter re-appropriates the text and its meaning, which has now been clarified, purified, even corrected; in a word: reconstructed.[104]

Communication

Here again it is not necessary to discuss the presuppositions, principles and main concepts of communication. It is sufficient to review

and Relativism (Philadelphia: University of Pennsylvania Press, 1986) 156 v.; Philisophical Profiles. Essays in a Pragmatic Mode (Philadelphia: University of Pennsylvania Press, 1986) 68 v.

[102] H.-G. Gadamer, Wahrheit und Methode (Tübingen: Mohr, 1960) 255.

[103] H.-G. Gadamer, Wahrheit und Methode, 279.

[104] P. Ricoeur, Hermeneutics and the Human Sciences (Cambridge: Cambridge University Press, 1978) 209 v.; From Text to Action. Essays in Hermeneutics II (Evanston: Northwestern University Press, 1991) 270 v.

the aspects that clarify what we mean by hermeneutic communication as the common denominator of all pastoral work.

While the hermeneutic dimension of all pastoral work consists in bridging the distance between past and present, the communicative dimension consists of bridging the distance between the participants in pastoral work in the present. The hermeneutic process itself may be a factor in creating this distance or enlarging it. The attempt to understand a text never leads to one, single meaning, but results in a never-ending, dynamic process of constantly changing meanings. Sometimes the meanings can be allowed to stand side by side, because they tend to complement rather than contradict each other. Sometimes, however, the pluralism of meanings can lead to conflicting interpretations, which demand further treatment by means of dialogue, argumentation and debate, once the hermeneutic arsenal is exhausted.[105]

The actors in the dialogue can be several people, but can also be one person in dialogue with him or herself. In the case of dialogue with others, we speak of interpersonal communication. In the case of dialogue with oneself, the communication is intrapersonal. It may be that he or she takes different positions and different roles at the same time. It may also be that he or she carries on a conversation with different autobiographical selves at various times of his or her life. Naturally, the changing positions in time and space can also be combined.[106] Both forms of communication, interpersonal and intrapersonal, are dialectically related: in interpersonal communication the person faces a real other, who represents for him or her one of his or her own multivoiced selves, whereas in intrapersonal communication he or she encounters aspects of himself or herself as though he or she were in conversation with one or more real others in the past or present.

The aim of this communication can be on three different levels. On the first level, the intent is simply to give the other (the real other or

---

[105] Cf. P. Ricoeur, *Hermeneutics and the Human Sciences*, 15-16.

[106] G. H. Mead, *Mind, Self, and Society* (Chicago: University of Chicago Press,1934); H. J. M. Hermans and H. J. G. Kempen, *The Dialogical Self. Meaning as Movement* (New York: Academic Press, 1993); H. J. M. Hermans and E. Hermans-Jansen, *Self-Narratives. The Construction of Meaning in Psychotherapy* (New York: Guilford Press, 1995)

one of my own selves) information concerning my beliefs (cognitions), feelings (affections), values (attitudes), and action tendencies (volitions), while the other conveys corresponding information to me. On the second level, the intent consists of an exchange of perspectives, meaning that the two partners in the dialogue stand in each other's shoes, as it were, or crawl into each other's skin, so that, from the perspective of the other, each can process the cognitions, affections, attitudes and volitions that the other communicates. This results in the understanding of the other. On the third level, there is an attempt to reach agreement, with an eye to the question of which cognitions, affections, attitudes and volitions are true, right and authentic. It is possible that a shared answer to this question, one that satisfies everyone, cannot be found, or at least not right away, and this is not necessarily a bad thing, although it may be frustrating; for the desire for consensus is subordinate to the desire for truth.[107]

Hermeneutic Communication as Common Denominator

It is not difficult to see that hermeneutic communication functions as the common denominator of the seven special functions, which we have not examined in detail thus far. Let us look at each one individually and in the process indicate the various paradigms from which the hermeneutic communication is shaped or ought to be shaped: liturgy and preaching from the ritual paradigm, catechesis from the teaching/learning paradigm, church development from the paradigm of community and organizational development, social ministry from the paradigm of social welfare, mission from the paradigm of cultural anthropology, pastoral counseling from the paradigm of therapeutic counseling, and spiritual direction from the paradigm of the self.[108]

Liturgy and preaching can be seen as a form of hermeneutic communication in which the ritual paradigm predominates. In the celebration of the word and the sacraments, the traditional texts play a central role and are interpreted according to their meaning for the

[107] Cf. J. A. van der Ven, *Practical Theology, an Empirical Approach*, 50-51; *Formation of the Moral Self* (Grand Rapids: Eerdmans, 1997) Chapter 1.

[108] Cf. J. A. van der Ven, *Practical Theology, an Empirical Approach*, 41-46; *Ecclesiology in Context*, 377- 379.

present. A separate problem is that the pastor must be aware that the texts can be interpreted in varying ways, thereby leading to divergent and even contrasting meanings, and that participants in the celebrating community may represent any and all of these contrasting meanings. Based on the principles and methods of the ritual paradigm, the pastor must then set in motion a communication, and he or she must do it in such a way as to create a sense of engagement and reconciliation in his or her listeners, but without creating an unhealthy harmony or forced unity of thought.

Catechesis is the field of pastoral activity par excellence in which the divergence of scriptural and other traditional meanings of texts can by systematically and methodically examined. The teaching/learning paradigm offers every possible opportunity for carrying out the hermeneutic process step by step as well as for systematically rehearsing and actually putting into practice communication about divergent interpretations.

Church development is inherently determined by the dialectical tension between the vertical dimension of hermeneutics (time) and the horizontal dimension of communication (space). The members of the congregation form the people of God, participate in the movement of Jesus and try to build and improve on the house of the Spirit because they experience themselves as called by the scriptures to be what they are and to do what they do, and to do this together in communion, which is to say through communication. Whenever a congregation runs into difficulties, the cause can be traced to deficiencies in hermeneutic understanding and/or communication. This hermeneutic communication has to be developed in keeping with the paradigm of community and organization development.

Social ministry appears to be less obviously based on hermeneutic communication than the preceding three functions. Yet hermeneutic communication is no less relevant. The activities that are undertaken to liberate individuals and groups from situations of poverty, oppression and alienation are, or ought to be, legitimated by a religious inspiration and orientation, which has its origin in texts from the religious literature and traditions. We saw earlier that the specific domain of the pastor, relative to the domains of other professionals, is religion. This does not preclude the pastor from moving into other domains as well, but always from an explicitly religious background and matrix (chapter III, section 1). In conjunction with the social welfare paradigm, social ministry is deeply marked by hermeneutic communication.

In the present day, the mission function is essentially determined by the dialogue about texts and their interpretations between representatives of the Christian religion and the other world religions. Drawing on the paradigm of cultural anthropology, this hermeneutic communication contributes to intercultural and especially interreligious dialogue, in theory and in practice.

Pastoral counseling is characterized by helping conversation with respect to texts that stem from the client's own past and his or her cultural and religious tradition. Pastoral counseling can be said to be a therapeutic way of processing secular and religious self-narratives with the help of a professional counselor. Especially the intrapersonal dimension of communication, in which the person dialogues with his or her multivoiced self, characterizes this ministry of self-reconciliation.

Lastly, spiritual direction by its very nature consists of clarifying the meanings of texts for one's own life or that of one's group in and through intrapersonal and interpersonal conversation. Here, the intrapersonal conversation with oneself is stimulated by the conversation with the individual spiritual director and/or in a group of spiritual directees. From the paradigm of the self, the directees search for personal truth and meaning in the texts they communicate about.

3.2. The Special Functions

Up till now we simply took the seven special functions of the pastor for granted, without further discussion. Nevertheless, as noted in the previous section, there are a number of problems and reservations associated with this classification. This is because different authors have proposed different divisions into levels, dimensions or sectors and have localized different functions in them. In the literature one

---

[109] R. Volp, "Praktische Theologie als Theoriebildung und Kompetenzgewinnung bei F. D. Schleiermacher," *Praktische Theologie heute*, eds. F. Klostermann and R. Zerfass (München: Kaiser, 1974) 52-64; B. Kaempf, "La théologie pratique D. F. Schleiermachter," *La théologie pratique*, eds. B. Reymond and J.-M. Sordet (Paris: Cerf, 1993) 7-19.

therefore encounters a variety of different lists, from lists with two to lists with six categories.

The simplest system is that proposed by Schleiermacher, who starts from the basis of the local congregation and distinguishes two main functions: worship ('Kirchendienst') and organization ('Kirchenregiment'), which also covers the maintaining of relations with society and the state.[109]

Lists of three functions are the most numerous, although they are based on a broad range of different principles of categorization. One of these, which again is based on the local congregation, consists of the following three-way classification: shepherding, communicating and organizing.[110] Another three-way classification that begins from the viewpoint of the local congregation is: kerygma (preaching), didache (catechesis), paraclesis (pastoral care). These are described as the three forms of pastoral work through which the basic form is realized, which is the local congregation gathering together.[111]

Taking the congregation as the starting point for a system of classification of functions brings with it the danger that these functions will be restricted to the domain of the church. This, however, runs counter to the principle described in Chapter I, namely, the presence of religion at the macrolevel of the society, the mesolevel of the church and the microlevel of the individual. This last principle, in varying forms, is encountered as the basis for a number of classifications.

In some systems of classification, society and the individual change places, and the three levels are again divided into several functions, as in the following list: individual level: diaconate and pastoral care; church level: preaching and liturgy; societal level: religious education and church development.[112] These sequence is also followed in the next list, which nevertheless differs substantially from the preceding one: individual level: pastoral care, religious education, spirituality; church level: church development, catechesis, liturgy, preaching; societal level: diacony, evangelization, volunteer education.[113] Here we

---

[110] S. Hiltner, *Preface to Pastoral Theology* (New York: Abingdon Press, 1958); R. Zerfass, *Praktische Theologie heute* (München: Kaiser, 1974).

[111] J. Firet, *Het agogisch moment in het pastoraal optreden*, 54-122.

[112] D. Rössler, *Grundriss der Praktischen Theologie* (Berlin: De Gruyter, 1986).

[113] G. Heitink, *Praktische theologie. Geschiedenis, theorie, handelingsvelden*, 241.

see that the same principle of classification can lead to entirely different lists.

Starting from the same division into three levels, the church level can also be put in first place, followed by the individual and societal levels, resulting in yet another set of categories: church level: church development, spirituality, koinonia, diakonia; individual level: pastoral care and rites of passage; societal level: church and society, social movements.[114]

The Gütersloh *Handbuch der Praktischen Theologie* also bases itself on the three aforementioned levels, in the familiar sequence: individual, church and society. The authors place this sequence along one axis and project on to it a second, perpendicular axis with the following categories: proclamation/communication, education/socialization, pastoral care/diaconate, leadership/organization. The framework produced in this way contains 12 cells representing 12 sectors of pastoral work.[115] This does, however, result in a great deal of overlap. The category of individual and group counseling, for example, is dealt with at the individual, church and societal levels.[116]

The three-level sequence can be treated in yet another fashion, by starting with the societal level, followed by that of the individual and finally the church. Again these levels can be situated along one axis, onto which another, perpendicular axis is projected, this time with the following six categories: communication, learning, experience, care, service and ideology critique. The result is a matrix with 18 cells that portrays the rich and complex whole of pastoral work.[117] Here again there is considerable overlap, owing to the fact that the categories contained in the six-way classification are logically inadequate.

There are also lists with four sectors. These appear to be more or less limited to the perspective of the church, although this does not prevent them from differing considerably among themselves. The Berlin *Handbuch der Praktischen Theologie* uses ecclesiological

---

[114] P. Zulehner, *Praktische Theologie*, Band I-IV (Düsseldorf: Patmos, 1989).

[115] P. Bloth et al., *Handbuch der Praktischen Theologie* (Gütersloh: Gütersloher Verlaghaus Gerd Mohn, 1981).

[116] Cf. F. Haarsma, 1982 424

[117] G. Dingemans, *Manieren van doen. Inleiding tot de studie van de praktische theologie*, 147.

structure as the starting point for its classification: the church as a social formation ('Sozialgestalt'), a service formation ('Dienstgestalt'), a juridical formation ('Rechtsgestalt') and a community formation ('Personalgestalt')[118], a scheme which certainly does not neglect the relationship of the church to society.

Another, almost classical four-way division is: kerygma, leitourgia, koinonia and diakonia .[119] When a fifth component is added, the list becomes: kerygma, leitourgia, koinonia, diakonia, paideia.[120]

Elsewhere, I myself presented an entirely different list of five pastoral functions that are considered to be mutually irreducible: pastoral counseling, catechesis, liturgy, proclamation and diacony. These five sectors are then placed along a horizontal axis, onto which is projected a vertical axis divided into four ecclesial functions: identity, integration, policy and administration. The combination of the five pastoral and the four ecclesial functions creates a matrix in which all the cells are oriented towards one goal: church development.[121]

Lists also exist that are based on a six-part division, such as the one presented in the renowned Catholic *Handbuch der Pastoraltheologie* that came about under the stimulating leadership of Karl Rahner. It lists the following sectors: proclamation, which is subdivided into missionary, congregational and catechetical proclamation; liturgy, especially the Eucharist; the administration of the sacraments; church discipline; Christian life, which is divided into, among others, family life and professional life; and, finally, caritas. The authors of this list are aware of the many questions that it may raise. Thus, they themselves point to the overlap between Christian life and caritas, between liturgy and the administration of the sacraments, and between church discipline and the administration of the sacraments. Their answer to this question is that they are simply concerned with the practical goal of describing the functions of the church that actually occur in the life of the church. The authors are also aware that the sequence of the items

---

[118] H. Ammer et al., *Handbuch der Praktischen Theologie* (Berlin: Evangelische Verlagsanstalt, 1974).

[119] F. Haarsma, *Kirchliche Lehre* (Freiburg: Herder, 1970).

[120] J. W. Fowler, *Weaving the New Creation. Stages of Faith and the Public Church* (San Francisco: Harper and Row, 1991) 178 v.

[121] J. A. Van der Ven, *Ecclesiology in Context*, 81-82.

on this list may lead to questions as well. Should not the Eucharist be placed at the beginning and are not all other functions subordinate to it? Their answer is that the church has always considered itself as the church of both the word and the sacrament. On these grounds the first three functions or sectors belong together, with the Eucharist at the centre. The last three functions or sectors proceed from the first three. They take the love that has been celebrated and brought to a culmination point in the liturgy of word and sacraments and carry it out into other domains of life. Church discipline is considered a necessary condition that allows this process to occur. Once church discipline is guaranteed, love can be manifested in Christian life and in caritas. Against this background, the authors note, the six functions can be reduced to three: proclamation, Eucharist and love.[122]

It is clear from this overview that the authors of this six-part classification are right when they note, with reference to the choices and the sequence of sectors and functions that make up pastoral work: "This question is dark and difficult".[123] The same, indeed, is true of all systems of classification.

Whichever system one chooses and for whatever reasons, the resulting list of sectors and functions will certainly not be able to stand up against the most obvious criticism which follows from applying criteria that are valid for any list: exhaustiveness, consistency, logical strength, and mutual exclusion. Exhaustiveness means that the whole field of pastoral work is covered by the list of functions and that there are no activities left over that are not covered by the list. Consistency signifies that the chosen principle of classification is applied in the same way to all items on the list. Logical strength points to the need for making divisions that are logically adequate, and mutual exclusion means that there is no overlap between items.

The foregoing gives us some clues as to what a system of classification should look like, and traps to avoid. What we can not and need not do is to apply a pre-determined principle in such a consistent and

---

[122] K. Rahner, "Die grundfunktionen der Kirche. Theologische und pastoraltheologische Vorüberlegung," *Handbuch der Pastoraltheologie*, Band I, eds. F. X. Arnold, K. Rahner, V. Schurr and L. Weber (Freiburg: Herder, 1964).

[123] K. Rahner, "Die Grundfunktionen der Kirche. Theologische und pastoraltheologische Vorüberlegung," 217.

logical way as to derive a number of mutually exclusive functions that cover all pastoral activities. It should be noted in advance that the functions that we propose do partially overlap and do not completely do justice to all pastoral activities. What we do need to do is to identify the most important functions that make up the actual practice of pastoral work in western countries in the second half of the nineteen nineties, at least as we now perceive and analyze this work. We will then localize these functions on a continuum that we construct from the three levels of religion which we defined in Chapter I, with the macrolevel of the society and the microlevel of the individual as the two ends of the continuum and the mesolevel of the church in the middle. The advantage of working with a continuum is that we need not allocate the various functions exclusively and discretely to one or the other of the three levels, but can localize them anywhere between and across the levels. Moreover, we can indicate the extent to which the functions stretch from one level to another, as the arrows in the following figure show.[124] In this manner, we can describe the seven functions as follows:

macrolevel society	mesolevel church	microlevel individual
	<——— liturgy/preaching ———>	
	<——— catechesis ———>	
	<—— church development ——>	
<—— social ministry ——>		
<—— mission work ——>		
		<—— pastoral counseling ——>
		<—— spiritual direction ——>

[124] Cf. D. Browning, "Auf dem Wege zu einer Fundamentalen und Strategischen Praktischen Theologie," *Praktische Theologie und Kultur der Gegenwart. Ein internationaler Dialog*, eds. K. E. Nipkow, D. Rössler and F. Schweitzer (Gütersloh: Kaiser, 1991) 21-42; K. E. Nipkow, "Praktische Theologie und gegenwärtige Kultur. Auf der Suche nach einem neuen Paradigma," *Praktische Theologie und Kultur der Gegenwart. Ein internationaler Dialog*, eds. K. E. Nipkow, D. Rössler and F. Schweitzer (Gütersloh: Kaiser, 1991) 132-154; G. Heitink, *Praktische theologie. Geschiedenis, theorie, handelingsvelden*, 240- 241.

From this perspective, we allocate three functions around the mesolevel of the church in the middle of the continuum: liturgy, including preaching, catechesis, and church development. These three functions are not restricted to the mesolevel of the church but extend also into the societal and individual levels.

In liturgy and preaching the members of the congregation are not addressed solely as a community, but also as individual people who, through the celebration of the liturgy, express in the face of God the needs and desires that are part of their human existence. However, they are also addressed as members of communities and institutions outside the church and as such are called on to engage with people and groups in society who are suffering and who require material or spiritual support and assistance.[125]

The function of catechesis is not merely to introduce and convey the richness contained in the traditions of the church, but to establish relations between these traditions and the questions of the participants as individuals, as well as between these traditions and the problems of society, including the suffering of certain groups in the society.[126]

In church development, concern for the welfare of the congregation, of course, ranks first and foremost. This includes the identity, integration, policy and administration of the local community. What must always be borne in mind, however, is that the church does not exist for its own sake, but that, as the people of God, the movement of Jesus and the community of the Spirit, it looks beyond its own boundaries and takes up the cause of all groups and individuals who are 'different',

---

[125] R. Grimes, *Beginnings in Ritual Studies* (Washington, 1982); *Ritual Criticism* (Columbia: University of South Carolina Press, 1990); A. Scheer, "De beleving van liturgische riten en symbolen," *Pastoraal tussen ideaal en werkelijkheid*, ed. J. A. van der Ven (Kampen: Kok, 1985); H. Pieterse, *Communicative Preaching* (Pretoria, 1987); G. Dingemans, *Als hoorder onder de hoorders* (Kampen: Kok, 1991).

[126] C. Hermans, Vorming in perspectief (Baarn: Gooi en Sticht, 1993); A. de Jong 1990, *Weerklank van Job,* Theologie en Empirie, 8 (Kampen: Kok, 1990); H.-G. Ziebertz, *Moralerziehung im Wertpluralismus* (Kampen, Weinheim: Kok, 1990); *Sexualität im Wertpluralismus* (Mainz: Matthias Grünewald Verlag, 1991); *Empirische Religionspädagogik*; Th. Groome, *Sharing Faith. A Comprehensive Approach to Religious Education and Pastoral Ministry* (San Francisco: Harper, 1991).

JA VAN DER VEN

whether it be because of the social class they belong to, the culture they come from or the religion they belong to.[127]

Next, we allocate two functions to the field that spans church and society: social ministry and mission. We situate them between the two levels because if they were to be limited to the church, we would not do justice to the particular objectives and tasks confronting the pastor in these two sectors. However, if they were to be situated exclusively at the level of society, they would in the long run lack the foundation that is necessary for accomplishing the goals and tasks of these two functions.

Social ministry is aimed at the poor in society who suffer for lack of material and spiritual resources, both individual and collective, and therefore are denied a dignified existence. For the church as the movement of Jesus and — as an extension hereof — the church of the poor, or at least with the poor — the situation of the poor represents a categorical responsibility.[128]

In conjunction with social ministry, mission has as its purpose intercultural and interreligious dialogue and the concrete realization of such dialogue in the tangible practice of liberating cultural and religious minorities, who more often than not belong to the lowest classes of society, from the many forms of need from which they suffer. This includes liberation from economic oppression, political alienation, social isolation and cultural and religious dominance.[129]

---

[127] A. Baart and B. Höfte, *Betrokken hemel, betrokken aarde. naar een praktische theologie van lokale kerkopbouw* (Baarn: Gooi en Sticht, 1994); N. Shawchuck and R. Henser, *Managing the Congregation. Building Effective Systems tot Serve People* (Nashville, 1996); J. S. Dreyer, "Die moderne gemeente en haar funksionering: die belang, aard en benutting van praktijkkennis," *The dynamics of the Modern Church*, eds. J. S. Dreyer and H. Pieterse, (Lynnwoodrif: Verba Vitae) 221-247; J. A. van der Ven, *Ecclesiology in Context*.

[128] H. Steinkamp, *Sozialpastoral* (Freiburg, 1991); C. Dudley and J. Carroll, "Congregational Self-Images for Social Ministry," *Carrier of Faith: Lessons from Congregational Studies*, eds. C. Dudley, J. Carroll and J. Wind (Westminster, 1991). T. van den Hoogen and P. van Gerven, "Gemeenteopbouw in de spiegel van de diakonie," *Praktische Theologie*, 18, no. 4 (1991) 414-435; H. Hasslinger, *Diakonie zwischen Mensch, Kirche und Gesellschaft. Eine praktisch-theologische Untersuchung der diakonischen Praxis unter dem Kriterium des Subjektseins des Menschen*. Studien zur Theologie und Praxis er Seelsorge, no. 18 (Würzburg: Echter, 1996).

[129] A. Camps, L. Hoedemaker, M. Spindler and F. Verstraelen, *Oecumenische inleiding in de missiologie* (Kampen: Kok, 1988); R. van Rossum, "Jezus uniciteit in

Finally we allocate pastoral counseling and spiritual direction to the area between church and individual. In both functions, concern for the welfare and happiness of the individual, of course, is foremost. However, if the structural link with the church were broken, both the quality of the work in these sectors and the church itself would suffer.

Pastoral counseling is aimed at the cognitive, affective and volitive unblocking of the powers of the individual, which are essential to the further development of the self. This development concerns the aims of human life, which consist of self-esteem and dignity, love and justice[130], for which religion provides the necessary inspiration and orientation.[131]

Spiritual direction is concerned with religious transformation within the relation between God and the individual person. Central to this task are the clarification of the individual's religious autobiography and the development of a conversion process that encompasses cognitive, affective and volitive aspects and that demands a process of continuous disciplined practice.[132]

How are these functions related to one another? This is an important question, for although all are made up of their own specific tasks

---

missionair perspectief," *Tijdschrift voor Theologie*, 28, no. 3 (1988) 272-288; B. Klein Goldewijk, Praktijk of principe. Basisgemeenschappen en de ecclesiologie van Leonarde Boff (Dissertation Nijmegen University, Kampen: Kok, 1991); D. Bosch, *Transforming Mission* (New York: Orbis Books, 1991); F. Wijsen, *There is Only one God. A Social- Scientific and Theological Study of Popular Religion and Evangelization in Sukumaland*, Northwest Tanzania (Kampen: Kok, 1994); D. Pittman, R. Habito and T. Muck, eds., *Ministry and Theology in Global Perspective. Contemporary Chalenges for the Church* (Grand Rapids: Eerdmans, 1996).

[130] Cf. P. Ricoeur, *Soi-même comme un autre*. English Translation: *Oneself as Another*.

[131] G. Heitink, Pastoraat als hulpverlening (Kampen: Kok, 1977); H. Clinebell, *Basic Types of Pastoral Care and Counseling. Revised and Enlarged*; R. Wicks, R. Parsons and D. Capps, *Clinical Handbook of Pastoral Counseling*, Volume 1 (New York: McGraw-Hill, 1985); H. Vossen, *Vrijwilligerseducatie en pastoraat aan rouwenden* (Dissertation Nijmegen University, Kampen: Kok, 1985); M. van Knippenberg, *Dood en religie* (Dissertation Nijmegen University, Kampen: Kok, 1987); R. Wicks and R. Parsons, *Clinical Handbook of Pastoral Counseling*, Volume 2; J. Savage, *Listening and Caring Skills in Ministry* (Nashville: Abingdon Press, 1996).

[132] Confer O. Steggink and K. Waayman, *Spiritualiteit en mystiek* (Nijmegen: Gottmer, 1985); R. Wicks, *Handbook of Spirituality for Ministers*.

and activities, all are in principle carried out by one and the same pastor or perhaps a small team of pastors and laity, who have a very real and practical interest in understanding these relationships.

The point which I emphasized earlier in this section is that the various functions differ in terms of the divergent paradigms which underlie them. Thus, for liturgy, including preaching, it is the ritual paradigm that is decisive, for catechesis the learning/teaching paradigm, and for church development the paradigm of community and organizational development. Social ministry is guided by the social welfare paradigm and mission by the cultural-anthropological development paradigm. Pastoral counseling is structured according to the therapeutic counseling paradigm and spiritual development according to the paradigm of self-development. The theological orientation and inspiration as well as the theological content of these functions remains undamaged, but are modeled on the structures and processes inherent in the various paradigms. At this point I can not go into greater detail on the theological aspects of these functions, and for a discussion thereof in terms of the aforementioned paradigms, the reader is referred to the relevant handbooks and other publications which I have mentioned in relation to the various functions.

The general rule which I wish to bring out here is that it is not only possible but also necessary and important to view the relations among the various functions from the point of view of their mutual paradigms. The reason why this is necessary and important is that looking at a function from a paradigm other than its characteristic one provides an opportunity to see new aspects in that function and thus to set in motion certain processes that may be fruitful and productive for that function. It is proposed, for example, that pastoral counseling, liturgy, social ministry and spirituality be regarded from the perspective of the teaching/learning paradigm[133], and that the ritual paradigm be applied to pastoral counseling[134] and catechesis.[135] Similarly, the

---

[133] Th. Groome, *Sharing Faith. A Comprehensive Approach to Religious Education and Pastoral Ministry* 137 v.

[134] M. van Uden, Rouw, *religie en ritueel* (Baarn: Ambo, 1988).

[135] P. McLaren, "Evaluating Competence for Professional Practice," *Educating Professionals. Responding to New Expectations for Competence and Accountability*, eds. L. Curry, J. Wergin (San Francisco: University of California Press, 1993).

cultural-anthropological paradigm can be applied to liturgy/preaching, catechesis, church development and so on, the paradigm of therapeutic counseling to spiritual direction, and the paradigm of self-development to pastoral counseling. This sort of 'paradigm crossing' should be encouraged, all the more in that it can help the individual pastor to establish a greater cohesion among the various functions which he performs.

3.3. The Second-Order Functions

In the previous sections, we have mentioned the importance of the commitment and participation of church members for the life and work of the church. From the vision of the church as the people of God, its mission as the movement of Jesus, and its imagination as a community of the Spirit, the active engagement of the church's members as the pillars, the very subjects of the church, can not be overrated. This commitment and participation also extend to the domain of ministry. The professional pastor is not the only one who bears responsibility for pastoral work, nor does he bear the highest responsibility. He is called upon to carry out the functions discussed above as adequately as possible in cooperation and collaboration with other professional pastors as well as active lay people.

Within this shared responsibility and cooperation, it is up to the professional pastor, together with others, to prepare pastoral volunteers to carry out these functions. This preparation consists of three separate tasks: the recruitment of pastoral volunteers, training of volunteers, and providing of guidance and support. I refer to these tasks as second-order functions, because the seven functions that were looked at earlier return here at a higher level, but now in the sense of recruitment, training and guidance. In other words, the pastor must recruit, train and provide guidance for pastoral volunteers for each of the three church-related functions (liturgy/preaching, catechesis, church development), for the two church/society-related functions (social ministry, mission), and for the two church/individual-related functions (pastoral counseling, spiritual direction). The combination of the three tasks involved in the preparation of volunteers with the seven functions results in a total of 21 subtasks.

Second-order functions

	Recruitment	Training	Guidance
Liturgy/preaching	*	*	*
Catechesis	*	*	*
Church development	*	*	*
Social ministry	*	*	*
Mission	*	*	*
Pastoral counseling	*	*	*
Spiritual direction	*	*	*

Of course, this outline is not meant to suggest that every pastor must always be responsible for all of the 21 subtasks. The pastor, together with his or her professional colleagues and the pastoral volunteers, will make choices among these subtasks, but in the process it is helpful to bear this outline in mind so as to be aware of the choices that are being made and why, and of which subtasks are being left to others.

4. Reflective Ministry

Having described the general and special functions of the pastor in the preceding section, we now proceed to clarify these functions in terms of reflective ministry. As we have seen in Chapters I and II as well as in the present part, pastoral work is becoming ever more complex and dynamic. As a result the pastor is increasingly forced to rely on his or her own initiative, own judgement and self-guidance. The epistemology of technical rationality that underlies the major professions is absent here. Instead of a technical and technocratic interpretation of the pastoral profession, we need an approach that is based on practical rationality and focusses on ministry as a reflective profession, on pastoral work as reflective practice and on the pastor as a reflective practitioner.[136]

---

[136] Cf. D. Schön, *The Reflective Practicioner. How Professionals Think in Action* (San Francisco: Jossey-Bass, 1983); *Educating the reflective Practicioner* (San Francisco: Jossey-Bass, 1987).

In this section we therefore pose the question: what is reflective ministry? We approach this question from the concept of 'reflective practice'. First, we will look at the relationship between 'practice' and 'reflection' in terms of 'reflection in practice' and 'reflection on practice' and elaborate on the teleological dimension within both 'reflection in practice' and 'reflection on practice' (section 4.1). Then we will apply the term 'reflective practice' to the general and special functions of the pastor (section 4.2).

4.1. Practice and Reflection

In looking at the relationship between practice and reflection, we take the perspective of American pragmatism, as developed by the great American philosophers of the Golden Age of American philosophy at the beginning of this century, in particular, Charles S. Peirce and John Dewey. The adjective, 'American', is by no means superfluous here, at least for European ears. In Europe the term pragmatism is often associated with 'mere pragmatism', implying that moral considerations, matters of principle or theoretical aspects are set aside, and that in deciding on the course of action to be followed as well as in assessing these actions afterwards, the pragmatist is guided solely by the power of the facts. American pragmatism as a philosophy, on the other hand, is something quite different. The description of facts and of situations does occupy an important place, but is nevertheless only one aspect of a much more complex approach to reality, in which experiential, conceptual, moral and transformational aspects play an important role, as we shall see. In analyzing the term 'practice' from the point of view of American pragmatism, I follow the lead of several contemporary authors with whom I share the view that this approach offers a way of deepening our understanding of the 'practice of ministry'. It is interesting to note that these authors are to be found not only on the American continent — for instance Browning[137], Chopp[138],

---

[137] D. Browning, *A Fundamental Practical Theology. Descriptive and Strategic proposals* (Minneapolis: Fortress Press, 1991).

[138] R. Chop, *Saving Work. Feminist Practices of Theological Education* (Westminster: Abingdon Press, 1995); *Christian Moral Imagination. A Feminist Practical Theology and the Future of Theological Education. Internal Paper* (Emory University, Atlanta, 1996).

West[139], Soneson[140], Lasalle-Klein[141], Gelpi[142] — but also in Europe. Thus Volp[143] established a fundamental connection between his interpretation of Schleiermacher and Peirce more than twenty years ago, and Bastian[144] applied Peirce's semiotics, which is at the core of the latter's pragmatism, to the practice of religious communication. I have recently taken a similar semiotic approach[145], and have also applied a few of Dewey's insights to practical theology.[146]

In the following, I will approach the relationship between practice and reflection from three points of view: the experiential point of view, by which 'reflection in practice'can be clarified, the experimental point of view, by which 'reflection on practice'can be interpreted, and the transformational point of view, by which the teleological dimension of both 'reflection in practice' and 'reflection on practice'can be understood. The first I take from Peirce, the second from Dewey, and the third from West, who has given a brilliant analysis of American pragmatism.

Reflection in Practice

The first perspective, the experiential, draws attention to the fact that the term, 'practice', simply denotes the experiences of the practitioner

[139] C. West, *The American Evasion of Philosophy. A Genealogy of Pragmatism; Prophetic Thought in Postmodern Times. Beyond Eurocentrism and Molticulturalism.* Volume I; *Prophetic Reflections. Notes on Race and Power in America. Beyond Eurocentrism and Multiculturalism.* Volume I.

[140] J. Soneson, *Pragmatism and Pluralism. John Dewey's Significance for Theology* (Minneapolis: Fortres Press, 1993).

[141] R. Lassale, *The Jesuit Martyrs of the University of Central America. An American University and the Historical Reality of the Reign of God* (dissertation, Graduate Theological Union, Berkeley, California); *Making Sense of the UCA Model for Christian Education. Thoughts on Practical Foundations for Theology in the America* (Internal Paper Jesuit School of Theology at Berkeley, California).

[142] D. Gelpi, *The Devine Mother. A Trinitarian Theology of the Holy Spirit,* 17-44 (Lanham: University Press of America, 1987); *The Turn to experience in Contemporary Theology* (New York: Paulist Press, 1994).

[143] R. Volp, "Praktische Theologie als Theoriebildung und Kompetenzgewinnung bei F. D. Schleiermacher," 52-64.

[144] Bastian, Kommunikation. *Wie Christlicher Glaube Funktioniert* (Stuttgart-Berlin: Kreuz-Verlag, 1972).

[145] J. A. Van der Ven, *Ecclesiology in Context,* 104 v.

[146] J. A. Van der Ven, "Die qualitative Inhaltsanalyse," *Paradigmenentwicklung in der Praktischen Theologie,* Theologie and Empirie, 13, eds. J. A. van der Ven and H.-G. Ziebertz (Kampen, Weinheim: Kok, 1993) 113-164.

in the course of his or her work. These experiences relate to himself or herself, to other persons, groups of persons, situations, processes, structures, etc. This is true also of the pastoral practitioner in the various functions that he or she carries out in the course of his or her work.

From the point of view of Peirce's pragmatism, it is important to realize that these experiences do not refer to a merely passive experiencing, as though the person in question were merely 'undergoing' the experience. On the contrary, the expression, 'to have experiences', is understood here in the active sense, as something that we do, not something that is done to us. We make experiences. This active involvement encompasses three aspects, as Peirce notes: evaluations, actions, and general tendencies.[147]

First, that experiences are laden with evaluations is evident when one looks at the fact that in our experiences within our practice, we not only perceive people and things through the senses, but also develop feelings about them. We experience joy or sorrow, fear or anger, gratitude or disappointment when we are in the presence of and interact with people and things. We experience these feelings because we are attentive and at the same time these feelings make us attentive. However, these attentive experiences are not simply aroused by vague feelings, but are mediated by images. These images are carried around in our memory and are reactualized, as it were, in concrete experiences. It may also be, however, that our experiences spontaneously and unconsciously, preconsciously or semi-consciously construct new images from various memory fragments. The significance of these images lies simply in that they are part of a network of images and occupy a special place in that network.

The processing of these images within experience is important because it fulfils three functions: abduction, deduction and induction. Although these terms sound scientific, and although they do occupy a prominent place in scientific theory and methodology, we are concerned here with the analysis of daily experience in daily practice. We can illustrate these three functions using the example of Columbus. As the young Columbus sat on the shore and watched the ships

---

[147] D. Gelpi, The Devine Mother. *A Trinitarian Theology of the Holy Spirit*, 17-44.

approaching, he noticed that he saw first the tips of the masts, then the masts, then the hull. From this specific experience Columbus inferred the abduction that the earth must be round. From this insight he inferred the deductive prediction that he could reach the Orient by sailing west instead of east. Eventually, Magellan's crew provided inductively the data to verify Columbus's predictive hypothesis.[148] In their experience of daily practice, people are constantly going through these processes. From their perceptions of other people and themselves they abductively infer a case, from which they deductively infer hypothetical predictions and then inductively test them. This is true of the pastor as well. He or she also goes through continuous processes of abduction, deduction and induction, from a profane as well as a religious perspective, with regard to situations he or she and others are in.

Evaluations within experience involve sensory processes, feelings, cognitions (images), and logical frames, and extend from passive sensations to active, abstract inferences.

Continuing our analysis of experience in daily practice, we note that the individual not only responds with evaluation, but also with decisive reaction. The actions which I perform in the course of this decisive reaction lend a sharp concreteness to my experiences. I react in this way or the other by doing this and not doing that. I make a choice, conscious or not, from among several alternatives. When the pastor is approached by someone whom he or she finds threatening, because he or she has been injured materially or spiritually by that person in the past and predictively assumes that the same thing will happen again, he or she has two possible ways to respond: fight or flight. The making of such a choice, based on the evaluations that take place as part of the experience, is part of the whole of experience itself.

Analysis of these experiences also reveals a third and final aspect which has to do with the characterization of the personal self that makes the evaluations and performs the actions. How does the self experience itself in these experiences? This question can sometimes be very much in the foreground ('focal self'), at other times more in

---

[148] D. Gelpi, *The Turn to Experience in Contemporary Theology*, 31-32.

the background ('matrix self'). To answer this question we look at the aspect of general tendencies. This means that the self which evaluates and acts does so from within a certain continuity, a certain habit, which leads the observer to say: "This is typical of him or her." These general tendencies make it possible to retrospect into the past of the self, introspect into the actuality of the self, and prospect into the future of the self. This is not to say that habits do not change. While habits result from evaluation and decisive action, these evaluations and decisions either corroborate old habits or (re)construct new ones. Consequently, the self is constantly changing. "In either case the self is modified. Old habits are perfected and strengthened through repetition: practice makes perfect. New habits are established through innovative decisions".[149] Reflection on these tendencies and habits is one of the characteristics of the self. Through the internal dialogue that the self carries on with itself, it is able to travel through time, as it were, to gain an understanding of its own time and to give shape to the dialogue with the 'different selves in time' in a critical fashion. This is also how the term 'conscience' can be understood: as the 'critical self in dialogue with itself'. The self is an interpreting subject, but at the same time an interpreted object.[150] Each self is a self-defined and self-defining process.[151]

This description of the three aspects contained in the experiences of daily practice is of the utmost importance for the analysis of ministry as reflective practice. It is clear from what we have just seen that reflection, at least in the sense of the inferential processes that are part of it, is not separate from practice nor, even less so, elevated above it, but forms an intrinsic part of this practice. In other words, reflection is something that happens within practice. The signficance of Peirce's analysis is that he puts an end to the Cartesian split between the 'res extensa' and the 'res cogitans' and the Kantian dichotomy between 'practical reason' and 'pure reason', in which so many present-day European theologians, and Latin American liberation theologians, are

---

[149] D. Gelpi, The Devine Mother. *A Trinitarian Theology of the Holy Spirit*, 36.

[150] V. Colapietro, *Peirce's Approach to the Self* (New York: State University of New York Press, 1989) 66, 91, 94.

[151] D. Gelpi, The Devine Mother. *A Trinitarian Theology of the Holy Spirit*, 37.

still caught up in their relation to experience and practice respectively, at least according to Gelpi.[152]

Reflection on Practice

The second perspective from which I wish to approach the relationship between practice and reflection is an experimental one. The aspects of our daily practice that come to the fore from this angle are implicit in what was said previously about the analysis of experience, but it is nonetheless useful to explicitate it here. The analysis so far has been about 'reflection in practice', and we are now turning our attention to 'reflection on practice', without, however, losing sight of 'reflection in practice'. For the fundamental insight that I wish to convey is that 'reflection on practice' has its roots in, arises from and returns to 'reflection in practice'. One could say that 'reflection on practice' is merely an explicitation and extension of certain aspects of 'reflection in practice'.

For the experimental perspective I refer to Dewey's analysis of the cycle of problem raising and problem solving, as it occurs in everyday practice, including that of the pastor. This analysis reveals several phases in this process.[153]

In the first phase, one experiences a situation which is so unsettled or indeterminate that one feels confused, and experiences the situation as obscure and strange. One is taken by surprise, as it were, and confronted with such a complexity of vagueness, questions, doubts, hesitations, that one initially does not know a way out. As one undergoes the situation, it triggers all kinds of feelings, above all of discomfort and uneasiness, rather than activating a number of clear images to which one is able to accord an appropriate meaning within a larger network of images. In other words, the fullness of the aspects which we saw in the analysis of experience is lacking here, at least partially.

---

[152] D. Gelpi, *The Turn to Experience in Contemporary Theology*, 9-51.

[153] J. Dewey, *How We Think*; *Logic: The Theory of Inquiry*, The Later Works. Volume 12 (Chicago: University of Chicago Press, 1986); *The Moral Writings of John Dewey*, Edited by James Gouinlock, Revised edition (New York: State University of New York Press, 1994) 257 v.; C. Wales, A. Nardi and R. Stager, "Emphasizing Critical Thinking and Problem Solving," *Educating Professionals. Responding to New Expectations for Competence and Accountability*, 178-211.

There is sensation and there is feeling, but there are no clear images, no network of images, no inferential processes of abduction, deduction and induction. Consequently, one is also prevented from decision and action. And certainly such a situation does not contribute to the self-defining process of the self.

The second phase centers around the question of how this confusion can be diminished. Dewey's answer is that the only way out of this situation is for the person to make a choice from the whole complex of uncertainties, questions, doubts and hesitations, to fix on one of these uncertainties, questions and difficulties and elevate it, as it were, to the status of a problem. Of course, the choice itself already forms a problem. The person is now directly confronted with the choice problem: how am I going to handle the situation, which problem will I tackle? The choice may be determined by a variety of factors, but these always have to do with the interaction between the person who is in the situation and the situation. There are no 'objective' or 'neutral' factors that lead to problem raising, only interactional factors.

The third phase is problem setting. This, too, is crucial. How I look at and formulate the problem, once I have selected it as the problem, determines to a large extent the strategies that I will use to find alternative solutions and, ultimately, a definitive solution. A well-formulated problem already contains half the solution. It indicates which prior experiences are relevant for dealing with the problem, and which abductions, deductions and inductions that one has developed in the past may be helpful for what aspect of the problem, and for what purpose. It also suggests the kind of support, guidance or advice I will need from others, and also to what degree the problem can be solved only in cooperation with others. It provides information about the relation between the weight of the problem and my own ability to carry that weight.

The fourth phase consists in the actual determination of possible solutions to the problem. It is important to carefully trace the various processes that are involved in this. First of all the situation is analyzed as carefully as possible in order that one may identify as clearly as possible which factors may improve or be detrimental to the situation. For the clearest possible diagnosis, these factors are set out side by side, and the conditions which have brought these factors into play are explicitated. In this way, one or more ideas for possible solutions automatically suggest themselves. Such an idea arises because one anticipates the possible consequences that will ensue if the idea is put into effect in the particular situation. The more information is collected about the factors and conditions of the situation, the more clearly the idea can be defined and the more clearly the actions that would result in a real solution suggest themselves. At the beginning such an idea springs up in the form of a sudden thought or a suggestion that flashes through one's mind. This becomes an idea only when it is examined with reference to its 'functional fitness', its ability to solve the problem.

This examination takes place in the fifth phase, which follows the basic pattern of abduction, deduction and induction that was described earlier. In the process, one constantly makes use of the experiences that oneself or other people who are involved in solving the problem have had in the past. From the previous experiences, one infers insights and applies them to the problem (abduction); from the application one infers hypothetical predictions (deduction), and from one's experiential familiarity with the situation one makes estimates with regard to the reliability of those predictions (estimate induction). The examination is not limited to one possible solution, but includes a number of alternatives. For each alternative, complex (and sometimes unconscious) processes of abduction, deduction and (estimate) induction take place. The outcome of the examination is a decision concerning the choice of the most desirable, or in some cases the least undesirable, problem-solving strategy.

After the examination and determination, the sixth phase consists in performing specific actions which are aimed a solving the problem. These actions take place in time, which is simply to say that they may take a longer or shorter period of time to carry out, depending on the extent and complexity of the problem and of the quantity and quality of people who are affected by it. This phase shows whether the selected problem-solving strategy is actually effective and to what extent it contributes to the solution of the problem. It is here that the true process of induction takes place.

The last phase is that of evaluation. The object is to determine whether one is satisfied with the chosen approach or whether the cycle must be gone through again because the selected problem-solving strategy did not produce the results one had hoped for. It is on the basis of the whole of this cycle of seven phases, culminating in the evaluative phase in which the decision may be taken to go through the entire cycle again, that I speak of the 'experimental nature of practice'. Practice is not the object of experimentation, but implies experimentation. Practice is, to a greater or lesser extent, an experiment.

Thus far I have approached the relationship between practice and reflection from two perspectives: the experiential and the experimental. From the discussion, it is clear how closely the two are linked. The aspects of experience that were first described in a synchronous sense in the experiential perspective (evaluations, including inferences, actions and general tendencies of the self), return in a diachronous sense in the experimental perspective, which is relevant specifically when the situation is complex and confusing.

The Teleological Dimension in the Reflection in/on Practice

The last perspective from which I will approach the relationship between practice and reflection is what I will call the transformational perspective. This perspective is present in the elements that we have already reviewed in the analysis of the experiential and experimental perspectives. From the experiential point of view, the evaluations, actions and general tendencies contain a teleological orientation. And from the experimental perspective, the raising, setting and solving of problems and evaluation of problem-solving imply an ultimate standard. What is this ultimate standard? For an answer, I refer to Peirce, who states that there are three functions of the human person: "to work out his [or her] own nature and impulses, to aid others, and to contribute to the fulfillment of the destiny of his [or her] generation." The reference to the destiny of one's generation can be understood to mean determining our function at least partially in terms of our time and place, the spatio-temporal context, as Colapietro has remarked.[154]

The experiential and experimental nature of the relation between practice and reflection forms the infrastructure for the transformational orientation that is also present in this relation. This transformational

---

[154] V. Colapietro, *Peirce's Approach to the Self*, 41.

orientation contains a tension between two aspects: the absolute standard and the spatio-temporal context. The first represents the ideals of the intrinsic dignity of human beings, the love between human beings and the existence of a just society. The second points to conditions of an economic, political, social and cultural nature that impede the realization of these ideals. In American pragmatism, the term 'practice', including its core, 'reflection', refers precisely to the bringing to consciousness of this tension, the process of making this tension communicable and reducing it through the active shifting of boundaries, under the societal conditions under which we live, in the direction of the aforementioned ideals. The term transformation makes this explicit, and according to the various areas in which the transformation needs to occur, one can speak of different kinds of transformation: economic, political, social and cultural, in particular educational and religious transformation, as well as individual transformation.[155] In order to prevent the notion of transformation from becoming an empty phrase, some advocate what Dewey, for example, calls 'social experiments' or 'cultural experiments'. The description of these experiments can also be a way of intervening in the public discussion about societal problems.

This transformational nature of practice, in which the tension between ideals and restrictive societal conditions is made explicit, without falling into the trap of wishful thinking, on the one hand, or embittered cynicism, on the other, draws attention to the tragic dimension in all practice, even though this dimension is usually ignored in descriptions of pragmatism. This tragic dimension has to do with intractable constraints, irreconcilable values, choices between conflicting goods, limited options, the lesser evil (in connection with which one always has to ask: lesser evil for whom? who are the victims?) The theologian, Reinhold Niebuhr, too, is sensitive to the 'Nature and Destiny of Man', the tension between the wilful self and fateful circumstances, between human volition and historical limits.[156] The notion of the tragedy inherent in practice, particularly from a

---

[155] C. West, *The American Evasion of Philosophy. A Genealogy of Pragmatism*, 218.

[156] C. West, *The American Evasion of Philosophy. A Genealogy of Pragmatism*, 159.

transformational point of view, can and must not be lacking in the analysis of the practice of reflective ministry.

In the prophetic pragmatism of Cornel West, the transformational nature of practice and the notion of tragedy are related to each other in a creative way. West uses the adjective, prophetic, because it refers to the Jewish and Christian tradition of prophets who passionately criticized societal evils and abuses and opposed the suffering which those at the bottom of the societal order had to endure: "The mark of the prophet is to speak the truth in love with courage — come what may".[157] This means never giving up on new possibilities for human agency, both individual and collective. West combines the adjective, 'prophetic', with the term, 'pragmatism', however, in order to raise awareness that prophetic idealism can only be realized step by step in a reformist way. At the same time he points to the evil in individual and collective life of which the religious traditions remind us, and to the disappointment, doubt and despair that are awakened by the experience of evil. It is precisely these traditions which are capable of making a distinction between inescapable and transformable evil, thereby transcending the opposition between Sisyphean pessimism and utopian perfectionism. They describe the drama of human existence in terms of the tension between hope, on the one hand, and the sense of defeat and disillusionment, on the other. They point to the freedom of human beings to determine their own actions and, at the same time, to the fact that actions can not be undone.[158] They point to the meaning of life and the absurdity of the human condition.[159] Prophetic pragmatism, drawing on the religious traditions, promotes the possibility of human progress and the human impossibility of paradise.[160]

Overall, the relationship between practice and reflection from the experiential, experimental and transformational perspective can be described as follows. First, from the experiential perspective, we speak

---

[157] C. West, *The American Evasion of Philosophy. A Genealogy of Pragmatism*, 233.

[158] C. West, *Prophetic Thought in Postmodern Times. Beyond Eurocentrism and Multiculturalism*, Volume I, 31-58.

[159] C. West, *Prophetic Reflections. Notes on Race and Power in America. Beyond Eurocentrism and Multiculturalism*, Volume I, 49.

[160] C. West, *The American Evasion of Philosophy. A Genealogy of Pragmatism*, 229.

of reflection in practice. The reflective processes that take place in practice are: the inferential processes (abduction, deduction, induction) that occur in evaluation, the more or less conscious choice processes with regard to actions, and the self-defining processes that take place around the individual's own self. Second, from the experimental perspective, we can speak of reflection on practice. This reflection on practice can be divided into two processes: the experimental analysis of the reflective processes that are active in the practice itself, and the experimental evaluation of these processes. Finally, from the transformational perspective, we can speak of a teleological orientation in the reflection in practice and the reflection on practice. This orientation contains a tension between two aspects: a complex of ethical ideals and the societal constraints that impede their realization. Inherent in this tension is a fundamental tragedy.

4.2. Reflective Practice in Ministry

At the beginning of this section we asked: what is reflective ministry? We are now in a position to answer this question, and to apply the three perspectives (experiential, experimental and transformational) from which we approached reflective practice (reflection in practice, reflection on practice, teleology) to the general and special functions of ministry (section 3). We described the general function in terms of hermeneutic communication. Hermeneutic communication, we noted, is the common denominator that is present in the special functions, i.e., the church-related functions (liturgy/preaching, catechesis, church development), the church/society-related functions (social ministry, mission), and the church/individual-related functions (pastoral counseling, spiritual direction). Describing the general function in terms of the three perspectives implies, at the same time, interpreting the special functions, in which the general function is concretely manifested, in terms of these three perspectives. This applies also to the 'second-order' functions that relate to the recruitment, training and guidance of pastoral volunteers to prepare and support them for carrying out the special functions. We will make this description concrete by using an example, let us say a session of a liturgy preparation group that focuses on the sermon for the following Sunday (in this case about the meaning of the Song of Solomon for human sexuality), or a catechet-ical group on the same subject, a pastoral counseling group, or a spir-itual direction group.

Reflection in Ministry

We begin with reflection in ministry. In the practice of hermeneutic communication it is possible to distinguish the same three aspects that are characteristic of practice in general, namely, evaluation, action and general tendencies of the self, as we showed from the experiential point of view.

Evaluation is the first aspect: the pastor perceives the hermeneutic communication that he or she engages in with others (sensation). In the process he or she experiences certain feelings (joy, anger, disap-pointment) and also brings up certain images from which he or she produces labels to indicate (just for himself or herself) the two sub-groups he or she is working with (the group which underlines "God is love" and the group which stresses "God is justice"). With the help of these images he performs certain inferential processes consisting of: abductive discovering (for example: "Because in the Song of Solomon human sexuality is divine, this specific act of truly human sexuality is divine"), deductive reasoning (for example: "Human sexuality contributes to human flourishing and happiness"), and induc-tive testing (for example: "The sexual doctrine of the Catholic Church does not satisfy").

Based on these evaluations, the pastor is faced with a choice problem with respect to his or her actions: does he or she allow the hermeneutic communication to proceed apace or does he or she inter-vene? If he or she allows it to proceed, he or she is refraining from acting, but to refrain from acting is also a form of action.[161] If the pas-tor intervenes, he or she can do two things. Based on a renewed text/context correlation he or she may, for example, attempt to defend the sexual doctrine of the Catholic Church or he or she may criticize and reject it. In the process the pastor may come face to face with another choice problem: whether or not to try to obtain the support of

---

[161] G. H. Von Wright, *An Essay in Deontic Logic and the General Theory of Action* (Helsinki: Acta Philosphica Fennica, 1968).

other members of the group in his or her attempt to defend the sexual doctrine of the Catholic Church or in his or her criticism and rejection of it.

In the actions the pastor performs, his or her self also plays a role, sometimes in the foreground ('focal self'), sometimes more in the background ('matrix self'). He or she asks himself or herself whether the actions he or she is performing correspond with the way he or she sees and values himself or herself in light of his or her own past. Are the planned or soon-to-be-planned actions a result of certain hermeneu-tic-communicative habits that he or she has developed in the past and, if so, ought these to be continued or broken off and replaced by new habits? The self of the pastor, his or her hermeneutic-communicative self, his or her professional self, are at stake, and along with them his or her personal identity. For the pastor must also ask himself or herself personally what he or she, for example, actually thinks of the contrast between the Song of Solomon and the sexual doctrine of the Catholic Church.

Reflection on Ministry

From the experimental perspective, with the help of which we inter-preted reflection on practice, we can apply the aspects that we have just looked at in relation with the experiential perspective to analysis and evaluation. What the pastor does — to stay with the example of the Song of Solomon — is to analyze what exactly is the hermeneu-tic-communicative problem that arises as a result of the contrast between the Song of Solomon and the sexual doctrine of the Catholic Church (phases 1, 2 and 3), what alternatives for action exist — for instance non-intervention, or defending the Song of Solomon or the sexual doctrine of the Catholic Church — and which actions will pro-duce which effects (phase 4), which choices he or she should make and for what reasons, for example, fidelity to the biblical text, respect for the human dignity in sexuality, or fear of church authority (phase 5), what effects his or her intervention will have, such as widening the gap between Bible and doctrine, condemnation or approbation from members of the group, enhancing or detracting from his or her reputa-tion for hermeneutic communication and his or her personal credibility (phase 6), and finally whether he or she assesses this effect as positive or negative and whether he or she must repeat the cycle (phase 7).

The Teleological Dimension in the Reflection in/on Ministry

From the transformational perspective, with the help of which we studied the teleological dimension, the hermeneutic-communicative practice of the pastor likewise needs to be explicitated according to various aspects. Let us assume that the pastor is trained in a constructive-critical approach to culture and religion based on the prophetic traditions in Judaism and Christianity and also personally feels comfortable with this approach. When he or she is then confronted with — to return once more to the Song of Solomon — a contrast between the interpretation of the biblical text and the sexual doctrine of the Catholic Church, he or she realizes that he or she is in a field of tension between, on the one hand, the ideal of the liberation of sexuality from subjugation and tutelage through the religious theme of creation and, on the other hand, the constraints that condition his or her hermeneutic-communicative task. These constraints may be of a social kind, in so far as some members of the group are socialized to be so faithful to the church that they will tolerate no criticism of church authority, regardless of how firmly it may be founded in scripture. The constraints may also be institutional, since the pastor must fear for his or her job and livelihood if, for example, he or she were to give a sermon the following Sunday defending the dignity of human sexuality against the sexual doctrine of the Catholic Church. From a reformist point of view, he or she will seek a prudent compromise in which he or she attempts to make a few, careful steps forward, but at the same time he or she will not be able to rid himself or herself of a deep sense of tragedy.

In summary, the most important aspects of reflective ministry can be clarified by looking at them in terms of the three perspectives (experiential, experimental, transformational) that we have identified as being relevant to the relation between reflection and practice in general: reflection in ministry, reflection on ministry, and the teleological dimension within the reflection in/on ministry. The reflective quality of the pastor's general and special functions, as well as the second-order functions, can be clarified from the basis of hermeneutic communication, which forms the common denominator of the pastor's practice.

5. Reflective Competence for Ministry

Having examined the main aspects of the model of reflective ministry, it is now time to describe the most important aspects of the reflective competence that a pastor must possess in order to be capable of reflective ministry. This description can be seen as a more detailed concretization of that which remained implicit in the analysis of the model of reflective ministry. We distinguished between reflection in practice and reflection on practice and between reflection in ministry and reflection on ministry. From this distinction we try to answer two questions: what is competent reflection in ministry (section 5.1) and competent reflection on ministry (section 5.2)?

5.1. Competent Reflection in Ministry

The term 'competence' can be used in two different senses. The first sense is the legal or juridical capacity to act or refrain from acting. This is not something that only falls to judges or magistrates, but applies to anyone who, in a legally defined capacity of some kind, can assert certain rights, for example, spouses with regard to one another, parents with respect to their children, or heirs among themselves. The second meaning is completely outside any legal or juridical frame of reference. It refers to the the set of abilities required to execute a function, fulfil tasks and perform actions or series of actions. It entails the presence of the knowledge, insight, skills and attitudes needed to carry out the functions, tasks and actions concerned. Both of these meanings have relevance for the pastor. In order to do his or her work, the pastor needs the requisite legal authorization to allow him or her to properly carry out the tasks and activities in question. Likewise, he or she needs a set of professional abilities to perform these tasks and activities effectively, that is, in such a way that they achieve the desired objectives that are intrinsically contained therein. Aristotle would say: the pastor needs the professional abilities to perform these tasks and activities in a manner corresponding to the intrinsic standards of excellence. A person who possesses the technical skills to play a Beethoven sonata, but has no understanding of the musical structure and dynamic, does not have the competence to perform the composition according to its intrinsic standard of excellence. In this section, I restrict myself to the second meaning of competence. This is not to say that the first meaning is not important for the work of the pastor, for it certainly is, but a discussion of this aspect is not necessary in the present context of education for ministry.[162]

I will now describe the competent reflection in ministry in two stages. The first stage refers to the components of this competent reflection, the second to the difference between general and special competent reflection in ministry.

Components of Competent Reflection in Ministry

From among the set of abilities of which competence consists, I distinguish four components, which I mentioned above in passing: knowledge, insight, skills and attitudes. What does each of these components signify and what do they consist of? What is knowledge, what is insight, what are skills, what are attitudes? To answer this question one needs a theory or theories from which to draw definitions or at least descriptions. Without such theories any description will perforce be arbitrary in some way.

a.   Knowledge refers to the abilities to reproduce narratively and conceptually structured information. These abilities have to do with the apperception of information, the recognition of information and the actualization of information.[163]

b.   Insight relates to the abilities to produce narratively and conceptually structured information. The difference between knowledge and

---

[162] Cf. A. van de Spijker, *Pastorale competentie* (Heerlen: Poimen, 1984); A. Reijnen, *Terugblik met het oog op de toekomst*. Lezing gehouden op het symposium 'Pastorale vorming van de toekomst — Toekomst van de pastorale vorming' (May 31, Heerlen, 1996); G. Heitink, *Praktische theologie. Geschiedenis, theorie, handelingsvelden*, 295 v.

[163] E. de Corte, *Onderwijsdoelstellingen* (Leuven: Universitaire Pers Leuven, 1973) 157.

insight is that the first refers to the reproduction of information and the second to the production of information. The abilities inherent in the latter have to do with the interpretative production of information, the convergent production of information, the evaluative production of information and the divergent production of information. I take these descriptions of knowledge and insight from the Flemish educational psychologist De Corte, who owes the difference between reproduction and production to Guilford's structure-of-intellect model, which is based on factoral-analysis research into the nature of human intelligence.[164] However, where De Corte defines knowledge simply in terms of the reproduction of information and insight in terms of the production of information, I have added the qualifying concept of narratively and conceptually structured information. This distinction between narratively and conceptually structured information I borrow from the doyen of American cognitive psychology, Jerome Bruner, who has pointed to the irreducibility and complementarity of the two processes underlying information and information processing: narration and conception.[165]

c.   Skills refer to the abilities to appropriately use social methods and techniques which apply to specific aspects of concrete situations in which the professional performs his work. The difference between physical and social methods and techniques is that the first proceed from a subject/object relation and the second from a subject/subject relation. This subject/subject relation contains ethical aspects which must be respected if these social methods and techniques are to be properly used. These ethical aspects relate to the goals as a function of which the methods and techniques are utilized, and the values and norms within which the goals themselves are embedded. They also have to do with the human dignity of both the professional worker and his or her clients as human subjects, as I have said. Finally, they also relate to the soundness of the social methods and techniques, for instance, their effectiveness and efficiency. By emphasizing these ethical aspects, it is possible to reduce the resistance to social methods

---

[164]   E. de Corte, *Onderwijsdoelstellingen*, 136 v.

[165]   J. Bruner, *Actual Minds, Possible Worlds* (Cambridge: Harvard University Press, 1986); *Actions of Meaning* (Cambridge: Harvard University Press, 1990).

and techniques which is frequently expressed in a preference for the term 'social arts' over 'social methods and techniques', with the former refering to the unique expression of the professional worker's personal individuality.[166] And, indeed, in so far as methods and techniques contribute to indoctrination, coercion and technocratic change, they must be rejected precisely because of the lack of any social quality.[167]

d.   Attitudes are the affective-evaluative orientations which the professional has at his or her disposal in order to perform his or her work in an appropriate way. The term 'orientation' refers to the particular style or manner in which the person relates to persons or things. 'Affective' means that in these orientations, affects or feelings play a central role. These may be negative as well as positive affects (gladness and gratitude, sorrow and anger), and they may be directed at oneself, at other people or at things (pride, care, loyalty). 'Evaluative' means that these affects are associated with particular beliefs and values that are valued positively or negatively according to the nature of the feelings (self-love, fidelity, patriotism). That the professional has these attitudes at his or her disposal in the work he or she does means that he or she has both aspects at his or her disposal: the affects as well as the beliefs and values. Both together make up the attitudes.[168]

The aforementioned components of competence (knowledge, insight, skills, attitudes) now need to be related to the general and special competence of the pastor. The general competence concerns the common denominator that is present in all of the functions that the pastor performs, namely, hermeneutic communication. The special competence has to do with the special functions the pastor carries out, i.e., the church-related functions (liturgy/preaching, catechesis and church

---

[166] M. van Beugen, *Sociale technologie en het instrumentele aspect van agogische actie* (Assen: Van Gorcum, 1971) 42 v.

[167] Cf. W. Bennis, K. Benne and R. Chin, *The Planning of Change*, Second Edition (New York: Holt, Rinehart and Winston, 1971) 9-107.

[168] M. Fishbein, *Readings in Attitude Theory and Measurement* (New York: Wiley, 1967); M. Fishbein and I. Azjen, *Belief, Attitude, Intention and Behavior* (New York: Addison-Wesley, 1975).

development), the church/society-related functions (social ministry, mission), and the church/individual-related functions (pastoral counseling, spiritual direction).

General Competent Reflection in Ministry

The general competence of the pastor consists in hermeneutic-communicative competence. This is made up of four components, which are illustrated here with the help of several examples.

a.   Knowledge: The pastor is capable of the reproductive apperception, recognition and actualization of basic, narratively and conceptually structured information in the fields of hermeneutic theory and communication theory. Examples: the ability to recognize the differences between two homilies based on the relation between text correlation and text/context correlation hermeneutics; the ability to indicate the differences between three groups of speech acts (descriptives, expressives, regulatives) and their relevance for pastoral conversation and catechetical instruction.

b.   Insight: The pastor is capable of the interpretative production, convergent production, evaluative production and divergent production of basic, narratively and conceptually structured information in the fields of hermeneutic theory and communication theory. Examples: the ability to critically evaluate an article in which the hermeneutic assumptions and conclusions are inconsistent and mutually contradictory; the ability to produce an essay on religious communication in which aspects of information theory and semiotics are combined in an original way.

c.   Skills: The pastor has the ability to use social methods and techniques in the domain of hermeneutics and comunication. Examples: the ability to produce an original interpretation of a pericope from one of the Gospels clarifying its meaning for today's unchurched college students; the ability to listen to people's ambivalence with regard to certain aspects of the story of Jesus'resurrection in terms of the emotions they implicitly and explicitly express, and to help them communicate this ambivalence to other group members.

d. Attitudes: The pastor has the ability to use his or her hermeneutic and communicative attitudes, i.e., his or her personal affective-evaluative orientations with regard to hermeneutical and communicative beliefs and values, in such a way that it contributes to his or her parishioner's religious development. Examples: the ability to express his or her own feelings with regard to a specific biblical text, as he or she personally perceives and receives this; the ability to express his or her own spirituality in order to advance a parishioner's communication in which attitudes regarding religious themes like God's presence, creation or liberation are explored and clarified.

Special Competent Reflection in Ministry

Having described the components of the pastor's general competence, we can now proceed to describe the components of the pastor's special competence, which relates to the seven sectors I identified in section 3, i.e., the three church-related functions (liturgy/preaching, catechesis and church development), the two church/society-related functions (social ministry, mission), and the two church/individual-related functions (pastoral counseling, spiritual direction). Thus, we speak of one general competence (hermeneutic communication) and seven special competences (the seven special functions). This distinction seems to me more logically adequate than that proposed by Heitink[169], who speaks of three general competences (hermeneutic, hermeneutic-liturgical and agogic-communicative) as well as three special competences (pastoral, educative, community building/church building). In describing the seven special competences I will adhere to the breakdown into knowledge, insight, skills and attitudes. I will confine myself to general descriptions and a few examples, which will be taken from the respective disciplines associated with the special functions, i.e., the liturgical sciences, catechetics, practical ecclesiology, practical social ethics, missiology, poimenics, and spirituality theory.

a. Knowledge: The pastor is capable of the apperception, recognition and actualization of basic, narratively and conceptually structured

---

[169] G. Heitink, *Praktische theologie. Geschiedenis, theorie, handelingsvelden*, 301-302.

158   J.A. VAN DER VEN

information from the special disciplines, i.e., the liturgical sciences, catechetics, practical ecclesiology, practical social ethics, missiology, poimenics, and spirituality theory. Examples: the ability to describe the differences between an exegetical-instructional, kerygmatic, rhetorical, narrative or existential approach to preaching[170]; the ability to give well-structured information about exclusivism, inclusivism and pluralism with regard to interreligious dialogue, including the arguments and counter-arguments[171]; the ability to compare the kerygmatic, counseling and communicative approaches within pastoral care.[172]

b. Insight: The pastor is capable of the interpretative production, convergent production, evaluative production and divergent production of basic, narratively and conceptually structured information about the special disciplines, i.e., the liturgical sciences, catechetics, practical ecclesiology, practical social ethics, missiology, poimenics, and spirituality theory. Examples: the ability to write an original essay on the relevance of a cultural-anthropological approach to Christian liturgy in comparison with a purely historical approach[173]; the ability to read a paper which aims at a critical evaluation of social ministry policies by liberal, conservative, charismatic and fundamentalist congregations[174]; the ability to develop a criteriology for a program of spiritual exercises with special emphasis on the relation between freedom, leadership and spiritual authority.[175]

c. Skills: The pastor is able to use social methods and techniques in the domain of liturgy/preaching, catechesis, church development, social ministry, mission, pastoral counseling and spiritual direction. Examples: the ability to develop a homily from inscription hermeneutics[176]; the ability to design a funeral liturgy for a young person who

---

[170] Cf. G. Dingemans, *Als hoorder onder de hoorders*; H. Pieterse, *Communicative Preaching* (Pretoria: University of South Africa Press, 1987).

[171] Cf. P. Knitter, *No Other Name? A Critical Survey of Christian Attitudes Towards the World Religions*; H. M. Vroom, *Religies en waarheid* (Kampen: Kok, 1988); J. Hick and E. Meltzer, *Three Faith One God* (New York: Orbis Books, 1989).

[172] M. van Knippenberg, *Dood en religie* (Dissertation Nijmegen University, Kampen: Kok, 1987).

[173] R. Grimes, *Ritual Criticism* (Columbia: University of South Carolina Press, 1990).

[174] J. Carroll, C. Dudley and W. McKinney, *Handbook of Congregational Studies*.

[175] R. Wicks, *Handbook of Spirituality for Minister*.

[176] P. Ricoeur, "Naming God," *Union Seminary Quarterly* 34 (1978) 215-227.

committed suicide; the ability to use a taxonomy of educational objectives to develop a series of catechetical lessons[177]; the ability to use catechetical techniques of process and product evaluation[178]; the ability to apply the policy cycle for church development[179]; the ability to use management techniques in church administration[180]; the ability to use community development techniques to implement an outreach program for third-generation migrants[181]; the ability to apply methods of pastoral planning regarding popular religion[182]; the ability to handle transference and countertransference in counseling the bereaved[183]; the ability to use proclamation methods (informing, sharing, confronting, contending) in spiritual direction.[184]

d.   Attitudes: The pastor is able to use his or her attitudes, i.e., beliefs and affects, with regard to the main themes in the different functions, in such a way that this contributes to his or her parishioners' personal and religious development. Examples: the ability to express his or her feelings and values regarding a pericope from the Bible on the subject of guilt in such a way that the suppression processes among the participants of a catechetical meeting are broken through[185]; the ability to share his or her personal beliefs with regard to the relation between the Christian religion and the other Abrahamite religions; the ability to express his or her emotions of shame and to distinguish between

[177] B. Bloom et al., *Taxonomy of Educational Objectives*, Handbook I, Cognitive Domain (New York: Longman, 1951); D. Krathwol, B. Bloom and B. Masia, *Taxonomy of Educational Objectives*, Handbook II, Affective Domain (New York: Longman, 1964).

[178] B. Bloom, J. Hastings and G. Madaus, *Handbook on Formative and Summative Evaluation of Student Learning* (New York: Longman, 1971).

[179] W. Dunn, *Public Policy Analysis. An Introduction* (Englewood Cliffs: Prentice Hall, 1981).

[180] N. Shawchuck and R. Henser, *Managing the Congregation. Building Effective Systems to Serve People.*

[181] H. Steinkamp, *Sozialpastoral.*

[182] F. Wijsen, *There Is Only One God. A Social-Scientific and Theological Study of Popular Religion and Evangelization in Sukumaland, Northwest Tanzania.*

[183] M. Basch, *Doing Brief Psychotherapy* (New York: Basic Books, 1995); H. W. Stone, *Brief Pastoral Counseling. Short-term Approaches and Strategies.*

[184] C. Taylor, *The Skilled Pastor. Counseling as the Practice of Theology* (Minneapolis: Fortress Press, 1991).

[185] A. Uleyn, *The Recognition of Guilt. A Study in Pastoral Psychology* (Dublin: Gill and Macmillan, 1969).

authentic and inauthentic shame in order to help his or her counselee
to clarify his or her own emotions of shame.[186]

5.2. Competent Reflection on Ministry

I now proceed to the description of competent reflection on ministry, in which the way the pastor employs his or her competence in
pastoral practice is the object of reflection.

Competent reflection on ministry will also be related to the pastor's
general function and seven special functions, and therefore we will
speak of general competent reflection on ministry and special competent reflection on ministry. Both of these will in turn be described in
terms of the components of competence, albeit this time in a 'meta-
reflective' mode, in which these components become the object of
reflection, i.e., meta-knowledge, meta-insight, meta-skills, and meta-
attitudes.

General Competent Reflection on Ministry

Let me begin once again with the components of general competence that concern the area of hermeneutic communication.

a.   Meta-knowledge: The pastor is capable of reflective reproduction
of the disciplinary structures in hermeneutic theory and communication theory. The structure of knowledge which this entails has two
sides. On the one hand, the pastor has an understanding of the structure according to which the narrative and conceptual information
is organized by scholars in both fields. On the other hand, the pastor
has an understanding of the structure according to which he or she
himself or herself organizes information in the field of hermeneutic
theory and communication theory. The structure of the discipline has
two sides, as it were, an 'objective' side, which relates to the academic disciplines, and a 'subjective' side, which relates to the deeper
web or network of this information within the person himself or
herself, in this case the pastor. The objective side can be called expert
knowledge, the subjective side craft knowledge. Meta-knowledge
consists of the reflective ability to dig up both kinds of knowledge

---

[186]   B. Williams, *Shame and Necessity* (Berkeley, 1993).

structures, compare them in terms of similarities and differences and relate them to one another. This is called the interactive approach, by which the expert knowledge and the craft knowledge come together.[187] The assumption is that the cognitive activities of scholars and practicing professionals, not to say all human beings, are essentially the same, but nevertheless, on account of differences in specialization and investment of time, produce different, yet complementary results. It is by developing knowledge about knowledge that one begins to identify these meta-cognitive activities.

For the pastor, the aim is to acquire knowledge about knowledge in the area of hermeneutics and communication. In the process, he or she must ask question such as: which scholarly conceptual models of hermeneutic communication are available, what are their characteristics, what are their theoretical advantages and disadvantages; and: from what conceptual models or combinations thereof does the pastor himself or herself proceed, which assumptions underlie them, which tacit, unconscious arguments does he or she use, and to what degree are his or her choices theoretically defensible? In order to answer these questions, the pastor needs to engage in the exchange of and confrontation with pluriform visions, contrasts and contradictions. These questions must be adequately dealt with for a dynamic 'knowledge management' to be possible.[188]

As important as this 'knowledge management' is, the relating of the 'objective' side (expert knowledge) and 'subjective' side (craft knowledge) is a far from simple business. This is above all because, as research shows, professional practitioners have difficulty in articulating their subjective structures of knowledge. And this in turn is because strategies for adequately representing these subjective structures of knowledge as yet exist only in incipient form. Research into strategies for codifying these structures has begun, but is still in the early phases. These subjective structures can be tracked down and identified in particular by means of narratively and conceptually structured interviews, in which attention is paid to the following elements:

---

[187] P. Bergen, *Docenten scholen docenten* (Nijmegen: Katholieke Universiteit Nijmegen, 1996).

[188] Cf. J. Brunner, *The Culture of Education*, 60 (Cambridge: Harvard University Press, 1996)

assumptions, theses/hypotheses, arguments, counter-arguments, expected results, expected consequences, normative standards, operative values and norms, evaluations, perceived facts, perceived situation, perceived context.[189]

b. Meta-insight: The pastor is capable of the reflective production of the disciplinary structures in hermeneutic theory and communication theory. This ability allows the pastor, after the reproduction and interaction of the objective disciplinary structures (expert knowledge) and subjective disciplinary structures (craft knowledge), to construct his or her own disciplinary structure.This process of construction does not occur for its own sake, but with an eye to clarifying and rendering dynamic the problematic situation in which the pastor finds himself or herself, in order to direct the processes contained in the problematic situation in such a way that the desirable transformational quality can be brought about. This is important because in this way the processes of problem raising, problem setting and problem solving can be nourished that are characteristic of the experimental dimension of practice, from which we interpreted 'reflection on practice' (section 4). They contribute to 'inventing' the future, a future for which, owing to the complexity and dynamic change that characterize the church and the society, no 'master models' or 'master narratives' any longer exist.[190] What is needed is the competence to experiment with recombining elements from different knowledge areas[191], which requires recognition of rules, patterns and analogies. Only through pattern completion, pattern transformation and pattern association can change take place in an appropriate way.[192] This competence implies both logical and analogical thinking. Raising, setting and solving a problem require that the case which is seen as the problem be understood in terms of prior

---

[189] Cf. N. Verloop and Th. Wubbels, "Recente ontwikkelingen in het onderzoek naar leraren en lerarenopleiding," *Pedagogische Studien* 71 (1994) 168-186; F. Korthagen, "Reflectie en de professionele ontwikkeling van leraren," *Pedagogische Studien* 69 (1992) 112-123.

[190] Cf. B. Shore, *Culture in Mind. Cognition, Culture, and the Problem of Meaning* 129, 142.

[191] B. Shore, *Culture in Mind. Cognition, Culture, and the Problem of Meaning*, 151.

[192] B. Shore, *Culture in Mind. Cognition, Culture, and the Problem of Meaning*, 348 v.

schemes. The case is adapted to these schemes by processes of assimilation, so that it fits into these schemes, but at the same time the schemes accommodate to the case.[193] In assimilation it is convention that dominates, in accommodation it is invention. In other terms, 'inventing' the future only occurs in a dialectical process of convention and invention.

c.   Meta-skill: The pastor is capable of critical reflection about the use of social methods and techniques in the domain of hermeneutics and communication and about these methods and techniques themselves. Here, too, one can speak of an 'objective' side (expert knowledge) and a 'subjective' side (craft knowledge). The 'objective' side refers to the way in which scholars organize the methods and techniques in terms of their outer structure, meaning how they are organized relative to each other, and their inner strcture, meaning how each is internally organized, their qualities, in which situations they can be applied and in which they can not, and what the effects and side-effects may be. The 'subjective' side refers to the manner in which the pastor himself or herself experiences the methods and techniques that he or she uses, how he or she himself relates them to one another and structures them, which qualities he or she finds attractive and how he or she deals with the negative side-effects. The meta-skill we are talking about here consists in the pastor's ability to relate the 'objective' and 'subjective' sides to each other in a dialectical manner in order to develop a creative reconstruction process in himself. This is important in order to do justice to the complex and dynamic situations in church and society in which the pastor performs his or her functions on a daily basis.

d.   Meta-attitude: The pastor is capable of critical reflection on his or her personal feelings and beliefs in the domain of hermeneutics and communication. In order to understand this meta-attitude as fully as possible, I draw extensively on Kegan's ideas about critical attitude development in his *The Evolving Self* (1982) and *In Over Our Heads* (1995). The focus is on interpersonal and intrapersonal development.

---

[193] J. Piaget, *Introduction à l'épistémologie Génetique*. Tome III. German Translation: *Die Entwicklung des Erkennens III. Das biologische Denken. Das psychologiche Denken. Das soziologische Denken* (Stuttgart: Metzler, 1975) 77v.

Kegan is certainly not the first and not the last author to explore this field, as is evident from the work of Selman (1980), Kohlberg (1981), Hoffmann (1993) and Fowler (1981), but his particular accomplishment is to have explicitly taken into account the context of modern western society in elaborating his concept of attitude development.

In the field of interpersonal and intrapersonal attitude development, Kegan distinguishes five developmental orders of consciousness, of which it is primarily the last two that are of interest to us here. For the sake of completeness I will briefly describe the first three. In the first order, the child from the ages of 2 to 6 has the interpersonal ability to recognize that persons exist separately from itself as well as the intrapersonal ability to differentiate between inner sensations and outside stimulation. In the second order, the child from the ages of 6 to 10 years has the interpersonal ability to take the perspective of other persons and manipulate them in order to reach its own goals, and the intrapersonal ability to regulate internal impulses and identify enduring qualities of the outer self. In the period of the teenage years and beyond, the adolescent has the interpersonal ability to respect another's beliefs and emotions and be aware of shared feelings, and the intrapersonal ability to internalize another's beliefs and emotions and feel and express authentic empathy.

The fourth and fifth order go considerably further, and form a necessary condition for developing the pastor's reflective competence with regard to his or her attitudes. In the case of the fourth order, the person in question transcends the immediate experiences he or she has undergone and continues to undergo. This transcending process is made up of four basic insights: I am not made up of my own experience, I am not made up of the other's experience, the other is not made up of of his or her own experience, and the other is not made up of my experience.[194] A person in the fourth order has the ability to reflect on his or her own and the other's experiences. This reflection is about the relationships in which one is engaged, and consists of asking whether this is the kind of relationship one really wants to engage in, based on one's own beliefs, needs, values and norms, whether one

---

[194] R. Kegan, *In Over Our Heads. The Mental Demands of Modern Life* (Cambridge: Harvard University Press, 1995) 128.

should invest more in it and ask more of it, whether one should complement, adjust or correct it, or ultimately give it up. Underlying these
questions is the assumption that the self is co-constructor of this relationship. One is aware that it is one's own work and that one has 'to
own his or her work'. The person in question recognizes and accepts
that one is a self-initiating, self-correcting, self-evaluating person in
one's relationships, not only in relation to other people but also in relation to himself or herself. The person has the feeling that his relationships have to be guided by one's own visions and that one also has
responsibility for what happens in them, both externally and inter-
nally.However, these visions are not static or fixed, even though they
are the object of reflection. We are not our experiences, feelings,
beliefs and attitudes; we have experiences, feelings, beliefs and attitudes, as we learn from the non-directive approach pioneered by
Rogers, who favored the client's self-support, from Ellis' rational-emo-
tive therapy (RET) and from the object relations psychology of Kohut
and others.[195] In short, a person in the fourth order of consciousness
has a sense of self- regulation, an awareness of self-direction. He or
she sees himself or herself as a project.

The fourth order of consciousness is followed by the fifth order,
which again relativizes the assumptions, claims and statements which
characterize the fourth order. In the fifth order, one is aware that the
construction of one's own experiences, emotions, beliefs and attitudes
does not start from nothing, but molds and shapes what is already
there. One is aware of the setting, the situation, the context which
co-determine the choices one makes, the relationships one enters into,
the work one does, the love one engages in. The fifth order is characterized by going beyond absolutism and fanaticism, aknowledging and
accepting the factors which condition one's life, and proceeding from
there in order to re-create, re-construct and trans-form it. In short, the
self in the fifth order is a contextualized self. The self is a co-project.

I have said that the fourth and fifth orders are necessary conditions
for the pastor's reflective competence with regard to his or her attitudes to come into being, but we must be aware that this statement is
more the expression of a desired state than the description of a fact.

---

[195] R. Kegan, *In Over Our Heads. The Mental Demands of Modern Life*, 234 v.

Empirical research tells us that more often than not, people have a sense of 'being in over one's head' rather than of being a responsible and self-directing, adult self. Around one half to two thirds of the adult population appear not to have really reached the fourth order of consciousness.[196] Many remain stuck in immature attitudes of authority and dependence, others overreact by repeatedly entering into irrational conflicts with authority, and still others suffer from burn-out syndrome.

Leaving the third order and going toward the fourth and fifth orders means leaving behind what Kohlberg calls conventionalism, which operates in conventional religion and conventional morality.[197] It means leaving what Kegan calls the family religion, the family faith: "we move from being 'brought up in the faith' to become ourselves spiritual adherents to that faith".[198] What the fourth order "requires is that we construct a new relationship to the family or the religion".[199] And what the fifth order requires is that when we construct a new relationship, we take into account that we do that in a specific situation, a specific setting, a specific context. Ricoeur would say that this requires 'wisdom in situation'[200], which also from a pragmatist perspective includes an awareness of the tragic sense of life.[201]

An important aid for moving from the third order to the fourth and fifth orders is what is known as autobiography reconstruction. This reconstruction takes place through clarification of feelings and beliefs that the person has carried with him or her from the first years of life and that are influenced by the positive and negative experiences he or she has had since then. This clarification takes shape by critically sifting through the narratives and fragments of narratives that the person recounts about himself or herself and his or her history, and that others have told and still tell about him, and then connecting them in such a way as to create one, complex whole which adequately reflects both the 'idem' identity and the 'ipse' identity of the person . The 'idem' identity relates to the notion that one is still the same person

[196] R. Kegan, *In Over Our Heads. The Mental Demands of Modern Life*, 188-191.
[197] Cf. J. A. van der Ven, *Formation of the Moral Self*.
[198] R. Kegan, *In Over Our Heads. The Mental Demands of Modern Life*, 267.
[199] R. Kegan, *In Over Our Heads. The Mental Demands of Modern Life*, 270.
[200] P. Ricoeur, *Soi-même comme un autre*, 240 v.
[201] C. West, *Prophetic Thought in Postmodern Times. Beyond Eurocentrism and Multiculturalism*, Volume I, 31 v.

that one was in the past, while the 'ipse' identity has to do with the idea that one is the author of one's own life and will remain so.[202]

Special Competent Reflection on Ministry

I will now go over the description of the components of special competent reflection on ministry, relating to the various special functions that the pastor performs. Again, I distinguish between metal-knowledge, meta-insight, meta-skill and meta-attitude.

a. Meta-knowledge: The pastor is capable of the reflective reproduction of the disciplinary structures in the theories which refer to the different functions, i.e., liturgy science/homiletics, catechetics, practical ecclesiology, practical social ethics, missiology, poimenics, and spirituality theory. What I said with regard to the meta-knowledge within general reflective competence also applies here. The aim must be to dig up both the 'objective' side and the 'subjective' side of the structures of knowledge within these disciplines, compare them in terms of similarities and differences and relate them to one another.

b. Meta-insight: The pastor is capable of reflective production of the disciplinary structures in the theories which refer to the different functions, which are, again, liturgy science/homiletics, catechetics, practical ecclesiology, practical social ethics, missiology, poimenics, and spirituality theory. Just as in the case of meta-insight within general reflective competence, the object here, too, is the construction of one's own theory, accounting for both the objective and the subjective sides, in order to produce a structure appropriate to the problematic situation in which the pastor finds himself or herself.

c. Meta-skill: The pastor is capable of critical reflection on social methods and techniques and on the use of these methods and techniques in the different functions, i.e., liturgy/preaching, catechesis, church development, social ministry, mission, pastoral counseling and spiritual direction. Again there is an 'objective' and a 'subjective' side, which refer respectively to the scholarly theories of social methods and techniques and those of the pastor. The meta-skill that is central

---

[202] P. Ricoeur, *Soi-même comme un autre*, 113 v.

to reflective competence is the ability of the pastor to continuously move back and forth from the systematic description of these methods and techniques in books and articles, on the one hand, and his or her own, personally structured experiential knowledge concerning the practical desirability and usefulness of the methods and techniques, on the other. To develop this meta-skill, the pastor must continuously and systematically practice the work of 'mining oneself'.

d.   Meta-attitude: The pastor is capable of critical reflection about his or her personal feelings and beliefs in the domains corresponding to the different functions, i.e., liturgy, catechesis, church development, social ministry, mission, pastoral counseling and spiritual direction. Again, the evolution from the third order of development to the fourth and fifth orders is crucial. In the fourth order, the pastor discovers that he or she can initiate his or her own relationship to the work he or she performs, invest energy in it in the way he or she wants, and direct it in the direction he or she wishes. The pastor becomes self-directive in liturgy, catechesis and church development, he or she owns his or her work in social ministry and mission, and develops his or her own project in pastoral counseling and spirituality. In the fifth order, however, he or she also discovers that his or her feelings and ideas, projects and programs are situation-bound and contextualized. He or she develops wisdom in creating liturgy, preaching, spiritual guiding, he or she accepts from within the people he or she works with in pastoral counseling and mission, and tries to make gradual changes from there. The pastor does not construct his or her feelings and beliefs, his or her acting and working from scratch, but re-constructs and trans-forms them.

Summary

We began chapter III by first establishing the religious domain as the professional domain of the pastor, albeit in a relation of interdependence with other domains, and noting that the church in an evangelical sense is the context in which his or her action occurs. We then distinguished between the pastor's general function and his or her seven special functions. The general function, which can be seen as the common denominator of the seven special functions, is hermeneutic communication. The seven special functions are divided into three groups: church-related functions (liturgy/preaching, catechesis, church development), church/society-related functions (social ministry, mission), and church/individual-related functions (pastoral counseling, spiritual direction). After that the reflective character of these general and special functions was clarified by looking at the analysis of 'practice' in the American philosophy of pragmatism, particularly that of Peirce, Dewey and West. Three aspects were stressed: reflection in practice, reflection on practice and the teleological dimension in both the reflection in practice and the reflection on practice, which we clarified from three different points of view, i.e., the experiential, experimental and transformational. From this analysis we described reflection in ministry, reflection on ministry and the teleological dimension within the reflection in/on ministry. Lastly, the reflective quality of the competence which is needed in order to perform reflective ministry in an adequate way was examined. The components of competent reflection in ministry, i.e., knowledge, insight, skills and attitudes, were described, as were the four components of competent reflection on ministry: meta-knowledge, meta-insight, meta-skills and meta-attitudes.

CHAPTER IV

EDUCATIONAL CONDITIONS FOR
REFLECTIVE MINISTRY

In chapter I we described the function of religion at the macrolevel of society, the mesolevel of the church and the microlevel of the individual, and saw how complex and dynamic the function of the pastor has become within that domain. In chapter II we indicated that the traditional models of training for the ministry are no longer sufficient, because they are too much focussed on the microlevel of the individual and/or do not sufficiently take account of the complexity and dynamics at the macrolevel and mesolevel. We therefore called for a training that goes 'beyond therapeuticalism' and 'beyond managerialism'. Against this background, in chapter III we described a model of ministry in terms of reflective ministry, that functions in the domain of religion at the levels of society, church and individual. In the process we also looked at the functions and competences that comprise this reflective ministry. In this part, these lines will now be carried through into a discussion of the educational conditions for reflective ministry.

Introduction: Educational Anthropology and Psychology

Preparatory to the description of these educational conditions, consideration needs to be given to some preliminary questions. These can not be exhaustively dealt with here, but we will review them briefly nonetheless. These concern the educational anthropology and educational psychology that form or should form the basis for education for ministry. We will also consider the nature of the curriculum that students need to have followed as a prerequisite for the education for ministry program.

Educational Anthropology

Anyone who reflects on education in general and on education for ministry in particular will have to think about the educational

anthropology on which this education is, or should be, based, because
the purpose of this education is not the training of more or less intel-
ligent animals, but the formation of fellow human beings. For this
reason certain educational approaches, if indeed they can be called
that, will not be considered, for example, approaches that are consciously or unconsciously used with the aim of indoctrination or pious
manipulation. Such processes can be recognized by their aims and their
content. The aims are of a low-cognitive and high-affective and high-
attitudinal level, while the content is characterized by doctrinal closed-
ness.[1] Similarly, a merely behavioristic approach can be ruled out,
because there the actions of the future minister would be seen solely
in terms of a stimulus-response reaction. In this way his freedom of
action would be taken away, robbing him of the very thing that makes
human beings human.[2] Even a purely information-theoretical approach
will not suffice, because here everything which has meaning is reduced
to information. This would reduce the future pastor from an 'animal
significans' or 'homo symbolicus' to an 'animal computans' or 'homo
informaticus'.[3] In other words, the freedom of the future minister must
not be impeded either by deformation from the outside in (indoctrination, manipulation), or by deformation from the inside out (behaviorism, computationalism). Instead, this freedom must be fostered and
encouraged. Not only an ontological aspect is at stake here, but also
a cultural one. In the preceding sections we saw how important self-
direction is for reflective ministry in today's western culture, and the
self-steering capacity that this entails cannot be developed by such
approaches. Freedom is important for the pastor as human being as
well as for the pastor as pastor.

In the anthropology that serves as the foundation for that insight,
the primary focus must be on two dimensions: first, human beings
actualize themselves in interaction with their natural and social environment and not separately from it, and, second, in this actualization,
the physical, neural, sensory, cognitive, emotional, spiritual and behavioral aspects of being human form an interactive, complex whole. This

[1] Cf. J. A. Van der Ven, *Formation of the Moral Self*.
[2] Cf. B. Skinner, *About Behaviorism* (New York: Knopf, 1974).
[3] Cf. J. Bruner, *Actions of Meaning* (Cambridge: Harvard University Press, 1990);
The Culture of Education (Cambridge: Harvard University Press, 1996).

is not the place to elaborate on these ideas, and I therefore confine myself to referring to a few authors who, from the fields of neurophysiology and cognitive psychology, provide the coordinates for the sort of educational anthropology that serves as the foundation for what follows. These are, in the field of neurophysiology, especially Damasio[4], and, in the field of cognitive psychology, especially Lazarus[5] with regard to the meaning of emotions, Kegan[6] on the development of interpersonal and intrapersonal attitudes, and Johnson[7] on the higher mental processes like morally intuitive thinking.

Educational Psychology

From the educational anthropology of which we have sketched here the briefest outline, some preliminary remarks are in order as well with regard to the more specific teaching/learning aspects in the field of educational psychology that underlies or ought to underlie the education for ministry.[8]

The supervision literature often refers to two key teaching/learning principles: learning by doing and learning by experience. Apart from the fact that, at least in Peirce's analysis, the two concepts, 'doing' and 'experience', imply each other, if they are not identical, as we have seen (chapter III section 4.1), these terms can be not only refined but also amplified from the point of view of educational psychology. The two concepts, 'learning by experience' and 'learning by doing', can be specified by what Bandura calls, on the one hand, 'observational learning' and, on the other hand 'enactive learning'. Learning by experience and learning by doing take place first of all through observational learning, that is to say, one acquires knowledge, insight, skills and attitudes by watching others and imitating what they do,

[4] A. Damasio, *Descartes' Error. Emotion, Reasons, and the Human Brain* (New York: State of New York University Press, 1994).

[5] R. Lazarus, *Emotion and Adaption* (New York: Oxford University Press, 1991).

[6] R. Kegan, *In Over Our Heads. The Mental Demands of Modern Life.*

[7] M. Johnson, *The Body in the Mind* (Chicago: The University of Chicago Press, 1987); *Moral Imagination. Implications of Cognitive Science for Ethics* (Chicago: The University of Chicago Press, 1993).

[8] S. Bolhuis, *Leren en veranderen bij volwassenen. Een nieuwe benadering* (Bussum: Couthino, 1995) 108 v.

whether or not one identifies with them in the Freudian sense. It is not hard to see that this form of learning is of great importance in education for ministry, particularly in practica, supervision and coaching, because there the instructor, supervisor or senior pastor functions as an influential model.[9] Learning by experience and learning by doing also occur through enactive learning, meaning that the student independently puts into practice what he or she has learned, and by perceiving the results of what he or she has done, develops, reinforces and expands the learning process by trial and error.[10] Both forms of learning, observational and enactive, are indispensable in the framework of education for ministry.

A third form of learning can also be distinguished, i.e., learning by reinforcement. Reinforcement means that certain behaviors by the learner are followed by behaviors by another person, for instance a parent or teacher, who thereby expresses that the behaviors of the learner merit reward or praise because they are positively valued. As a result these behaviors are more readily repeated and gradually result in permanent dispositions or capacities. In the training of pastors, learning by reinforcement is an important condition of learning, particularly in practica, supervision and coaching, and, above all, in the negative form, i.e., the extinction of previously learned reactions by the omission of positive reinforcement and by counterconditioning. In omitting positive reinforcement, the practicum leader or supervisor pays little or no attention to the input of the trainee or supervisee, because his or her input hampers the achieving of the goals previously set by the student himself or herself. The aim of counterconditioning is to eliminate learned reactions by eliciting reactions that are incompatible with the prior ones. Thus, a practicum leader or supervisor, when dealing with a student who is fearful of failing at a particular activity which he or she is required to perform, will speak with the student in a friendly manner and try to calm him or her down by directing his or her attention to positive aspects of the activity, thereby creating a sense of confidence and trust that forms a counterweight to

---

[9] H. Vossen, "Klinische Pastorale vorming als religieus-communicatief leerproces," *Praktische Theologie* no. 18, 2(1991) 176-196.

[10] A. Bandura, *Social Foundations of Thought and Action. A Social Cognitive Theory* (Englewood Cliffs: Prentice Hall, 1986).

the previous fear. Another form of reinforcement that is important in this context is self-reinforcement, in which the person consciously rewards and positively values himself or herself for performing a task to standards which he or she has set for himself or herself. Of course, it is important to cast a critical glance at these standards to determine to what extent they are in agreement with specified values and norms.[11]

There is yet a fourth form of learning that can be considered essential, namely, learning by insight. By this we do not mean the achievement of insight, in which insight is the result of learning, although the importance of this cannot be overstated. What is meant is learning that comes about through insight, which is to say that certain capacities or dispositions come about through the acquiring of insight. Insight in this case is not the result of learning, but rather insight leads to learning, in the form of certain abilities or attitudes. Thus, the verbal naming of problems leads more readily to solutions for the problems than when verbal naming is not done. Solutions are found even more readily when the problem is approached in an insightful manner, which means that one sees it as a problem (problem raising), formulates it as a problem (problem setting), and systematically reviews alternatives for solving it (problem solving). Problem-discovering learning and problem-structuring learning are highly reflective activities, especially when alternative hypotheses for solving the problem are formulated in a creative and imaginative way, and these alternatives are tried out and tested experimentally. Discovery learning strategies as well as joint problem-solving procedures are important in this context.[12]

One further form of learning that merits attention, because it bears on all of the preceding categories, is what can be called meta-learning or deutero learning. This consists of reflection about learning itself, in which the person observes, interprets, analyzes and evaluates the way in which he or she learns.[13] To do this, one needs to make use of meta-learning strategies, which enable one to determine to what extent the

[11] D. Jehu, *Learning Theory and Social Work* (London: Routledge, 1973). Dutch Translation: *Leertheorie en maatschappelijk werk*, 35-41 (Deventer: Van Loghum Slaterus, 1973).

[12] A. Knoers, "Supervisie en leertheorie," *Supervisie 1. Theorie en begrippen*, eds. F. Siegers, P. Haan and A. Knoers (Alphen aan de Rijn: Samsom, 1975) 138-153.

[13] R. Kegan, *In Over Our Heads. The Mental Demands of Modern Life,* 232.

four forms of learning we have distinguished, i.e., observational and enactive learning, learning by reinforcement and learning by insight, are suited to achieving the desired learning objectives, on the one hand, and to the learner's initial situation, in particular his specific learning style, on the other. Not everyone has the same learning style, and not everyone's learning style necessarily remains the same forever. The learning style may be characterized by attention to concrete experiences, reflective observation and interpretation, abstract conceptualization, or active experimenting, thus giving the learner a greater affinity for learning by experience, by reflection, by abstract conceptualization, or by doing. All of these forms of learning, however, form a cyclical whole that needs to be gone through in its entirety.[14]

What links these five forms of learning is that the learning is always 'learning in situ', meaning that it never takes place outside of a specific situation, setting or context. The knowledge one picks up, the insight one acquires, the skills one learns, the attitudes one develops, are always 'situated', 'conditioned' or 'concretely anchored' knowledge, insight, skills, attitudes. Even if one considers the acquisition of abstract concepts and theories as a central objective of the education for ministry program, one must bear in mind that the normal sequence of learning is from context-boundedness to decontextualization, not the other way around. And in connection with this decontextualization one must take into account that it takes place via proximate transfer to distant transfer.[15]

The Theological Curriculum as Prerequisite

Finally, we will outline here the curriculum that should serve as a prerequisite for the more specific education for ministry. This curriculum consists of courses and seminars in the following subjects which, at least from my point of view, which is shaped by the five-year

---

[14] Cf. D. Kolb, *Experiential Learning* (Englewood Cliffs: Prentice Hall, 1984).

[15] L. De Klerk, "Een metacognitieve benadering van de doelstellingen in het onderwijs," *Pedagogisch tijdschrift* 15(1990) 152-161. P. Simons, *Leren denken, denkend leren*. Referaat tijdens het symposium "Een goede raad, de leraar tussen onderwijs en arbeidsmarkt" ter gelegenheid van het afscheid van Prof. Dr. A. Knoers als voorzitter van de onderwijsraad (Den Haag: ABKO, 1992) 13-27.

theology curriculum at the Divinity School of the Catholic University of Nijmegen, should be required of every student entering the education for ministry program.

The discussion of educational conditions for reflective ministry that follows should therefore be understood as being predicated on the assumption that students who enter the education for ministry program will have already completed the courses and seminars in this list of prerequisites. As the following scheme indicates, this list consists of four parts: philosophy, social sciences, theological methodology, and the theological disciplines. Both the third and the fourth part (methodology and theological disciplines) cover four groups of methodologies and disciplines: literary, historical, empirical and systematic.

The Theological Curriculum as Prerequisite to the Education for Ministry Program

I. Philosophy
History of philosophy, ethics, metaphysics, philosophical anthropology, social philosophy, philosophy of religion

II. Social Sciences
Psychology, including psychology of religion, sociology, including sociology of religion, introduction to the world religions

III. Theological Methodology
Literary methodology, historical methodology, empirical methodology, systematic methodology

IV. Theological Disciplines
Exegesis Old Testament, exegesis New Testament, history of church and theology, fundamental theology, dogmatic theology, theological ethics, including social theological ethics, spirituality, liturgy, practical theology, including practical ecclesiology, theology of religions/missiology

---

Thus far we have spoken, without further discussion, of educational conditions in the plural. In the literature one at times encounters the view that there is only one condition, which covers the whole of training for ministry, namely: supervised ministry. However, this one condition is then understood as a relatively complex one, encompassing internship and supervision, plus, in some cases, theological reflection as well, with supervision and theological reflection then being conceived of as one whole.[16] In this part we proceed on the assumption that the competence that the pastor must possess cannot be realized from only one condition, not even in an initial sense. We have broken this competence down into competent reflection in ministry and competent reflecion on ministry. In both forms of competent reflection we distinguished between four components: in competent reflection in ministry between knowledge, insight, skills and attitudes; in competent reflecion on ministry between meta-knowledge, meta-insight, meta-skills and meta-attitudes. Moreover, we distinguished between general and special competencies. In order to cover all of these different aspects of competence, even if it be only in an initial sense, a number of conditions must be met, and these will be reviewed in the following order: courses and seminars (section 1), practica (section 2), internship (section 3), supervision (section 4), coaching (section 5), theological reflection (section 6), and action research (section 7).

A final remark concerns the credits associated with the curriculum as a whole and its elements. The description of the elements of the curriculum is not meant to imply anything about the duration of any of these elements. Nor does it imply that every student in the program must take part in each of the parts of the program. The following, therefore, is descriptive only and says nothing about the number of credits that should be associated with each of the parts of the curriculum or about the total number of credits that students must obtain.

1. Courses and Seminars

The majority of the education for ministry programs justifiably assume that courses and seminars will be a standard part of the curriculum, although they may vary in number and kind. On the basis of chapter III, it can be said that the aim of the courses consists primarily in one of the four components that we have distinguished in

---

[16] P. Moriarty, *Field Education Program. Franciscan School of Theology* (Berkeley: University of California Press, 1988).

competent reflecion in ministry and competent reflection on ministry, i.e., knowledge and meta-knowledge (chapter III, section 5). The goal of seminars, however, consists in one of the other components, i.e., insight and meta-insight. This goal consists in the 'objective' side (expert knowledge) and the 'subjective' side (craft knowledge) of the structures of the discipline being dialectically related to one another, in such a way that an original construction is produced. The objective side has to do with the structures in the heads of the academic experts, the subjective side with the structures in the heads of the students (chapter III, section 5).

One can hardly devote too much time to the meta-cognitive strategies (meta-knowledge, meta-insight), because research shows how difficult it is for professional practitioners to uncover and clarify their own knowledge structures and conceptual structures, to reflect critically on these and to develop them further independently. It is all the more crucial, then, for students who have yet to be initiated into the profession, to learn this process of explicitation systematically.[17]

General Courses

hermeneutics
religious communication theory

Special Courses

pastoral-liturgical sciences/homiletics
catechetics
practical ecclesiology
practical social ethics
practical missiology
poimenics
theory of spiritual direction

---

[17] Cf. N. Verloop and Th. Wubbels, "Recente ontwikkelingen in het onderzoek naar leraren en lerarenopleiding," *Pedagogische Studien* 71(1994) 168-186; J. Kessels, F. Korthagen, Th. Somers and Th. Wubbels, *The Relationship between Theory and Practice: Back to the Classics*. Paper presented at the Annual Meeting of the American Research Association (New York: State of New York University, 1996).

The same thing applies a fortiori to them as it does to, for example, professional teachers, namely, that the process of 'mining oneself' is impeded by feelings of fear, anxiety, helplessness, loneliness, meaninglessness and hostility, and that professional self-inquiry is readily experienced as resulting in deficiency or as a sign of deficiency.[18] With regard to this meta-cognitive strategy, a distinction must also be made between general and special competence. The result is the following list.

In the list of special courses and seminars, extra consideration should be paid to what we called in the previous part 'crossing paradigms' (chapter III, section 3.1). This means that, for example, in the course and seminar on 'Liturgical Sciences', attention is devoted to the relevance of the ritual paradigm for catechesis, church development, social ministry, pastoral counseling and so on. Similarly, in 'Practical Social Ethics', some time is devoted to the meaning of the community development paradigm for liturgy and spiritual direction, and so forth.

General Seminars

hermeneutics
religious communication theory

Special Seminars

pastoral-liturgical sciences/homiletics
catechetics
practical ecclesiology
practical social ethics
practical missiology
poimenics
theory of spiritual direction

---

[18] A. Cole, *Reflection in the Margins. From Research On Teachers to Research On Contexts and For Teachers*. Paper presented at the Annual Meeting of the American Educational Research Association (San Francisco: University Press, 1995).

2. Practica

One way or another, the majority of education for ministry programs provide room for the practice and acquisition of skills. Sometimes practical exercises are held within the courses and seminars, sometimes special practica are set up. From research we know that practica which are not structurally connected with internship, supervision and coaching, appear to be ineffective. They have to be curricularly integrated with internship, supervision and coaching. With this integration of internship, supervision and coaching, we will deal further on.

From the point of view of chapter III, it must be said that the goal of the practicum is the acquisition of the skills that are needed to enable the student to make use of appropriate social methods and techniques (chapter III, section 5.1). At the same time, the meta-skill that is described in connection with reflective competence is also important (chapter III, section 5.2). Here, too, the distinction must be made between general and special competence. The result is the following list.

General Practica

hermeneutics
religious communication

Special Practica

liturgy/preaching
catechesis
church development
social ministry
mission
pastoral counseling
spiritual direction

Along with the practicing of skills, a number of education for ministry programs allocate time for practica that are intended specifically to provide an opportunity for clarification and development of attitudes, especially religious attitudes. These form an intrinsic part of the pastor's competence (chapter III, section 5.1). Considerable attention should also be devoted to the development of meta-attitudes (chapter III, section 5.2). The practica are aimed at the development of personal attitudes ('personal development') as well as religious attitudes ('religious development'). In the former it is autobiography reconstruction that occupies a central place, in the latter religious autobiography reconstruction.

Practica in Spiritual Formation

personal development
religious development

These last two practica are important for the development and clarification of the student's personal and religious identity. They may take place in the setting of the theological school or in a setting outside the school, like a center for clinical pastoral education or a center for spiritual development. The advantage of a setting outside the school is that the students can take part in the practica as boarders for several consecutive or non-consecutive weeks at a time, an arrangement which favors the spiritual learning process.

3. Internship

Internship forms the part of the education for ministry program where the student comes into direct contact with pastoral practice. In this internship, which Fielding calls 'field education', as distinct from earning one's living in 'field employment' or doing voluntary work without supervision in 'field service', four stages can be distinguished.[19]

The first stage of field education is the student's participation in a parish simply as a member of that parish or as if he or she were a

---

[19] C. Fielding, *Education for Ministry* (Dayton: American Association of Theological Schools, 1966) 227-235.

member. That is, he or she does not participate in a quasi-ecclesiastical or proto-ministerial function. He or she takes part in church services in the same way that all other parishioners take part, sings in the choir along with all the other members of the choir, and participates in working groups and committees just as all other members take part in meetings and activities. Fielding adds that supervision in this stage "can be best undertaken by laymen or faculty members not identified with the practical field".[20]

In the second stage, the student takes a first step toward professional involvement. He or she has the status of a student, but the role of a pastor. He or she does not participate in the parish work as such, but in the pastoral activities of the parish. This means that, under the direct guidance of (one of) the parish pastor(s) he or she carries out pastoral tasks in the true sense of the word, such as delivering a sermon, conducting a catechetical group, counseling a person in grief, proposing a project in social ministry. Supervision should now be in the hands of a person who has been trained as a supervisor. Fielding adds: "An experienced and mature pastor will hardly take exception to the judgment that parish experience cannot by itself equip him [or her] to supervise the process described in our chapter on supervision".[21] If such an experienced and mature pastor does supervise the student, without having been trained in supervision, then this is called pre-professional supervision. In the training of psychotherapists, this sort of supervision occurs frequently, with the most experienced therapists acting as supervisors.[22]

In the third stage, the student takes full responsibility for the pastoral work he or she does. Whereas the first two stages are determined by participation in parish work and pastoral activities respectively, the third stage is characterized by pastoral leadership: "He [or she] is not a student for the ministry, but a minister in the ministry entering upon a student's role".[23] As far as supervision of the tasks he or she performs is concerned, the same thing applies as in the second stage: it should be provided by a professionally trained supervisor.

[20] C. Fielding, *Education for Ministry*, 237.
[21] C. Fielding, *Education for Ministry*, 239.
[22] F. Siegers and D. Haan, *Handboek supervisie* (Alphen aan de Rijn: Samsom, 1988) 153.
[23] C. Fielding, *Education for Ministry*, 241.

The fourth stage is characterized by specialization. The student obtains qualifications in one or more forms of specialized ministry. According to Fielding, specialization in ministry is of two kinds: "Some is required by the situation, e.g., hospital, jail, university, inner city, etc. Other specialities are refinements of normal skills required in the ministry of the local church, e.g., preaching, education, counseling, care of the aged, youth work, evangelism, etc.".[24] Here again supervision must meet professional standards.

In various education for ministry programs, the directors attempt to select places for internship that will offer optimal opportunities for the student's learning process. In this connection it is good to keep in mind Fielding's admonition that "it is not important to find an impressive and smoothly running parish for field education. Disorganization in community and personal life and frustration in parish life are typical of what Christian ministry is expected to deal with. The need is for a good supervisor and a field of ministry, not a place where most problems appear to be solved and costing reconciliation, hard work, and frustration unnecessary".[25]

In other words, parishes selected for internship must satisfy three conditions: they must provide an opportunity to experience fully the complexity and dynamics that determine today's ministry, sufficient learning opportunities must be present, and the student must be able to receive adequate supervision and coaching. I add parenthetically that, based on the more recent literature, I make a distinction that Fielding does not and that is absent in a number of education for ministry programs, but that is managed well in other programs, namely the difference between supervision and coaching, which I will come back to further on (see sections 4 and 5 below).

These conditions can be met by establishing or shaping 'laboratory parishes', much like the 'laboratory school' established by Dewey in the pragmatist tradition.[26] With his 'laboratory school', Dewey sought to create a link between the school and the university in order to train good teachers, an experiment that was later continued in the so-called

---

[24] C. Fielding, *Education for Ministry*, 243.
[25] C. Fielding, *Education for Ministry*, 240.
[26] C. West, *The American Evasion of Philosophy. A Genealogy of Pragmatism*, 84.

'Professional Development Schools'. These, however, did not deliver on the expectations that were placed in them, probably due to the fact that there was a lack of support through research, that innovation strategies were too much top-down, while these were moreover too strongly oriented to the microlevel of the individual teacher.[27] These considerations would have to be taken into account in any attempt to establish 'laboratory' or 'experimental' parishes.

Two remarks of an administrative nature are in order. The first is that it is recommended that a clearly worded contract be concluded in connection with each work placement, so that both parties, the theological school and the parish, know their rights and responsibilities and what they can expect from the other. Such a contract should specify the goals of the placement, formal conditions (compensation, insurance, house rules) and substantive conditions (quality guarantees).[28] The theological school should develop a standard contract form that meets these requirements, as has been done in a number of American theological schools.[29]

Secondly, it is advisable that an inspection committee carry out regular inspections (for instance once every three years) of the conditions and quality of the work placement on behalf of the theological school. The object is not to verify whether the terms of the contract are being met, but to improve the quality by means of inspection. Such a committee can consist of four or more people, of whom two represent the theological school, one the parishes, and one the group of interns or former interns. Such inspection committees are customary, for example, in the training of general practitioners in the Netherlands.

Internship Differentiation

Up till now we have been speaking, by way of example, of internship in the setting of a parish. The pastor, however, can perform his or her various functions in a number of different settings: not only in

[27] N. Verloop and Th. Wubbels, "Recente ontwikkelingen in het onderzoek naar leraren en lerarenopleiding," *Pedagogische Studien* 71 (1994) 168-186.

[28] B. de Vries, *Overeenkomsten bij stages* (Nijmegen: ITS, 1984).

[29] R. O'Gorman and B. Tucker, *The Field Education Manual. A Study of Some 27 Field Education Manuals According to Nine Categories* (Chicago: University of Chicago Press, 1995) 8-10.

a parish, but also in monastries, hospitals, schools, media, social welfare agencies, mental health agencies, or in a mission setting. For this reason differentiation is needed between internships, and students need to make a choice. In the programs of most theological schools they must choose from among three to five settings.[30] The differences between the various settings are nevertheless relatively minor compared with the differences between functions. In a nutshell, the student must learn the functions, but he or she only needs to be introduced into the settings, although the administration of the various institutions that make up these settings may tend to reverse this priority. Put another way, after a certain settling-in period, a pastor who is skilled in pastoral counseling will be capable of adequately performing the function of pastoral counselor in any setting, be it the parish, school or hospital. The following is an exemplary list of various settings along with the various functions that the pastor may perform in them.

Internship Differentiation

Parish: liturgy, catechesis, church development, social ministry, mission, pastoral counseling, spiritual direction

Monastery: spiritual direction

Hospital: liturgy, pastoral counseling

School: liturgy, catechesis, social ministry, pastoral counseling, spiritual direction

Media: liturgy/preaching, catechese, social ministry, mission

Agency for Social Welfare: social ministry

Agency for Mental Health: pastoral counseling

Mission Setting: mission in first-world countries, mission in third-world countries

Analogously to what was said above about the teaching or experimental parish, the development of the teaching or experimental monastery, hospital, school, media, agency and mission setting also merits serious consideration.

[30] R. O'Gorman and B. Tucker, *The Field Education Manual. A Study of Some 27 Field Education Manuals According to Nine Categories*, 10-11.

4. Supervision

In a general sense supervision is considered to be the opportunity for the student to relate two kinds of experiences to one another in a systematic and methodical way, i.e., learning and working. While working and reflecting on working, the student learns, and while learning he or she performs his or her work better.

Supervision is not appropriate for all kinds of work, but only for work which satisfies certain characteristics. First, the work to be supervised aims at offering a service (help, guidance, education, treatment) to fellow human beings. Second, it does so in a reflective-professional way, meaning that it makes critical use of scientific knowledge and insights, skills and attitudes. Third, it is relational, meaning that the core of the profession consists in the adequate handling by the professional of the relationship with the client and of his or her own person within that relationship. Fourth, it is methodical work, which is to say that the professional is consciously aiming to achieve a specific objective and is concerned with working effectively and efficiently. Finally, the work is performed autonomously, which demands of the professional a large degree of self-direction.[31] Certainly, the work that the pastor does clearly meets these criteria (service-oriented, professional, relational, methodical, self-directive), and is thus work that can be considered for supervision, just like the work of the general medical practitioner, social worker, psychotherapist, nurse and teacher.

Supervision entails two different integration processes. The first concerns the processes within the person of the supervisee, and consists in relating his or her cognitions, affects and action tendencies to one another in such a way that a structured whole develops. The second concerns the developing consciousness of the interdependency between the professional's profession, the professional institution and the societal context.[32] Both integration processes are necessary conditions for working in a reflective-professional way.

Often supervision is considered to be the very core of the education for ministry program. Sometimes 'supervised ministry' is simply

---

[31] F. Siegers and D. Haan, *Handboek supervisie*, 25-32.
[32] F. Siegers and D. Haan, *Handboek supervisie*, 262 v.

identified with 'education for ministry'.[33] Where this is the case, however, it puts the programs in question sharply at odds with education
programs for other helping professions where supervision is seen as
one of the parts of the curriculum. In the training for social case-work,
for example, supervision is one component along with courses and
seminars, practica and training settings. This is also the case in the
training of psychotherapists, where courses and seminars, practica and
learning therapy are all part of the curriculum along with supervision.
Supervision is not supposed to cover all objectives at once, and the
supervisor should not be responsible for the achievement of all goals;
indeed he or she can not possibly fulfil such a responsibility.[34]

In the present section, therefore, we do not treat supervision as the
core of the education for ministry program, but as one component
within that program, albeit an extremely important component. We
can distinguish individual supervision, triadic supervision (supervision
with two supervisees) and group supervision.[35] All of these forms must
occur with sufficient frequency that the learning effect does not suffer
from overly long intervals between supervision sessions.[36] In the case
of group supervision, the number of supervisees should be limited to
three[37], although groups of four supervisees are seen occasionally.[38]
Groups of more than three or four supervisees are rare in the Netherlands[39], while, in the United Kingdom, a group of three supervisees
is seen as the very minimum and that of seven as the maximum.[40] In
putting together the groups it is important to bear in mind the principles
of homogeneity as a means of ensuring support and of heterogeneity

---

[33] W. Zijlstra, *Klinisch pastorale vorming. Een voorlopige analyse van het leer- en
groepsproces van zeven cursussen*, 233.

[34] P. Haan, "Pastorale supervisie van buiten getoetst,"in *Ontginingswerk. Klinische
Pastorale Vorming. Een overzicht. Bijdragen aan Dr. Wybe Zijlstra* (Kampen: Kok,
1985) 194-200; "Veranderingen in de maatschappelijke context: hebben deze de opleiding voor pastorale supervisie iets te zeggen?" in *Jaarverslag 1994 van de Raad voor
Klinische Pastorale Vorming in Nederland* (Kampen: Kok, 1994) 36-39.

[35] F. Siegers and D. Haan, *Handboek supervisie*, 113-139.

[36] N. Jagt and N. Leufkens, *Supervisie: praktisch gezien, kritisch bekeken* (Deventer: Van Loghum Slaterus, 1990) 43.

[37] N. Jagt and N. Leufkens, *Supervisie: praktisch gezien, kritisch bekeken*, 106.

[38] P. Haan, "Pastorale supervisie van buiten getoetst," 197.

[39] N. Jagt and N. Leufkens, *Supervisie: praktisch gezien, kritisch bekeken*, 106.

[40] P. Hawkins and R. Shohet, Supervision in the Helping Professions (London,
Jossey-Bass Publishers, 1990) 99.

as a means of promoting confrontation.[41] Without going into detailed historical and systematic observations, some fundamental distinctions are in order so as to clarify the concept of supervision.

Administrative Supervision, Staff Supervision, Field Instruction

It is important to remember that supervision historically originates from two different traditions, namely, social case-work and psychiatry. In the field of education for ministry, we have seen that the New England group grew out of social work and the New York group out of psychiatry (chapter II, section 1), but the same applies also for training programs for a number of other helping professions which consist essentially of the adequate handling of social interaction with the client and of one's own person in that interaction. In the training of social case workers, the supervisor initially functioned as an administrator who ensured that the (future) social worker performed his or her work satisfactorily. Later, the function of educational supervisor was added to that of administrative supervisor. This consisted mainly in providing consultation for volunteers in social case work. Later still, the function of trainer of volunteers was supplemented by that of trainer of future professional social workers.[42]

In psychiatric training, the teaching analysis came first, later supplemented by theoretical courses and seminars, and still later rounded out by the supervised analysis. Gradually a consensus developed that the goal of this supervision of analyses that the student performed with his clients was a learning process that was aimed at constantly raising the standards of the exercise of the psychiatric profession. This did not prevent the regular recurrence of the classic question: How much attention should the supervisor devote to the personal problems of the supervisee before the supervision turns into analysis or psychotherapy?[43]

The result was that a number of questions were raised about the role of the supervisor that are still heard today, namely, in the field of social

[41] F. Siegers and D. Haan, *Handboek supervisie*, 124.
[42] D. Haan, "Supervisie als coöperatief leerproces. Achtergronden van Amerikaanse supervisieliteratuur," 115- 137.
[43] F. Siegers and D. Haan, *Handboek supervisie*, 43.

case-work: does the supervisor fulfil (1) the function of 'administrative supervisor', who officially examines the professional's work within the institution for social case work, (2) the function of 'staff supervisor', who performs the consultation work within the institution for social case work, or (3) the function of 'field instructor' who, as a resident college faculty member, introduces the student to the field of social work and directs his or her learning process, and, in the field of psychiatry: (4) does the supervisor fulfil the function of a therapist?

The difference between the 'administrative supervisor', the 'staff supervisor' and the 'field instructor' is of particular importance in the education for ministry program as well.[44] It would appear that only the function of 'field instructor' is relevant, at least in so far as the supervision is carried out by a college faculty member and under the authority of the college. This, incidentally, is far from always the case, because the theological institutions do have not direct access to the ecclesial institution and have no authority there, and many pastoral supervisors therefore come directly from the church and consequently function in the capacity of a 'staff supervisor' vis-à-vis the student. But even when the supervisor acts as a 'field instructor', as is the case in the theological institutions in the Netherlands, one must bear in mind that intentionally or unintentionally, he or she also possesses certain traits of the 'staff supervisor' and even the 'administrative supervisor'. The theological institutions, at least the Catholic and some Protestant ones, are so dependent on the ecclesiastical authorities that, in the assessment and evaluation of the student's supervised learning process, they use (are required to use) criteria that are dictated to them by the church. In effect this means that there are two contracts, one with the student as supervisee and one with the ecclesial institution, and that the different values and norms, objectives and standards, contents and methods must be explicitly brought into line with each other. For this reason it is essential to be clear on the expectations and norms of the parties to both contracts, i.e., the student and the ecclesial institution. It also means that the various information streams must

---

[44] P. Hawkins and R. Shohet, Supervision in the Helping Professions, 41 v.; P. Ballard, The Foundations of pastoral Studies and Practical Theology (Cardiff: Wales University Press, 1986) 37.

be carefully kept separate. In particular, no information should be exchanged with the ecclesial institution about the student unless the student is present or the subject has been previously discussed with the student and the student has given his approval.[45]

Supervision and Therapy

Not only do the functions of 'administrative supervisor', 'staff supervisor' and 'field instructor' threaten to become mixed up with one another, but running through the supervisor's role is also the function, disguised or not, of therapist, in this case the pastoral therapist. Such a confusion of roles is entirely understandable, since, as in all the helping professions, the managing of social interaction and of one's own person in that interaction is one of the main elements of the pastoral profession and thus also of pastoral supervision. And as we have seen, attitude formation, in which personal as well as religious emotions and beliefs play a central role, is a key function within the education for ministry program. Nevertheless, although therapy and supervision can not be neatly separated from each other once and for all time, their goals are quite different. In pastoral therapy, what one might call the 'personal person' of the pastor is central; in supervision, on the other hand, it is the person of the pastor, in so far as this person effects the pastoral profession he exercises and the pastoral work he performs. The pastor is, of course, the wounded healer, to use Henri Nouwen's beautiful expression. But pastoral therapy has to do with the emotional processing of wounds which the 'personal person' of the pastor suppresses and is not yet able to reconcile and accept. Supervision, on the other hand, relates to a further stage: it is aimed at developing the pastor's (supervisee's) ability to take control of his woundedness as it were, in order that he can help other people help themselves. It is the professional responsibility of the supervisor to refer the supervisee to the pastoral therapist as soon as personal woundedness becomes an obstacle to the teaching/learning process of supervision and prevents it from progressing.

---

[45] F. Siegers, *Instellingssupervisie. Leren over werk in de context van leiden — begeleiden — (samen)werken* (Houten, Diegem: Bohn Stafleu Van Loghum, 1996) 169-205.

Three Orientations in Supervision

In order to widen the perspective that risks becoming too narrowly focussed by the discussion on the relationship between supervision and therapy, it may be expedient to indicate briefly that, in general, supervision should be carried out according to three different orientations, i.e., the profession, the person of the professional, and the institutional and societal context in which the professional does his or her work.[46] This background then allows us to adopt a position with regard to the aim of supervision within the education for ministry program.

In the first orientation, the profession itself — in this case the pastoral profession — is central. As noted above, a twofold integration takes place. First, the integration of cognitions, affects and action tendencies at the microlevel of the individual professional, and second, the integration of this professional in his or her work situation at the microlevel with the mesolevel of the professional institution and the macrolevel of society. The first form of integration can be seen as the goal of supervision in terms of attitude formation[47], based on the insight that the three aspects (cognitions, affects and action tendencies) belong to the classic attitude concept.[48] However, as far as the formation of attitudes is concerned, it is important to first differentiate clearly and sharply between these three aspects and then to integrate them. Integration is always a process of bringing together what first was differentiated. Integration implies differentiation. This insight was expressed by one of the leaders of the clinical pastoral education movement in the sixties, Thomas Klink, who says: "Supervision is rather a method of education designed to effect those personal changes which will permit the integration into practice of self-understanding, relevant theory, substantive knowledge, and functional skills".[49] However, the first form of integration is not enough. The second form that is necessary is the integration of the work of the professional at the microlevel, with the context of the professional institution at the

[46] F. Siegers and D. Haan, *Handboek supervisie*, 203-246.

[47] H. Korsten, H. Meertens and A. Reijnen, *Werken aan de basis. Opbouwwerk en Pastoraat*. Nijmegen, 76 v.

[48] E. Hilgard, R. Atkinson and R. Atkinson, *Introduction to Psychology* (New York: Harcourt Brace Jovanovich) 523

[49] Th. Klink, "Supervision," *Education for Ministry*, 196-217.

mesolevel and the societal context at the macrolevel. One could say that the first form of integration concerns the processes that occur in the person of the supervisee, albeit in interaction with the processes at the microlevel, mesolevel and macrolevel, while the second form concerns this interaction directly. In the first form the accent is on intrapersonal interaction processes, in the second form it is on institutional interaction processes. The organizing principle of this twofold integration is, as I said, the profession. Within this there is room for a plurality of approaches, provided that they can bring about the twofold integration on the basis of the profession. Some of these approaches are suggested by terms such as Rogerian, systems-theoretical, psychoanalytical, object-relational and Gestalt supervision.[50]

The second orientation, in which the person of the professional is central, is not characterized by such pluralism, although the counseling and experiential learning approach by Rogers, whose insights are fundamental to this orientation, does offer considerable inner space and freedom.[51] The emphasis is on learning and actualizing of the basic conditions that must be met in order to establish and maintain relations with other people. These basic conditions include the ability to be concrete, to understand empathically, to communicate respect, to demonstrate to the other that one accepts him or her, and to manifest oneself as transparent and authentic. In the learning process through which the supervisee acquires these basic conditions, the supervisee must examine how he or she experiences himself or herself, how he or she experiences his or her work and how he or she experiences the maintaining of the relationship of the other with whom he or she works. There is continuous reflection on, and feed-back about, the work situation. In this way the 'learning by doing' and 'learning by experience' which were discussed at the beginning of chapter IV are realized. In this process of experiencing and learning, the person of the supervisee is changed, and the supervisee is personally involved in this change process.[52] In such an experiential approach, knowledge,

---

[50] F. Siegers and D. Haan, *Handboek supervisie*, 153.

[51] Cf. C. Rogers, *Counseling and Psychotherapy; Clientcentered Therapy; On Becoming a Person.*

[52] H. Andriessen, *Leren aan ervaring en supervisie* (Nijmegen: Dekker en van de Vegt, 1975) 282-286.

theory, skills and attitudes are very close together. In pastoral supervision, for example, faith can be considered as knowledge, as theory, as a skill, and as an attitude, because all of these aspects imply one another within faith as self-understanding.[53]

In the third orientation towards supervision, the central focus is the institutional and societal context in which the professional performs his or her work. While psychology is dominant in the first two orientations, sociology is dominant in the third. Society-critical authors like Habermas, Giesecke, Mollenhauer and Oskar Negt, education-critical authors like Paulo Freire, and feminist authors like Lilian Rubin have been particularly influential. The emphasis is on emancipation from oppressive institutional and societal structures. What the supervisee must learn is to become personally aware of the practices of dominance and oppression that occur in the situations where people live and work, as well as of the associated processes of internalized dominance and oppression, and actually to create opportunities for emancipation, for example, with the help of 'critical role distancing'. The supervisee must also become aware of the circumstances in which helping can itself contribute to oppression. While the second orientation towards supervision is characterized by the experiential learning approach, in the third orientation it is the supervisor's cognitive transmission and the supervisee's cognitive development that are central, and there is much less room for the gathering and processing of experience, leading to the observation that "these are precisely the margins within which supervision can still take place. As soon as supervision becomes 'transmission', there is no room left for supervision".[54]

Characteristics of Supervision

Against this background it is now possible to adopt a position concerning the goal of supervision within the education for ministry program. This position should not be interpreted as being exclusivist. Rather, it is inclusivist, but without losing sight of the particular nature of pastoral supervision.

[53] H. Andriessen, *Leren aan ervaring en supervisie*, 305-307.
[54] F. Siegers and D. Haan, *Handboek supervisie*, 237.

First, supervision in the sense of 'field instruction' must be distinguished from 'administrative supervision' and 'staff supervision'. That is, in supervision as field instruction within the theological school, the learning process of the supervisee as future pastoral professional is central, and not the aims or concerns of the professional institution, i.e., the church. If these do interfere in the supervision, two dimensions will have to be clearly differentiated, that is, the dimension of the theological school in which the field instruction takes place, and that of the church, from whence the supervision is ascribed aspects of both administrative and staff supervision.

Second, supervision is not therapy, although some overlap may occur temporarily owing to the concern of supervision with the development of the person of the supervisee. It is important, however, that the supervisor refer the supervisee to a psychotherapist when more deep-reaching emotional blocks become apparent in the autobiography of the supervisee.

Third, supervision should not be viewed solely as a learning process, for psychotherapy, too, is a learning process, but rather as a teaching/learning process, that is, as a didactic or educational process centered around the interaction between the supervisor as teacher and supervisee as learner. However, it is a very special teaching/learning, didactic or educational process, because the way of teaching and the way of learning are peculiar. The way of learning is peculiar because it aims at the twofold process of integration, i.e., the integration of cognitions, affects and action tendencies at the microlevel of the individual professional, as well as the integration of the individual professional in his or her work situation with the mesolevel of the professional institution and the macrolevel of society. The way of teaching is peculiar because the supervisor facilitates this twofold integration process that is oriented towards the supervisee's learning and working in relation to each other.[55]

Fourth, in supervision each of the three above-named orientations (the profession, the person, the context) have a place, and each may be accented somewhat differently by different supervisees, different

[55] F. Haarsma, "Supervision: Ein Modell van Reflexion kirchlicher Praxis," *Praktische Theologie heute*, eds. F. Klostermann and R. Zerfass, 609-623 (München: Kaiser, 1974).

supervisors and in different program contexts.[56] The accent on one orientation must not be so strong, however, that the two other orientations are pushed into the background or even disappear from view. One wonders whether there is not sometimes a danger, in pastoral supervision, of the person of the supervisee becoming so central that the orientation towards the profession and the context are lost from view. Whereas the orientation towards the profession has never been completely neglected in the literature on supervision, in the newer literature there is an increased emphasis on the influence of the culture of the institution in which the professional carries out his or her work. By way of all sorts of conscious and unconscious codes, this culture significantly influences his or her perceptions, thoughts, experience and actions. It also determines the way in which the professional interacts with his or her clients and how they see him or her, and influences the faith that the professional has in his or her own profession and the identity he or she draws from it. Ethnographic analyses of the school culture, for example, are increasingly revealing the influence of this institutional culture, leading some authors to remark that the school supervisor must fulfil not only the functions of counseling, teaching and training, but also of cultural analyst and ethnographer.[57] And this is of course true of the pastoral professional, conditioned as he or she is by the culture of the church and the other settings in which he or she works. In other words, as far as possible, the three aforementioned orientations should be considered as being interconnected. From time to time it may be necessary to move from a more profession-oriented supervisor to a more person-oriented or more context-oriented supervisor and the other way around.

Fifth, the insight into the mutual interconnection between the three orientations is furthered by systematically and methodically reflecting about this interconnection. Some key questions are: What sort of influence is exerted by the profession on the person of the professional and by the person on the profession? How does the cultural context of the professional institution and of society at large influence the profession and the person of the professional? How does the person respond to

[56] N. Jagt and N. Leufkens, *Supervisie: praktisch gezien, kritisch bekeken*, 32-33.
[57] D. Waite, *Rethinking Instructional Supervision. Notes on Its Language and Culture* (London, Washington: Falmer Press, 1995) 101.

this influence and what kind of self-direction can he or she develop in this respect? By paying attention to the religious and ecclesial aspects of the professional's personal biography, the 'corporate identity' of the profession, the mission of the ecclesial institution and the 'civil religion' of the society, this reflection becomes theological reflection. Theological reflection thus constitutes an intrinsic part of supervision as 'field instruction'. It refers to the religious aspects of what is called earlier 'reflection in ministry'.

Supervision Contracts

Against this background it is important to establish a supervision contract in which the supervisor and supervisee each describe their rights and responsibilities and what they expect from each other. Such a contract should set out the objectives of supervision, the choice of individual and/or group supervision, the organization of the supervision sessions and their number and duration. The theological school should supply a contract form for this purpose.[58] If the church interferes in the supervision process in terms of its concerns, interests and goals, two seperate contracts should be made, clearly defining the rights and responsibilities of all parties.

Materials and Methods in Supervision

In stipulating the organization of the supervision sessions, an important consideration is what kind of material will be used and how. The preferred material used in the New England group, as we have seen, was the detailed description of the diagnosis and intervention in a particular case, in which the focus was on the patient or client, whereas the New York group preferred the verbatim and the verbatim analysis, in which attention was centered on the person of the pastor (chapter 2, section 1). The eventual dominance of the latter group in the clinical pastoral movement caused the case description to disappear almost entirely from view. The emphasis came to be placed on the verbatim and the verbatim analysis.

[58] R. O'Gorman and B. Tucker, *The Field Education Manual. A Study of Some 27 Field Education Manuals According to Nine Categories*, 9-10.

The verbatim and the verbatim analysis are characterized by two things. The first is that the pastor — the pastor in training — writes down from memory, as literally as possible, an account of the pastoral counseling that he or she held or — to take another example from ministry — the catechetical session that he or she conducted. The aim is not to produce a truly word-for-word account — that would be impossible — but rather a summary of the counseling or the catechetical session as the pastor remembers it. The second characteristic is that the supervisor — and in group supervision the fellow pastors — subject the verbatim to a close analysis, the purpose being to examine the way in which the pastor experienced the counseling or the catechetical session as well as the way in which he or she and his or her fellow pastors experience the counseling or catechetical session here and now. In an analysis of this kind, the feelings and attitudes of the pastor and the other pastors are expressed and can become the object of empathic and, at the same time, critical self-reflection and group reflection.

Based on the more general practice of supervision and the literature on the subject, the question may be asked whether the advantages of the verbatim are also accompanied by some disadvantages.

As far as the advantages are concerned, the verbatim and the analysis thereof are concerned first and foremost with the manner in which the pastor experienced the counseling, catechetical session etcetera. Even more strongly, the verbatim 'reveals' how the pastor experienced himself or herself as well as the people with whom he or she was speaking.[59] Next, the verbatim is not only an expressive medium of revelation, but also an effective learning tool. Precisely because it is a subjective account of the conversation, the verbatim analysis can put the pastor in touch with himself or herself and give him or her a deeper insight into himself or herself. Finally, the verbatim is also an effective tool for group learning. Through the shared analysis, the fellow pastors come to bear responsibility for the development of a deeper understanding of the counseling as well as for the catechetical session of both the pastor and themselves.

[59] W. Zijlstra, *Klinisch pastorale vorming. Een voorlopige analyse van het leer- en groepsproces van zeven cursussen*, 99.

There are disadvantages as well. The most important is that the pastoral counseling or catechesis session, as it in fact took place, is never considered. Only the pastor's subjective recollection is up for discussion. This recollection contains many selective elements, leaving out all the aspects that escaped the pastor's notice but that may have been significant. There are constantly things that evade the pastor's notice simply because the stimuli coming at him or her are so numerous that he or she must of necessity make a selection among them. One simply cannot avoid 'mnemotechnical forgetting': attention is always selective attention; there is no other kind. It may also be that the pastor selectively represses certain aspects in the Freudian sense, because they trigger personal protective mechanisms and defence systems in the pastor himself or herself. There are many ways of this sort of 'Freudian' forgetting, such as transference, countertransference, projection, compensation, denial, etc.[60] Who can guarantee that the analysis of the verbatim will see through and make up for the 'mnemotechnical' and 'Freudian' forgetting? Who can guarantee that the analysis wil not be equally affected by this sort of forgetting, this time on the part of the supervisor and the supervision group?[61]

Because of these drawbacks, the use of the verbatim today is on the decline in the general practice of supervision. But there are also more practical reasons at work: "In the past (10 to 20 years ago) verbatim accounts were a 'must'; at present they are used much less frequently. This is in part because the use of tape recordings has displaced the far more incomplete (and more distorted) 'verbatims' in supervision, partly because many supervisors and supervisees do not see the use of 'all that writing'. The preparing of verbatim accounts is indeed time-consuming, but as a learning exercise it may nevertheless be worthwhile to (have the supervisees) write one or more verbatims ... Nonetheless, verbatim accounts in our day have become more the exception than the rule".[62]

In certain education for ministry programs, tape recordings are indeed being used in place of verbatims. In some programs, this is one

[60] A. Uleyn, *The Recognition of Guilt. A Study in Pastoral Psychology.*
[61] J. A. Van der Ven, "Pastorale protocolanalyse I. Pastoraat in vernieuwing." *Praktische Theologie* 20, no. 5 (1993), 475-495.
[62] N. Jagt and N. Leufkens, *Supervisie: praktisch gezien, kritisch bekeken*, 83.

of the 'course requirements' for the pastoral counseling practicum: "Tape your session ... Always bring a tape of the last session with your client to every class".[63] The reason for this is that the professor who teaches this practicum wants to know what actually happened, so that he or she can base his or her supervision on it in a responsible manner. More than 30 years ago, one of the founding fathers of clinical pastoral education in the Netherlands, Willem Berger, already called for the use of tape recordings as a learning tool.[64] By this I do not mean to suggest that there are only two kinds of material that can be useful for supervision, i.e., the verbatim and the audio tape. These are only two items on a longer list, which also includes, for example, the oral account, the observation report, the daily logbook, the process note, the 'critical incident' report, the case description, role play, and the one-way screen.[65] In various ways, all of these are used in the present-day programs of theological schools.[66] In general, these types of material can be divided into three groups: the written account, the oral account, and tape recordings. The written account tends to favor reflection, the oral account experience and the tape recording actual performance.[67]

Differentiation in Supervision

Up till now we have spoken exemplarily of supervision in relation to the functions of pastoral counseling and catechesis. The pastor, however, fulfils a number of functions, as we have seen: church-related functions (liturgy, catechesis, church development), church/society-related functions (mission, social ministry), and church/individual-related functions (pastoral counseling, spiritual direction). The pastor carries out these functions alone or as part of a small team together

[63] *Guidebook of Information particular to the Graduate School of Religion and Religious Education. Annex Pastoral Counseling Practicum.* (New York: Fordham University, 1996,1997).

[64] W. Berger, *Op weg naar empirische zielzorg. Notities over een reis langs enige pastorale vormingscentra in de Verenigde Staten* (Nijmegen, Utrecht: Dekker en van de Vegt, 1965) 75.

[65] H. Andriessen, *Leren aan ervaring en supervisie,* 377-380; W. Berger, *Op weg naar empirische zielzorg. Notities over een reis langs enige pastorale vormingscentra in de Verenigde Staten,* 77-78.

[66] R. O'Gorman and B. Tucker, *The Field Education Manual. A Study of Some 27 Field Education Manuals According to Nine Categories,* 17-18.

[67] F. Siegers and D. Haan, *Handboek supervisie,* 291.

with pastoral volunteers (chapter III, section 3). Furthermore, supervisees do their internship in a variety of settings: parish, monastry,
hospital, school, media, social welfare agency, mental health agency,
or mission. When is differentiation of supervision necessary, and on
what principles should it be based?

Pastoral Supervision

The first principle we will discuss here is the relation between supervision in general and pastoral supervision. Herein lies a fundamental
theme that touches upon the core of supervision. Expressed in terms
of pastoral supervision, the problem is as follows: should one place
the primary emphasis on 'pastoral' or on 'supervision'? In the first
instance one will structure the supervision in accordance with the various pastoral functions and give full weight to the twofold integration
that determines supervision in its very essence and in which learning
to exercise the profession, in this case the pastoral functions, plays the
central role. In this way of thinking, the pastoral supervisor is a theologian and pastor, who is specialized in one or more pastoral functions and who has been trained in supervision. In the second instance,
the emphasis is on supervision as supervision, more or less independent of the exercise of that which is specific to the pastoral profession
and its various functions. In this approach the supervisor is primarily
a professional supervisor who is considered capable of preparing
supervisees for any profession and for any function. In the Netherlands
it is generally the first approach that is favored, and with good reason.
In some places in Germany, on the other hand, there is a movement
towards the second approach, but there it is less a matter of principle
than of market forces: supervisors who are not bound to any particular profession, for example psychologists, are recruited, hired and paid
to provide supervision for any profession or function.[68]

General and Special Pastoral Supervision

Having selected pastoral supervision over supervision in general, we
find that this pastoral supervision must be oriented towards the pastoral
functions that the pastor performs. In the foregoing we distinguished

---

[68] F. Siegers and D. Haan, *Handboek supervisie*, 185-189.

one general pastoral function and seven special functions (chapter III, section 3). Just as, based on this differences, we differentiated between general and special courses and seminars (chapter IV, section 1), as well as between general and special practica (chapter IV, section 2), so we now make a distinction between general and special pastoral supervision. In general supervision the focus is on the processes and structures of hermeneutic communication that the student will come across in his or her internship and on which he or she must give guidance. Of course these processes do not occur separately from the seven special functions, but are enacted within these functions. This means that the general supervision is oriented towards the work of the student in the seven functions, in so far as these seven functions are determined by processes and structures of hermeneutic communication. Consequently, there are two dimensions to general pastoral supervision.

General Pastoral Supervision

hermeneutics
communication

The next question we must consider is whether it is enough to create opportunities for the supervisee's various pastoral functions and/or work placements within the framework of general pastoral supervision, or whether it is necessary to create separate pastoral supervision opportunities for the different pastoral functions. From the analysis of the functions of the pastor, in which a distinction is made between a general function and seven special functions, we must say that simply making room in general pastoral supervision for the special pastoral functions does not adequately address the particularities of these functions, their presuppositions, principles, rules and methods. It is necessary to create separate opportunities for special pastoral supervision.

The last question that can be asked is whether these opportunities are to be oriented to the special functions we distinguished or to the settings of internship we mentioned. Indeed, one can create separate opportunities for each of the seven functions (liturgy, catechesis, church development, social ministry, mission, pastoral counseling, spiritual direction; see chapter III, section 3) or for each of the eight settings of internships we listed in the previous chapter (parish, monastery, hospital, school, media, social welfare agency, mental health agency, mission setting; see chapter IV, section 3). In the first case the choice is based on the professionality of the function, in the second on the work setting. It is clear that the first principle (professionality of the functions) is much more important for achieving the goal of supervision that we described at the beginning of this chapter than the second principle (setting of the functions) and thus should be given priority, as suggested earlier (chapter IV, section 3). We therefore propose the following forms of special pastoral supervision, from which the student should select three to five specialties corresponding to the choice of three to five placements (chapter IV, section 3).

Special Pastoral Supervision

liturgy/preaching
catechesis
church development
mission
social ministry
pastoral counseling
spiritual direction

At this point I would like to make another remark about the term, 'clinical supervision', which has played such an important role in the history of the clinical pastoral education movement. In the context of what has been said here about differentiation in supervision, the term, 'clinical supervision', is appropriate for supervision that takes place in the clinical setting or is concerned with the functioning of the pastor in the clinical setting, which applies primarily for the function of pastoral counseling within the hospital.[69] Of course, it is possible to use the term, 'clinical', in the metaphorical sense and hence to apply it to supervision in general.

---

[69] H. Andriessen, *Leren aan ervaring en supervisie*, 487-489.

A first metaphoric use of the term relates to observation of the supervisee's performance in situ by the supervisor, in which the observation can take place directly or with the help of a one-way screen. The actions of the supervisee become as it were the clinical object of the supervisor. This meaning is encountered in school supervision, where the supervisor is present in the classroom while the supervisee is teaching, and afterwards discusses his or her performance with him or her. In recent studies, clinical supervision is not identified with what might be called a post-observation conference design only, but with a pre-observation/post-observation conference design.[70] The advantage is that the observation in this clinical supervision provides the supervisee with relevant objective feedback.[71]

A second metaphorical use of the term 'clinical' relates to certain techniques that are utilized in the clinical setting and are transplanted from there to supervision, such as verbatims, process reports, observation reports, case studies.[72]

A last metaphorical usage has to do with the method that is central to supervision and that one can call the 'laboratory method', by which is meant that the performance of the pastor is put under a microscope, as it were, in order to analyze it in detail; after that, alternatives are looked for in a new 'laboratory situation' through a series of role plays.[73]

Strictly speaking, however, neither the particular form of observation, nor the techniques nor the methods can really be called clinical, as they are also frequently used by other professional groups outside the clinic. Andriessen rightly remarks that the use of the term to indicate pastoral supervision in general has only historical significance.[74]

I conclude this section with a remark that, in light of all that has been said thus far, is not insignificant. That a supervisor is more than

---

[70] C. Glickman and Th. Bey, "Supervision," *Handbook of Research on Teacher Education*, eds. R. Houston, M. Haberman, and J. Sikula (New York: Macmillan, 1990); R. Goldhammer, *Clinical Supervision. Special Methods for the Supervision of Teachers* (New York: Holt, Rinehart and Winston, 1966).

[71] D. Waite. *Rethinking Instructional Supervision. Notes on Its Language and Culture,* 118, 199.

[72] H. Andriessen, *Leren aan ervaring en supervisie*, 487-489.

[73] H. Andriessen, *Leren aan ervaring en supervisie*, 489-490.

[74] H. Andriessen, *Leren aan ervaring en supervisie*, 489-495.

a 'wise, experienced, senior pastor', to refer once more to Fielding, should be clear from the foregoing. In order to do his or her job adequately, the supervisor must have been trained in supervision. Furthermore, the theological schools should accord just as much importance to the hiring of professionally qualified supervisors as they now do to the list of academic publications of the faculty in the classic theological disciplines. There are two requirements for supervisor appointments: a Ph.D. in theology and a diploma from a recognized supervisor training program in field instruction, which is to be distinguished from administrative and staff supervision.

Precisely because of the different forms of supervision which we call for, it is advisable that the sitting faculty who are called upon to carry out supervisory tasks in this regard be given training with regard to those specific tasks. A general pastoral supervisor cannot adequately do this job. Without knowledge, insight and professional competence, special pastoral supervision cannot meet the required standards of quality. This applies equally for each of the special functions: liturgy/preaching, catechesis, church development, mission, social ministry, pastoral counseling and spiritual direction.

5. Coaching

Next to or even in place of supervision, there are a number of other forms of instruction and guidance which are explicitly and systematically concerned with the link between learning and working which is so characteristic of supervision. One of these forms is coaching, which is presented here as part of the education for ministry program along with supervision.[75] The relationship of dependence that is so characteristic of supervision and which shapes the interaction between supervisor and supervisee to a very large extent is absent in coaching. This is all the more striking since in particular forms of supervision, above all the psychoanalytically oriented forms, which still exert a certain influence on the clinical pastoral education movement, the authority of the supervisor and the distance between him or her and

[75] Th. Bergen, *Docenten scholen docenten.*

the supervisee are explicitly used as a learning object in the supervision interaction. Sometimes the supervisees' resistance to this dependence on the supervisor is so strong that there is an attempt to banish 'supervision' and replace it by 'paravision', which is supposed to indicate that the supervisor does not stand above ('super') the supervisee, but beside him or her (cf. the Greek 'para' in 'parakletos') in the capacity of a helper.[76]

Be that as it may, coaching is based on equality. It means that colleagues support and guide one another as colleagues, an arrangement which, as research shows, can have a positive effect on the functioning of the professional in question. Because coaching is also used with beginning professionals, I consider it here in the framework of the education for ministry program.[77] In that case coaching takes on the form of mentoring. Whereas coaching was originally based on the idea of consultation between professionals of equal status, mentoring is a form of coaching involving senior and junior professionals or professionals and interns. Some studies see coaching and mentoring as mutually exclusive, but the most recent studies place both forms along a continuum of peer relationships and view mentors and 'mentorees' as colleagues. One of the considerations here is that mentoring, as indeed coaching in general, encourages collegiality.[78] If we apply this to the area of ministry, mentoring can be seen as a form of coaching of the theology student by an experienced pastor in the parish, hospital or agency. Another possibility is for students to coach each other, alternately taking on the role of coach and coachee (collegial coaching).

The aims of coaching are to develop a collegial atmosphere, provide support, strengthen motivation, acquire knowledge and insight, and increase the coachee's ability to function as a professional. While the coach by definition is present when the coachee performs the predetermined professional activity and subsequently discusses the latter's performance with him or her, the nature and intensity of the

[76] E. Haight, "Paravision: A Model for Pastoral Supervision," *Journal of Supervision and Training in Ministry*, 15, 86-95.

[77] R. Raney and J. Rivers, "Professional Growth and Support Through Coaching," *Educational Leadership* (May 1989) 35-38.

[78] S. Conley, E. Bas-Isaac and R. Scull, "Teacher Mentoring and Peer Coaching. A Micropolitical Interpretation," *Journal of Personal Evaluation in Education* 19 (1995) 9: 7-19.

coach's input can vary, and can be described in terms of a continuum. The following activities by the coach, which gradually become increasingly non-directive, can be placed on that continuum: taking over, correcting, advising, supplementing, clarifying, reflecting and being available. The two extremes are taking over, meaning that the coach performs the activity in place of the coachee, and being available, meaning that the coach is open to any issue that the coachee himself brings up. In correcting, advising and supplementing, the coach's input successively declines. Clarifying and reflecting are central categories. Clarifying means that after observing the activity in question, the coach not merely describes but also analyzes and interprets, and also gives suggestions for improvement, always in dialogue with the coachee, for coaching is by its nature dialogical. Reflecting means that the coach only describes the observed activity.[79]

The effect of coaching can be enhanced by conceiving of it as a 'coaching cycle'.[80] The cycle can consist of the following phases: (1) pre-discussion by the coach and coachee(s) of the subject to be treated, which directly relate to the professional activity, (2) presenting/offering by the coach of a relevant, small-scale theory, (3) demonstrating by the coach the application of the theory so that through observational learning a form of model learning ensues, (4) application by the coachee of the theory in a simulated setting and observation by the coach (or peer coaches), (5) structured feedback by the coach including description, analysis and interpretation, (6) coaching for application in real practice situation, (7) application by the coachee in the real practice situation and observation by the coach, (8) structured feedback by the coach including description, analysis and interpretation, (9) post-discussion of the whole cycle.[81] In some cases it may be advisable to reduce this cycle to the phases 1, 2, 3, 7 and 8.

[79] H. De Jonghe, E. van Wezel and S. Veenman. *Het coachen van leerkrachten* (Hoevelaken: Christelijk pedagogisch studiecentrum 1996).

[80] P. Kalinauckas, "Coaching for CPD." *Continuing Professional Development*, ed. S. Clyne (London: Falma Press, 1995) 133-144.

[81] B. Joyce and B. Showers, "Improving Inservice Training. The Messages of Research." *Educational Leadership* (February 1980) 379-385; H. De Jonghe, E. van Wezel and S. Veenman. *Het coachen van leerkrachten.*

This approach assumes that the coach is adequately prepared and trained to fulfil this task. It requires disciplinary knowledge, methodological know-how, and communicative skills. The same requirements apply to peers coaching one another. It appears, incidentally, that the mutual observing and being observed, helping one another with analyses and being the object of one another's analyses is highly motivating for the peer coaches and fosters an atmosphere of fellowship and cooperation.

The effects of coaching, which up till now have been studied in the context of the school, can be described in terms of the goals which I listed earlier (chapter III, section 5.1). The coaching cycle leads to enhanced knowledge and insight, skill development, and the fostering of attitudes of self-confidence, collegiality, solidarity, risk taking and the courage to experiment.[82] Analogous effects can be expected to occur when coaching in the sense of mentoring is applied in the framework of the education for ministry program.

Differentiation in Coaching

Here we follow through on the line established previously. We looked for the common denominator among the seven pastoral functions, and found it in hermeneutic communication, which forms the general function of ministry (chapter III, section 3). Based on the difference between general and special functions, we made a distinction between general and special courses and seminars (chapter IV, section 1), general and special practica (chapter IV, section 2), and general and special pastoral supervision (chapter IV, section 4). Analogously to those distinctions, we here look separately at general and special coaching.

Just as general pastoral supervision is aimed at the exercising of the seven special functions, in so far as these are determined by the processes and structures of hermeneutic communication, so we now find that general coaching aims at ameliorating hermeneutic communication by the student. It thus comprises two dimensions: hermeneutics and communication.

---

[82] E. Roelofs, S. Veenman and J. Raemaekers, "Teamgerichte nascholing en coaching: Effecten op het didactisch handelen van leerkrachten in combinatieklassen," *Pedagogische Studien* 70 (1993), 352-367.

General Coaching

hermeneutics
communication

This general coaching can take on the form of mentoring as well as peer coaching. Sometimes the circumstances themselves will justify or demand mentoring or peer coaching or a combination of both.

Special Coaching

liturgy/preaching
catechesis
church development
social ministry
mission
pastoral counseling
spiritual direction

Given that coaching requires that the mentors, i.e., senior pastors, have appropriate training, it is expedient to consider from this point of view also the establishment of teaching or experimental parishes, hospitals, schools, agencies and mission settings (chapter IV, section 3).

6. Theological Reflection

It cannot be assumed as a matter of course that an education for ministry program will include a component bearing the name 'theological reflection'. Such a component fits into only two of the four training paradigms that are distinguished for professions in general. It does not fit into the training paradigms that are known as 'craft-oriented' and 'behavioristic'. In the first paradigm, the master/apprentice relationship, in which the craft is passed from one generation to the next, is central. Reflection, in this case theological reflection, has no place in this paradigm. The second paradigm centers on the skill approach, which is concerned with the routine application of procedures and techniques, without reflection. The third, personalistic paradigm is different. It is inspired by humanistic psychology and is aimed above all at the personal growth of the individual, which is encouraged particularly by reflection on intrapersonal and interpersonal experiences. The fourth, inquiry-oriented paradigm also accords an important place to reflection, albeit from a completely different perspective, characterized as it is by the self-directed raising, setting and solving of problems.[83] From the preceding chapters it can be inferred that in this book we advocate a combination of the last three paradigms, albeit not without at the same time transcending them in the direction of the reflective profession, that is, reflective ministry.

Anyone who dips into the abundance of literature on theological reflection has a hard time suppressing first of all a sense of astonishment at so much productivity, but also amazement at so much confusion. As far as productivity is concerned, a few years ago an annotated list of 69 titles was drawn up, consisting almost exclusively of books dealing directly or indirectly with theological reflection, along with the names of four centers that are developing special programs in theological reflection.[84] Certain titles are missing from the list[85], and other titles have appeared since.[86] But this enormous production has not really led to a clear insight into the essence and the aim of theological reflection and has perhaps actually raised the level of confusion.

---

[83] A. Knoers, *Leraarschap: Amb(ach)t of professie*. Afscheidscollege Nijmegen University (Assen: Van Gorcum, 1987; F. Korthagen, "Reflectie en de professionele ontwikkeling van leraren", *Pedagogische Studien* 69 (1992), 112-123.

[84] P. O'Conell Killen and J. de Beer, *The Art of Theological Reflection*. New York, 1994. 148-156.

[85] D. Browning, *Practical Theology: The Emerging Field in Theology, Church and World*; *A Fundamental Practical Theology. Descriptive and Strategic proposals*; R. Collins, *Models of Theological Reflection*; L. Mudge and J. Polling, *Formation and Reflection* (Philadelphia: Fortress Press, 1987); E. Farley, *Theologia: The Fragmentation and Unity of Theological Education* (Philadelphia: Fortress Press, 1983); B. Wheeler and E. Farley, *Shifting Boudaries. Contextual Approaches to the Structure of Theological Education* (Westminster: Abingdon Press, 1991); D.H. Kelsey, *To Understand God Truly. What's Theological About A Theological School*, 1992).

[86] R. Chopp, *Saving Work. Feminist Practices of Theological Education* (Westminster: Abingdon Press, 1995); R. Kinast, "Theological Reflection: Fad or Foundation?" *Seminary Journal* 2 (1996) 1, 11-15; J. Walsch, "Dialogue: Summary of Discussion on Theological Reflection Among East Coast Deans and Rev. Robert Kinast," *Seminary Journal* 2 (1996) 1, 16-18.

There is, of course, a more than just hypothetical risk that the presentation of the vision of theological reflection that follows will merely contribute to further confusion. However, it may be that one or two distinctions that are made here will help to clear the air somewhat.

The basic distinction we refer to here, is that between theological reflection in ministry and theological reflection on ministry, which relates to the religious aspects within the distinction we made earlier, i.e., reflection in ministry and reflection on ministry (chapter III, section 4).

Theological Reflection in Ministry

In connection with the analysis by Peirce, we saw earlier that reflection in ministry is based on the fact that the experiences the pastor makes in his or her practice relate to three different aspects, i.e., evaluations, actions and general tendencies of the self. As far as the evaluative dimension of these experiences is concerned, a plurality of sensations, feelings and images develop in the pastor's mind. On these sensations, feelings and images he or she conducts various kinds of inferential processes (abduction, deduction, induction). These evaluations may lead not only to evaluative responses, but also to decisive reactions or initiatory activities, in which the pastor makes a choice in his or her particular situation: for this and not for that, for that and not for this. In making these choices the pastor himself or herself is at stake, which is to say that, in these actions and reactions, he or she as a 'focal self' or 'matrix self' re-constructs the general tendencies which characterize him or her and have characterized him or her in the past.

Theological reflection in ministry relates to the religious aspects of the pastor's evaluations, actions and self-tendencies in the performance of his or her pastoral functions, i.e., liturgy/preaching, catechesis, church development, social ministry, mission, pastoral counseling and spiritual direction. These religious aspects may be associated with different types of chains between the pastor's evaluations, actions and self-tendencies. Let me list just a few of them.

The first type I call correlational in a Tillichian sense. The pastor meets a person who is asking questions about the predicament of human existence, its contingency and finitude. With the help of the sensations, feelings and images which develop in the pastor's mind and the inferential processes which indicate how he or she might or ought to react, he or she tries to place these questions in a perspective in which they can be answered on the basis of the Christian faith. In this pastoral action the pastor's own faith and spirituality are at stake. In this action he or she re-constructs his or her own religious self.

The second type I call hermeneutic. Whereas the correlational process begins with questions from the now and seeks to answer them on the basis of the Bible and the Christian tradition from the past, in hermeneutic work the pastor begins with religious texts from the past and subsequently inquires into their meaning for the present. In doing so, the pastor becomes aware of a range of sensations, feelings and images with regard to both these texts and the people he or she is in contact with. He or she also conducts different types of inferential processes with the help of which he or she performs the typically pastoral action, which is trying to bridge the distance between these texts from the past and the present situation. For that reason he or she consciously and intentionally inscribes those people's lives in the narrations these texts contain. Again, in this hermeneutic inscription, the pastor's self is at stake; in this process, he or she also inscribes his or her own 'focal self'or 'matrix self' into these texts.

The third type I call conversational. While the correlational and the hermeneutic processes primarily concern intrapersonal conversation, the realm of faith is naturally characterized to a large degree by interpersonal conversation. The two are dialectically related: in intrapersonal conversation one encounters, in oneself, the significant others with whom one is interpersonally in conversation, and by actually holding interpersonal conversation with these significant others one deepens the intrapersonal conversation in oneself and with oneself. Nonetheless, the two forms can be distinguished in an analytical sense and indeed should be. When the pastor enters into an interpersonal conversation about a religious topic (symbols, convictions, emotions, values, norms, rituals, communitarian topics) or guides and directs such a conversation, he or she coordinates the many sensations, feelings and images which arise in this conversation. From there he or she carries out specific inferential processes which lead him or her to a particular substantial or processual intervention. Again, in doing so,

the pastor 'reveals' both to himself or herself and to his or her partners in the conversation his or her personal religious feelings and convictions with regard to the topic. In the process the pastor re-constructs
his or her religious self.

In order to approach reflection in ministry in a methodical way, the
following questions may be asked: 1) What a) sensations, b) feelings,
c) images and d) inferential processes developed in the pastor's mind,
2) what actions, for example, correlational, hermeneutic and conversational, did he or she take and what actions did he or she not take,
and 3) which religious 'focal' self or 'matrix self' was at stake?

Theological Reflection on Ministry

The difference between theological reflection in ministry and theological reflection on ministry refers to the fact that theological reflection in ministry takes place in what Dewey calls a 'stream of consciousness', while theological reflection on ministry is triggered by a
situation of ambiguity and perplexity that blocks this 'stream of consciousness' because it confuses and paralyzes the pastor. In this situation, the "demand for the solution of a perplexity is the steadying and
guiding factor in the entire process of reflection".[87] In other words,
theological reflection on ministry refers to practice experiences that
arise out of a situation that the pastor experiences as ambiguous, per-
plexing, complex, confusing. These are experiences in which he or she
has the sense of being stuck, of having no way out, of seeing no
prospects for a solution. Theological reflection in ministry is of no
help here; in such a situation one needs more distance, greater detach-
ment, a higher level of abstraction, more degrees of freedom, in short:
' theological reflection on ministry'.

This theological reflection on ministry is served by going through
the seven phases of the experimental cycle that I have adopted from
Dewey in a free interpretation[88], as described earlier. These seven
phases, which can be seen as an extension of the so-called regulative

[87] J. Dewey, *How we Think*, 14.
[88] J. Dewey, *How we Think; Logic: The Theory of Inquiry. The later Works*; *The
moral writings of John Dewey*, 257 v.; C. Wales, A. Nardi and R. Stager, "Emphasizing
Critical Thinking and Problem Solving,", 193-211.

cycle of reflective professional action by Van Strien[89] on which some
practical theologians also have based themselves[90], are briefly summarized in the following (cf. Chapter III, section 4).

The first phase is that the pastor experiences a situation which is so
unsettled or indeterminate that he or she feels confused, and experiences the situation as obscure and alien. The second phase concerns
how to change the situation. According to Dewey, a way out can only
be found by making a choice from the whole complex of indetermi-
nacies, questions, doubts and hesitations, by fixing on one of these elements and elevating it as it were to the status of problem. After that
follows the third phase: problem setting. How the pastor conceives of
and formulates the problem, once he or she has selected it as the problem, determines to a large extent the strategies he or she will use to
find alternative solutions and, finally, a definitive solution. The fourth
phase consists in the actual determination of possible solutions to the
problem. For this, the pastor analyzes the situation as carefully as possible in order to determine what factors might improve the situation.
This automatically leads to an idea of one or more possible solutions.
The examination of these possible solutions occurs in the fifth phase.
In the process, the pastor continuously draws on past experiences, both
his or her own and those of other people who are involved in the solving of the problem. After examination, the sixth phase consists in the
performing of certain actions which are aimed at solving the problem.
This phase provides insight into whether the selected strategy will in
fact achieve its intended aim and to what extent it will contribute to
solving the problem.The last phase is characterized by evaluation. Here
the pastor must consider whether he or she is truly satisfied with the
chosen approach or whether the cycle must be gone through again.

This cycle of seven phases can serve as a set of reference points
with the help of which the theological reflection on ministry can be
conducted in a methodical fashion. Of course, one must take into consideration that although we distinguish seven phases, this division may

---

[89] P. Van Strien, *Praktijk als wetenschappelijke methodologie van het sociaal wetenschappelijk handelen* (Assen: van Gorcum, 1986) 19.
[90] G. Heitink, *Praktische theologie, Geschiedenis, theorie, handelingsvelden*, 205-
206; G. Dingemans, *Manieren van doen. Inleiding tot de studie van de praktische
theologie*, 116.

not coincide at all with the perception of the pastor in the situation, who may have the sense that the various phases are all mixed up and happening with no particular rhyme or reason. In other words, the cycle is a reconstruction after the fact, which can be useful in order to look back on what has taken place, as a way of imposing some order on their 'messy' reality.[91]

Theological reflection on ministry is concerned with what one could call 'meta-pastoral problems' that go beyond the self-evident plausibility and routine of daily pastoral praxis with its daily questions and problems, and calls these questions and problems themselves into question. Looking at the situation in the Netherlands, examples of such 'meta-pastoral problems', for which no easy answers exist, if there are any answers at all, include: creating a new liturgy in the context of modernity and postmodernity; the relation between youth, religion and the church; the dilemma of multiculturalism and religion between liberation and integration. These are not problems of conjuncture, but of structure.

The distinction that was made in the preceding sections between general and special functions, general and special courses, seminars and practica, general and special supervision and coaching, is no longer relevant here because the 'meta-pastoral problems' transcend the boundaries between functions. In the reflection on practice as we consider it here, it is precisely the relationships between the problems that arise in two or more functions that are of interest, that must be looked at and studied.

What distinguishes this kind of theological reflection from scientific approaches to these problems is that the students who engage in the reflection do so on the basis of their own, concrete professional experiences in their own concrete pastoral settings in parishes, agencies and the like. While working as interns, carrying out pastoral tasks of various kinds and taking responsibility for them, they are confronted in the most concrete way with the structural problems regarding, for example, liturgy in the context of modernity and postmodernity, youth and religion, or multiculturalism and religion between liberation and

---

[91] G. Teisman, *Complexe besluitvorming. Een pluricentrisch perspectief op besluitvorming over ruimtelijke investeringen* (Den Haag: VUGA, 1992) 119 v.

integration. Supervision and coaching are not the appropriate opportunities for dealing with these problems, because the length in time,
breadth in space, and depth in complexity of these problems is too
great. This kind of theological reflection requires some specific attitudes, which can be developed further in the course of the reflection
process: curiosity, open-mindedness, wholeheartedness, responsibility, and the courage of long-term thinking.[92]

For this reason students should not participate in this kind of theological reflection at the very beginning of their internship, but only
after they have completed, for example, the first half of it.[93] Furthermore, it should be borne in mind that students vary in their ability and
readiness to reflect in this way. Some people are characterized by an
internal orientation, which means that they are independent enough to
engage in imaginative, creative, critical, rational and even introspec-
tive thinking. Others have an external orientation, meaning that they
ask for guidance and direction from a teacher or a book, for instance.
For the latter, a gradual strategy is needed.[94]

Such a strategy could consist of a small number of instruction sessions in which Dewey's seven phases are explained using a concrete
example, followed by writing an extended paper, for which a small
number of tutoring sessions may be held to guide the student's writing process.

7. Action Research

In the preceding section we summarized again the phases of the
experimental cycle, freely adapted from Dewey, that was described in
chapter III, section 4. A particular phase can now be expanded upon
for educational reasons, as Dewey observes.[95] The phase we will look
at in greater detail is the sixth phase, in which one seeks to determine

---

[92] J. Dewey, *How we Think*, 29 v., 35 v.

[93] F. Korthagen, Reflectie en de professionele ontwikkeling van leraren, *Pedagogische Studien* 69 (1992), 112- 123.

[94] F. Korthagen, "The Influence of Learning Orientations on the Development of
Reflective Teaching," 35-50.

[95] J. Dewey, *How we Think*, 116 v.

whether the proposed strategy for solving a complex problem, a problem that is not conjunctural but structural in nature, does in fact produce the effect that it could reasonably be expected to produce. The data needed to answer this question can be obtained by carrying out action research. It is our position that in the education for ministry program, action research must be accorded due attention.

Certain readers will wrinkle their brows at reading this statement, for two very different reasons. Some will be of the opinion that research does not belong in a professional education program, since such a program is merely supposed to teach the students to apply the knowledge, insights and skills that they have acquired previously. It is not difficult to discern in this view the epistemology of technical rationality that we described in chapter II, section 2. This epistemology cannot provide a sound basis for the education for ministry program because the situation in which the pastor performs his or her work is so strongly determined by complexity and dynamic change that the straightforward application of knowledge, insights and skills simply is not sufficient.

Others will recognize the need for research in an education for ministry program, but will turn up their noses at the sort of research that is advocated here, i.e., action research. The only form of research that these people consider worthy of the name is pure or fundamental research or, at the very least, applied research. Pure research is generally said to be undertaken from no other motives than curiosity and the desire to contribute to the increase in human knowledge. It is called pure research — really the only true form of research — because this form of research is ostensibly uncontaminated by other drives or goals. Fundamental research is closely related to pure research in that it exposes the deepest structures of reality, without any foreseeable usefulness. The purpose is to discover natural laws or empirical laws as defined by John Stuart Mill. Natural laws describe uniformities in their simplest form and with the smallest possible number of propositions, for example "air has weight" or "pressure in one direction, not opposed by equal pressure in the opposite direction, produces motion". Empirical laws describe uniformities which we have not yet succeeded in reducing to simpler laws, such as "bodies expand with increasing temperature". Because such empirical laws are not always generally reliable, restrictions in time and space as well as any special circumstances must always be specified. In addition to natural and empirical laws there are also what Mill calls probabilities, which are also the object of fundamental research. These are known as probabilities because they are only approximately generalizable. They, too, must be specified as to time and space as well as special circumstances.[96] It would appear to be evident that in the human sciences — but to a certain extent perhaps in the natural sciences as well — one can speak only of probabilities and not of natural laws and empirical laws.[97] What links these three forms of fundamental research with pure research, however, is that they are aimed at the augmentation of knowledge. Applied research is then the form of research in which — generally speaking — these natural laws, empirical laws and probabilities are applied, but not with the direct aim of achieving a practical purpose, but to acquire knowledge about the application. Applied research, too, is and remains research: not the practical utility is foremost, but the acquiring of knowledge, or so the fundamental rule of the science of science tells us.[98]

Action research is a different matter. One could say that action research combines knowledge and utility.[99] As the term suggests, action research is concerned with human action that is essentially aimed at achieving a certain goal or set of goals and producing intended effects, so that a change is brought about in the status quo ante in the direction of the desired reality. In action research one tries to find out whether this change has in fact been brought about. Inasmuch as this change is not a phenomenon that takes place behind the backs, as it were, of the actors in the field that is being studied by this action research, but rather happens through the actors and indeed is brought about by them, action research is not concerned with 'objective processes' or 'neutral changes', but with changing human beings

[96] J. S. Mill, *A System of Logic Ratiocinative and Inductive*. Collected Works. Vol. VII. (Toronto: University of Toronto Press, 1973).

[97] J. A. Van der Ven, *Practical Theology: An Empirical Approach*, 26-32.

[98] A. Rip and P. Groenewegen, *Macht over kennis. Mogelijkheden van wetenschapsbeleid* (Alphen aan de Rijn, Samson,. 1980) 63-65.

[99] J. S. Dreyer, "Die moderne gemeente en haar funksionering: die belang, aard en benutting van praktijkkennis," *The Dynamics of the Modern Church*, eds. J. S. Dreyer, and H. Pieterse, 221-247 (Lynnwoodrif, University of South Africa Press) 235.

as subjects of these processes, who, as human beings, bring about and express this change. And inasmuch as the action researcher is a part of the field in which these human processes occur, he or she carries out his or her research not from the outside perspective of a neutral bystander, but from the inside perspective of an engaged and engaging participant. Were he or she not to do so, he or she could not adequately understand the true subject of his or her research, i.e., human actions.

For the sake of clarity, let us add that action research differs from experimental as well as quasi-experimental research. Experimental research that takes place in the laboratory and quasi-experimental research that takes place in a quasi-laboratory setting in the field are characterized by a pre-test — post-test control group design. This means that before treatment occurs, the research population is given a test to establish its cognitive, affective, attitudinal or action-related level, and after the treatment a post-test is given using the same measuring instruments. In order to account for any confounding variables that have nothing to do with the experiment as such but that could disturb it from the outside, such as occasional events, maturation, or mortality — the 'threats to validity' — one or more control groups are used to eliminate these variables.[100] The difference is that the action research is not "before and after", but "during-during-during".[101]

Action research also differs from the model of 'research and development', in that the latter is based on the epistemology of technical rationality, the presupposition being that there exists a body of scientific knowledge, resulting from fundamental research, and the only thing to be done is to derive from it certain absolute, solid principles and rules, with the help of which all kinds of technical applications can be developed. This technological development can then gradually take on a life of its own, the results of which are more or less beyond political control, as for example in the field of arms technology.[102]

[100] Th. Cook and D. Campbell, *Quasi-Experimentation. Design and Analysis Issues for Field Settings.*

[101] L. Cronbach, *Toward Reform of Program Evaluation. Aims, Methods and Institutional Arrangements* (San Francisco, University of California Press, 1980) 243, 272-295.

[102] A. Rip and P. Groenewegen, *Macht over kennis. Mogelijkheden van wetenschapsbeleid* (Alphen aan de Rijn: Samson,. 1980) 24, 130.

Other examples outside of the arms industry are information theory as
a fundamental discipline, and information technology, which produces
electronic payment cards and cordless telephones, or cognitive science
as a fundamental discipline and the development of software programs
like the one with which this text was produced. Action research is different because it does not have to do with the products of technological inventions, nor even with the actions of human beings ('actus
hominis') in so far as they make instrumental use of these inventions,
but with human actions ('actus humanus') that are aimed producing certain effects in certain situations in order to achieve certain goals. The
term 'certain situations' is essential, because action research takes very
seriously the setting in which people act and the context in which they
intervene. Action research, precisely because it is research into and on
human action, is local, situation-bound, contextualized research.[103]

The sixth phase of the experimental cycle, as described above,
demands some form of action research, because there is no other way
to determine whether, to what extent and in what manner the intended
effects of the selected problem-solving strategy have been achieved.
Within the framework of this cycle, action research can be described
more specifically as program evaluation research. The purpose of this
research is not merely to describe the actions of those involved nor the
processes they engage in, but to determine to what extent the situation
has been improved as a result of that action. This is the essential question for action research: has the intervention led to any improvement?
Here the normative dimension of reflection on practice once again
comes in, a normative dimension that even has a teleological purport
in the sense that values pertaining to the future of humanity and society are implied in it.[104]

In this form of program evaluation-oriented action research, it is
important to combine quantitative and qualitative methods of description, and to apply these to the various parties who are involved in
establishing the program and in its actual implementation. The focus

[103] D.J. Fox, *The Research Proces in Education* (New York: Holt, Rinehart and Winston, 1969) 97-100.
[104] L. Cronbach, *Toward Reform of Program Evaluation. Aims, Methods and Institutional Arrangements.* 62 v., 91 v.

is not only on individual people, like members of target groups, pastors, volunteers, administrative officers and so on, but also on the symmetric and asymmetric relations between these individual persons and their networks, such as groups, institutions and organizations, because these individuals and networks, in their various roles, influence each other in the same or analogous arenas within a kind of mutual, interactive dependence.[105] Methods may include the use of existing questionnaires or questionnaires designed specially for this evaluation, as well as methods of participative observation, interviews and group research as a means of gathering data about the target group and the actual course of the service rendered.[106]

Within the education for ministry program it is expedient that the students be versed in the most important principles, rules and methods of action research so that they can use them in phase six of their theological reflection paper which we described in the previous section. The goal would not be to learn to carry out pure, fundamental or applied research nor to learn to implement research designs like the survey design or the quasi-experimental design. What concerns us here is not the empirical methodology of research, but what Van Strien calls the regulative methodology of professional action.[107]

The introduction to action research within the education for ministry program could consist of a small number of instruction sessions in which the principles, rules and methods of action research are explained in terms of a concrete example, as well as carrying out an actual action research project and integrating the results into the paper on theological reflection. Some tutoring sessions could be held to guide the research process.

Summary

In this chapter we have looked at the details of an education for ministry program that fulfils the criteria of reflective ministry and

[105] G. Teisman, *Complexe besluitvorming. Een pluricentrisch perspectief op besluitvorming over ruimtelijke investeringen*, 49-78.

[106] P. Rossi and H. Freeman, *Evaluation. A Systematic Approach* (London: Sage Publishers, 1989); J. A. Van der Ven, *Ecclesiology in Context*, 473-475.

[107] P. Van Strien, *Praktijk als wetenschappelijke methodologie van het sociaal wetenschappelijk handelen* (Assen: van Gorcum, 1986).

reflective competence. At the beginning of this chapter, we formulated six educational principles that must be taken into consideration in the establishment of such a program. i.e., observational and enactive learning, learning by reinforcement and insight, meta-learning and learning in situ. Before taking the program, students must have completed prerequisite courses and seminars in philosophy, social sciences, theological methodology and the theological disciplines. The program itself consists of the following elements: courses and seminars, practica, internship, supervision, coaching, theological reflection, and action research. In the program a distinction is made between general and special courses, seminars, practica, supervision, and coaching. The general elements are concerned with hermeneutic communication, while the special elements concern the pastor's seven special functions which were defined earlier, i.e., the church-related functions (liturgy/preaching, catechesis, church development), church/society-related functions (social ministry, mission), and church/individual-related functions (pastoral counseling, spiritual direction). The student chooses three to five functions and their associated theories from among the special parts of the program. Finally, the description of the program does not imply any guidelines as to how many credits would be associated with the elements of the program. This is a matter to be decided individually by each theological school, and for which general rules are not appropriate.

CHAPTER V

GENERAL SUMMARY AND CONCLUSIONS

In the *Introduction* to this study on *Education for Reflective Ministry*, we show that the function of the pastor is marked by a profound ambiguity and that the pastor does not receive adequate guidance from the church and theology. The pastor, therefore, is forced to exercise self-responsibility and self-direction.

In *Chapter I*, entitled *Complexity and Dynamics of Religion*, the processes are described which characterize religion today in the western countries and which render complex and dynamic the situation in which the pastor carries out his functions.

A distinction is made between the religious processes at the macrolevel of society, the mesolevel of the church and the microlevel of the individual. The societal level is found to be strongly influenced by processes of partial and differential secularization (section 1).

At the mesolevel of the church, the factors are examined which determine the decline of the mainstream churches as well as the extent of church migration and religious migration. Mention is also made of the growing trend towards the volunteer-based church (section 2).

In looking at the religious developments at the microlevel of the individual, it is found that this development is increasingly characterized by processes of pluralization, individualization and fragmentation (section 3).

Along with the processes of secularization, processes of multculturalization also play a major role. Not only do these bring the western countries into contact with the other world religions inside their own borders, but they force society to confront the overwhelming poverty and alienation that are present among the cultural minorities and which constitute an immense challenge for the Christian religion as well.

Chapter II, The Need of a New Educational Perspective for Ministry, argues that the models for the training of pastors that have been used up till now are no longer capable of meeting the requirements engendered by the complexity and dynamics shaping the western countries and religion in those countries. These models are referred to as 'therapeuticalism' and 'managerialism'.

The model of therapeuticalism is no longer adequate, at least in a general sense, because it focusses too exclusively on the religious needs of the individual person and does not sufficiently take into account that the pastor's function extends also to the mesolevel of the church and the macrolevel of society (section 1).

The model of managerialism is no longer adequate because it does not sufficiently allow for the complexity and the dynamics that characterize the processes at the different levels (section 2).

In *Chapter III*, entitled *Reflective Ministry in Context*, the position is taken that in order to find a new perspective on education for ministry, it is necessary first to outline the essential function or functions which the pastor is called on to fulfil.

Against the background of the description of the processes which religion is undergoing in the countries of the west, and in order to stake out the terrain of the pastor relative to the areas in which other professionals are active today in these countries, the professional domain of the pastor is defined as the religious domain. This is not to say that the pastor can not, may not or should not operate in other cultural domains or in the economic, political or social domains, but that he or she always does so from the point of view of the interdependence of these domains with the religious domain and on the basis of a religious legitimation (section 1).

In this religious domain the religious institutions, collectively referred to as 'the church', occupy an important place at the mesolevel. The church's relationship to the processes taking place at the macrolevel of society and the microlevel of the individual is a dialectical one: the religious institutions influence these processes and are also influenced by them. It is from within this relationship of dialectical tension that the church functions as a context of ministry (section 2).

After the description of the religious domain and the church context, an attempt is undertaken to identify the one, fundamental function of the pastor. No such function appears to exist, given that he or she in fact performs many functions. Seven functions are distinguished, divided into three church-related functions (liturgy/preaching, catechesis, church development), two church/society-related functions (social ministry, mission), and two church/individual-related functions (pastoral counseling, spiritual direction). A common denominator among these seven functions is found in the concept of 'hermeneutic communication', which is referred to as the 'general function'. This is the function that is shared by the seven functions, which because of their particularities are called 'special functions'. A 'second-order function' is also distinguished, which consists of the recruitment, training and guidance of pastoral volunteers. It is called 'second-order function' because the pastor is called on to initiate the volunteers, in so far as necessary and feasible, into the general function and one or more of the special functions (section 3).

In the next section, the meaning of the term 'reflective ministry' is examined, particularly in relation to the more recent theories pertaining to social professions and professionalization. It is important to note that in the complex and dynamic society in which he or she functions, the reflective practitioner, i.e., the pastor, is called on to exercise a maximum of self-direction. This self-direction is inherent in the analysis of the concept of 'practice' based on the approach put forward by the American philosophy of pragmatism that had its golden age at the beginning of this century with Peirce, Dewey and, recently the black theologian, West. Against this background the distinction is made between reflection in ministry and reflection on ministry. Both forms of reflection imply a teleological dimension that makes ministry into transformatory ministry (section 4).

Finally, attention is given to the reflective competence which the pastor must possess in order to be able to carry out his or her reflective ministry. This reflective competence is broken down into the aspect of competent reflection in ministry and competent reflection on ministry. Both aspects are further broken down into four components. Competent reflection in ministry is found to consist of knowledge, insight, skills and attitudes, while competent reflection on ministry is divided into meta-knowledge, meta-insight, meta-skill and meta-attitudes. Both forms of reflection are related to the pastor's general function and special functions (section 5).

In *Chapter IV* the elements of a curriculum for the education for ministry program are described. A summary is given in the schema below.

This education for ministry program assumes a prerequisite five-year basic program in theology, which the student must have completed before beginning the education for ministry program. In addition to the classic and more modern theological disciplines, including theological methodology, this basic program also includes philosophical and social-scientific disciplines, as is usual in theological schools on the European continent.

Education for Reflective Ministry Program

General	Special
Courses	
	liturgical/homiletic sciences
	catechetics
hermeneutics	practical ecclesiology
	practical social ethics
communication theory	practical missiology
	poimenics
	theory of spiritual direction
Seminars	
	liturgical/homiletic sciences
	catechetics
hermeneutics	practical ecclesiology
	practical social ethics
communication theory	practical missiology
	poimenics
	theory of spiritual direction
Practica	
	liturgy/preaching
	catechetics
hermeneutics	church development
communication	social ministry
	mission
personality development	pastoral counseling
religious development	spiritual direction

General	Special
Supervision and Coaching	
hermeneutics	liturgy catechesis church development social ministry
communication	mission pastoral counseling spiritual direction
Internship	
Theological Reflection	
Action Research	

The education for ministry program itself consists of the following elements: courses, seminars, practica, supervision, coaching, internship, theological reflection, and action research. In the program a distinction is made between general and special courses, seminars, practica, supervision, and coaching. The general elements are concerned with hermeneutic communication, whereas the special elements relate to the pastor's seven special functions that are discussed in a previous section, namely, the church-related functions (liturgy/preaching, catechesis, church development), church/society-related functions (social ministry, mission), and church/individual-related functions (pastoral counseling, spiritual direction). In the scheme below, the general parts of the program are shown on the left side and the special parts on the right; the three elements at the end of the list, i.e., internship, theological reflection and action research, which are the common elements and are not divided into general and special parts, are in the middle.

From among the special parts of the program, the student must choose three to five special functions and their associated theories. The description of the program implies no guidelines as to the number of credits associated with the program or its elements. These are matters that each theological school must decide for itself.

In connection with the elements of the curriculum, it is noted that the theological schools must ensure that certain administrative measures are taken, in particular the drawing up of contracts in connection with internships, supervision and coaching.

The various parts of the education for ministry program that is summarized in the scheme on the preceding page do not aim at one and the same goal. The goals consist of the acquisition of the components of competent reflection in ministry (knowledge, insight, skills, attitudes) and competent reflection on miniostry competence (meta-knowledge, meta-insight, meta-skill, meta-attitude) which were defined in chapter III, section 5.

Matrix of Goals and Program Elements

	reflection in ministry				reflection on ministry			
	knowl	insight	skill	attitude	meta-knowl	meta-insight	meta-skill	meta-attitude
courses	*				*			
seminars		*				*		
practica			*				*	
pers./rel. dev.				*				*
superv/coaching	*	*	*	*				
theol. reflect	*	*	*	*	*	*	*	*
action research					*	*	*	*

In order to illustrate the various goals that are aimed at in the various parts of the program, a matrix has been constructed in which groups of parts of the program are related to groups of goals. This is not to say that the relations between goals and parts are exclusive; the asterisks represent only the relative emphasis on these relations.

From this matrix it becomes apparent that the courses and the seminars are aimed above all at the development of knowledge and meta-knowledge, and of insight and meta-insight, the practica in general at skills and meta-skills, the practica 'personal development' and 'religious development' at attitudes and meta-attitudes, supervision and coaching at knowledge, insight, skills and attitudes, theological reflection in ministry at knowledge, insight, skills and attitudes, theological reflection on ministry at meta-knowledge, meta-insight, meta-skills and meta-attitudes, and, lastly, action research at meta-knowledge, meta-inisght, meta-skills and meta-attitudes.

CONCLUSIONS

1. In the Introduction to this study it is remarked that there have been no substantial changes to the education for ministry program since the 1960s. Since then the processes of change affecting society, the church and the individual have led to a level of complexity and transformation that make changes to this program imperative. The present study points to the reflective ministry model as the direction in which these necessary changes must be made. This model consists of two forms of reflection: reflection in ministry and reflection on ministry. Reflection in ministry implies knowledge, insight, skills and attitudes. Reflection on ministry implies meta-knowledge, meta-insight, meta-skills and meta-attitudes.

2. The program that is elaborated in this paper is made up of courses, seminars, practica, supervision, coaching, internship, theological reflection and action research. In the program, a distinction is made between general and special courses, seminars, practica, supervision and coaching. The general elements relate to the pastor's general function of hermeneutic communication, while the special elements focus on the seven special functions, we distinguished, namely, church-related functions (liturgy/preaching, catechesis, church development), church/society-related functions (social ministry, mission), and church/individual-related functions (pastoral counseling, spiritual direction).

3. The integration of the program is guaranteed by various measures. First, ministry is situated in the religious domain, which does not mean that the pastor operates exclusively in this domain and not in the economic, political, social and cultural domains, but that his or her functioning in any domain is religiously informed and religiously legitimated. The religious domain brings unity into the pastor's special functions. It distinguishes his or her profession from that of other professionals. Secondly, the pastor's functioning takes place in the context of the church, which is to say within the dialectical tension between the church at the

mesolevel and society at the macrolevel as well as between the church at the mesolevel and the individual at the microlevel. The ecclesial context also brings unity into the pastor's special functions.Thirdly, the seven functions the pastor performs have a common denominator, i.e., hermeneutic communication, to which the general elements of the program refer. This also advances the integration of the program. Fourthly, it is advisable to develop paradigm crossing, by which the paradigms of some special functions are used to study other special functions and vice versa (chapter III, section 3). Fifthly, some parts of the curriculum are explicitly and intentionally aimed at advancing the integration of the program, especially supervision, coaching, theological reflection and action research. Lastly, the students are required to select three to five special functions for closer study, in order, among other things, to prevent them from falling into 'specialist's blindness'.

4. The pastor's spirituality is considered to play a constitutive part in the program, as can be seen from the following. First, spiritual direction, one of the pastor's seven functions, can be chosen by each and every student as part of the requirement for three to five special functions. Secondly, the parts of the program are aimed at developing not only knowledge, insight and skills, but also and especially attitudes. Attitudes generally refer to orientations within the person, in which feelings and convictions influence one another. Religious attitudes are seen as religious orientations consisting of the interaction between religious feelings and religious convictions. It is these religious attitudes that give the pastor the inspiration and motivation for his or her pastoral work, i.e., celebrating, preaching, catechizing, performing social ministry and mission activities, providing pastoral counseling and spiritual direction. He or she may interpret this religious inspiration and motivation in terms of God's call. Various parts of the program aim at the development of these religious attitudes. Lastly, two practica specifically seek to advance the pastor's personal development and his or her religious development. These practica may take place in a room-and-board arrangement outside the theological institution, so that the student has the opportunity to devote himself or herself as optimally as possible to deepening his or her religious commitment and engagement (chapter IV, section 2).

5. In 1774, when the first university chair for pastoral (or practical) theology was established in the theological curriculum at the University of Vienna, the duration of training for the education for ministry program was set at one year. In today's society, the modern professions require a training program of a quantitative duration and qualitative depth sufficient to allow for the dynamics and complexity of the processes in this society to be adequately dealt with. Since the 1960s, the duration of training programs for analogous professions, such as the general medical practitioner and psychotherapist, has been extended by a factor of three.Taking into consideration that students must choose three to five special functions for in-depth study, the education for ministry program as proposed in this paper will require a minimum duration of three years full-time equivalent.

6. The three-year education for ministry progam should be embedded in a new structure to be developed, which provides for various levels of pastoral functioning and various categories of pastors along with a continuum of professional competence[1]: the level of intern pastor, the level of assistant pastor, the level of associate pastor, the level of senior pastor/mentor, the level of pastoral supervisor. From this perspective, the education of pastors should be considered in terms of continuing professional education.[2] Analogously to the medical profession of the general physician, the professionally educated pastor should fullfill the obligation of spending at least 40 hours (1 credit) at an accredited scientific institution, participating in courses, seminars and/or practica in which new methods, principles and results of research are distributed and discussed from the point of view of their professional relevance.[3] Next to that he or she should spend about 160 hours a year (4 credits) reading scientific publications, which is about half a day per week based on an average working week of 55 hours.[4] For pastors it would

---

[1] W. McGaghie, "Evaluating Competence for Professional Practice," *Educating Professionals. Responding to New Expectations for Competence and Accoutability*, eds. L. Curry, J. Wergin et. al., 238 (San Francisco: Jossey-Bass, 1993).

[2] N. Bennet and R. Fox, "Challenges for Continuing Professional Education," *Educating Professionals. Responding to New Expectations for Competence and Accountability*, eds. L. Curry and J. Wergin, 262- 278.

[3] C. Houle, *Continuing Learning in the Professions*, 239.

[4] C. Houle, *Continuing Learning in the Professions*, 125.

be useful and indeed necessary to have an opportunity every year to familiarize themselves with new developments in the classic and more modern theological disciplines, philosophy and social sciences, as well as, and above all, with research pertaining to the pastor's general and special functions, and to explore these findings with a view to their practical meaning in the short and long term. Of course, it is important to bear in mind the factors that would spur the professional pastor on, in a positive sense, to participate in this continuing professional education, for example, stimulating his curiosity, drawing attention to the problems he encounters in his work and calling on teachers and instructors who can function as role models. Such continuing education is a requirement for enabling pastors to function adequately in today's complex and dynamic society in which religion plays such a plural, problematic and confusing role.

LITERATURE

ACTS URBAN CPE, 1996, Association of Chicago Theological Schools Urban Clinical Pastoral Education. *Papers: Mission Statement; Composition and Functional Roles; Historal Outline (1989-1996)*. Chicago.

AFFOLDERBACH M., and H. STEINKAMP, eds., 1985, *Kirchliche Jugendarbeit in Grundbegriffen. Stichworte zu einer ökumenischen Bilanz*. Düsseldorf/München.

AL W., W. BERGER, and B de LOOR, eds., 1979, *Ik bouw U een huis. Praktijkstudies over kerkverdamping, pastoraat en kerkopbouw*. Hilversum.

ALBERIGO G., 1984, "Het volk Gods in de gelovige ervaring," *Concilium* 20 6:31-43.

ALESHIRE D., 1980, "Eleven Major Areas of Ministry," *Ministry in America. A Report and Analysis, based on an In-Depth Survey of 47 Denominations in the United Sates and Canada, with Interpretation by 18 Experts*, eds. D.Schuller, P. Strommen, and M. Brekke, 23-53. San Francisco.

—, 1990, "ATS Profiles of Ministry Project," *Clergy Assessment and career development*, eds. R. Hunt, J. Hinkle, and H.N. Malony, 97-103. Nashville.

ANDERSON H., et al., 1992, *Family living in Pastoral Perspective. Vol. I Leaving Home. Vol. II Becoming married. Vol. III Regarding Children. Vol. IV Promising Again*. Louisville, Kentucky.

ANDRIESSEN H., 1975, *Leren aan ervaring en supervisie*. Nijmegen

—, 1978, *Pastorale supervision*. München/Mainz.

ANDRIESSEN H., and W. ZANDBELT, 1972, *Wacht bij het woord. Wegen tot pastoraat*. Nijmegen.

ANGENENT-VOGT M., and M. VAN HEMERT, 1994, "Jongeren en levensbeschouwing. Een literatuuroverzicht." *Kerkelijke documentatie* 121, 8 no. 4. Utrecht.

ARNOLD F.X., 1965, *Pastoraltheologische Durchblicke. Das Prinzip des Gott-Menschlichen und der geschichtliche Weg der Pastoral-theologie*. Freiburg/Basel/Wien.

AUER J., and J. RATZINGER, 1978, *Kleine Katholische Dogmatik. Band I - IX*. Regensburg.

AUDINET J., 1995, *Écrits de théologie pratique*. Ottawa.

BAART A., 1995, "De zogenaamde onbekwaamheid van de pastor," *Katholieken in de moderne tijd. Een onderzoek naar de 8-mei beweging*, eds. E. Borgman, B. van Dijk, and T. Salemink, 129- 151. Zoetermeer.

BAART A., J. BAKKERS, and B. de LOOR, 1985, *Maatschappelijke activering en opbouw van de kerk.*, Hilversum.

236   J.A. VAN DER VEN

BAART A., J. BAKKERS, and B. de LOOR, and B. HÖFTE, 1994, *Betrokken hemel, betrokken aarde. Naar een praktische theologie van lokale kerkopbouw*. Baarn.

BALLARD P., ed., 1986, *The Foundations of Pastoral Studies and Practical Theology*. Cardiff.

—, 1990, *Issues in Church Related Community work*. Cardiff.

BANDURA A., *Social Foundations of Thought and Action. A Social Cognitive Theory*. Englewood Cliffs.

BASCH M., 1995, *Doing Brief Psychotherapy*. New York.

BAUMAN Z., 1990, "Philosophical Affinities of Postmodern Sociology," *Sociological Review* 38 3:411-444.

—, 1994, *Postmodern Ethics*. Cambridge.

—, 1995, *Life in Fragments. Essays in Postmodern Morality*. Cambridge.

BÄUMLER C., and N. METTE, eds., 1987, *Gemeindepraxis in Grundbegriffen. Ökumenische Orientierungen und Perspektiven*. München/Düsseldorf.

BECKER H., B. EINIG, and P.-O. ULLRICH, eds., 1987, *Im Angesicht des Todes: ein interdisziplinäres Kompendium (vol I & II)*. St. Ottilien.

BECKER J.W., and R. VINK, 1994, *Secularisatie in Nederland*. Sociaal en Cultureel Planbureau. Rijswijk.

BELLAH R.N., 1975, *The Broken Covenant*. New York.

—, 1985, *Habits of the heart*. New York.

BENNETT N., and R. FOX, 1993, "Challenges for Continuing Professional Education," *Educating Professionals. Responding to New Expectations for Competence and Accountability*, eds. L. Curry, J. Wergin, et al., 262-278. San Francisco.

BENNIS W., K. BENNE, and R. CHIN, 1971, *The Planning of Change*. Second Edition. London/New York.

BERGEN Th., 1996, *Docenten scholen docenten*. Nijmegen.

BERGER P., 1963, "A Market Model for the Analysis of Ecumenecity," *Social Research* 30:77-93.

—, 1967, *The Sacred Canopy*. New York.

—, 1974, "Some Second Thoughts on Substantive versus Functional Definitions of Religion," *Journal for the Scientific Study of Religion* 13 2:125-133.

BERGER P., and Th. LUCKMAN, 1967, *The Social Construction of Reality. A Treatise in the Sociology of Knowledge*. New York.

BERGER W., 1965, *Op weg naar empirische zielzorg. Notities over een reis langs enige pastorale vormingscentra in de Verenigde Staten*. Nijmegen/Utrecht.

—, 1968, *Beoordeling en geschiktheid voor het priesterambt*. Diss. Nijmegen University. Nijmegen/ Utrecht.

—, 1975, "Het Amerikaans verschijnsel 'pastoral counseling' en zijn betekenis voor de pastoraal," *Helpen bij leven en welzijn*, 81-99. Nijmegen.

BERNSTEIN R., 1986, *Beyond Objectivism and Relativism*. Philadelphia.

—, 1986, *Philosophical Profiles. Essays in a Pragmatic Mode*. Philadelphia.

Beroepsprofiel leraar primair onderwijs op katholieke scholen, 1994, *Rapport in opdracht van de Bond van Besturen van Katholieke Scholen voor Basisonderwijs en de Katholieke Onderwijsvakorganisatie.* Den Haag/ Rijswijk. Uitgave Vereniging Samenwerkende Landelijke Pedagogische Centra.

BEYER P., 1994, *Religion and Globalization.* London.

—, 1994, *Religious Traditions and the Global Religious System. Theoretical Prolegomena to an Empirical Investigation. Paper presented at the Meeting of the Association for the Sociology of Religion.* August 3-6 1994. Los Angeles.

—, 1995, *The Religious System of Global Society. Paper presented at the Congress of the International Society for the Sociology of Religion.* June 26-30 1995. Quebec City.

BLOOM B., et al., 1956, *Taxonomy of Educational Objectives. Handbook I. Cognitive Domain.* New York.

BLOOM B., J. HASTINGS, and G. MADAUS, 1971, *Handbook on Formative and Summative Evaluation of Student Learning.* New York.

BLOTH P., et al., 1981, *Handbuch der Praktischen Theologie.* Gütersloh.

BOFF C., 1983, *Theologie und Praxis.* München.

BOFF L., 1985, *Kirche: Charisma und Macht.* Düsseldorf.

—, 1987, *Und die Kirche ist Volk geworden.* Düsseldorf.

—, 1987, "Leergezag en bevrijdingstheologen onder het oordeel van de armen," *Concilium* 23 4:5-6.

BOISEN A., 1945, "Cooperative Inquiry in Religion," *Religious Education* 40 5:290-297.

—, 1945, *Religion in Crisis and Custom.* New York.

—, 1960, *Out of the Depths.* New York.

BOLHUIS S., 1995, *Leren en veranderen bij volwassenen. Een nieuwe benadering.* Bussum.

BOOS-NÜNNING U., 1972, *Dimensionen der Religiosität.* Grünewald.

BOSCH D., 1991, *Transforming Mission.* New York.

BOUWER J., 1992, *Hermeneutics and Homiletics.* Amsterdam.

BOYER E.L., 1990, *Scholarship Reconsidered. Priorities of the Professoriate. The Carnegie Foundation for the Advancement of Teaching.* Princeton.

BREKKE M., 1980, "How Criteria for Assessing Readiness for Ministry Were Identified and Analyzed," *Ministry in America. A Report and Analysis, based on an In-Depth Survey of 47 Denominations in the United States and Canada, with Interpretation by 18 Experts,* eds. D. Schuller, P. Strommen, and M. Brekke, 525-563. San Francisco.

BROOKS HOLIFIELD E., 1979, "Ethical Assumptions of Clinical Pastoral Education," *Theology Today* 36 1:30-44.

—, 1983, *A History of Pastoral Care in America. From Salvation to Self-Realization.* Nashville.

238 J.A. VAN DER VEN

BROUWER R., 1995, *Pastor tussen macht en onmacht. Een studie naar de pro-fessionalisering van het Hervormde predikantschap. Pastores en Profiel. Supplement bij Pastor tussen macht en onmacht.* Diss. Utrecht. Zoeter-meer.
BROWNING D., 1976, *The Moral Context of Pastoral Care.* Philadelphia.
—, 1983, *Practical Theology: The Emerging Field in Theology, Church and World.* San Francisco.
—, 1987, *Religious Thought and the Modern Psychologies.* Philadelphia.
—, 1991a, *A Fundamental Practical Theology. Descriptive and Strategic Pro-posals.* Minneapolis.
—, 1991b, "Auf dem Wege zu einer Fundamentalen und Strategischen Prak-tischen Theologie," *Praktische Theologie und Kultur der Gegenwart. Ein internationaler Dialog*, eds. K.E. Nipkow, D. Rössler, and F. Schweitzer, 21-42. Gütersloh.
—, 1995, *Practical Theology and Congregational Studies. Paper for the Empirical Sector of NOSTER in the Netherlands.* Utrecht.
BRUNER J., 1960, *The Process of Education.* New York.
—, 1968, *Toward a Theory of Instruction.* New York.
—, 1970, *On Knowing. Essays for the Left Hand.* New York.
—, 1986, *Actual Minds, Possible Worlds.* Cambridge.
—, 1990, *Actions of Meaning.* Cambridge.
—, 1996, *The Culture of Education.* Cambridge.
BULTMANN R., 1965, *Theologie des Neuen Testaments.* Tübingen.
CAMPS A., L. HOEDEMAKER, M. SPINDLER, and F. VERSTRAELEN, 1988, *Oecu-menische inleiding in de missiologie.* Kampen.
CAPPS D., 1984, *Pastoral Care and Hermeneutics.* Philadelphia.
—, 1990, *Reframing. A New Method in Pastoral Care.* Minneapolis.
—, 1993, "Sex in the Parish: Social-Scientific Explanations for Why It Occurs," *Journal of Pastoral Care* 47:350-361.
CARROLL J., C. DUDLEY, and W. MCKINNEY, 1988, *Handbook of Congrega-tional Studies.* Nashville.
CHOPP R., 1995, *Saving Work. Feminist Practices of Theological Education.* Westminster.
—, 1996, *Christian Moral Imagination. A Feminist Practical Theology and the Future of Theological Education. Internal Paper.* Emory University. Atlanta.
CLINEBELL H., 1989, *Basic Types of Pastoral Care ad Counseling. Revised and Enlarged.* Canadian Edition. Second Printing. Burlington. Ontario.
CHRISTIAN-WIDMAIER P., 1988, *Krankenhausseelsorge und todkranker Patient.* Berlin.
COLAPIETRO V., 1989, *Peirce's Approach to the Self.* New York.
COLE A., 1995, *Reflection in the Margins. From Research On Teachers to Research On Contexts and For Teachers. Paper presented at the Annual Meeting of the American Educational Research Association.* San Francisco.

COLLINS R., 1984, *Models of Theological Reflection*. New York.

CONGAR Y., 1964, *Jalos pour une théologie du laïcat*. Paris.

——, 1965, "De kerk als volk Gods," *Concilium* 1 1:11-34.

——, 1968, *Vraie et fausse réforme dans l'église*. Paris.

——, 1970, *L'Eglise. De Saint Augustin à l'epoque moderne*. Paris.

CONLEY S., E. BAS-ISAAC, and R. SCULL, 1995, "Teacher Mentoring and Peer Coaching. A Micropolitical Interpretation," *Journal of Personal Evaluation in Education* 19 9:7-19.

COOK Th., and D. CAMPBELL, 1979, *Quasi-Experimenation. Design & Analysis Issues for Field Settings*. Boston.

CRONBACH L., et al., 1980, *Toward Reform of Program Evaluation. Aims, Methods, and Institutional Arrangements*. San Francisco.

DAMASIO A., 1994, *Descartes' Error. Emotion, Reasons, and the Human Brain*. New York.

De begeleiding in de praktijk., 1995, *Bijlage 4. Landelijk evaluatieformulier voor huisartsopleiders*. Nijmeegs Universitair Huisar teninstituut (NUHI). Nijmegen.

DE CORTE E., 1973, *Onderwijsdoelstellingen*. Leuven.

DE GRUCHY J., 1991, *Liberating Reformed Theology. A South African contribution to an ecumenical debate*. Cape Town.

DE JONG A., 1990, *Weerklank van Job*. Diss. Nijmegen University. Kampen.

DE JONGH VAN ARKEL J.T., 1987, *A Paradigm for Pastoral Diagnosing*. Pretoria.

DE JONGHE H., E. VAN WEZEL, and S. VEENMAN, 1996, *Het coachen van leerkachten*. Hoevelaken.

DEKKER G., 1987, *Godsdienst en samenleving. Inleiding tot de studie van de godsdienstsociologie*. Kampen.

DE KLERK L., 1990, "Een metacognitieve benadering van de doelstellingen in het onderwijs," *Pedagogisch tijdschrift* 15:152-161.

De lerarenopleiding in vogelvlucht, 1996, Universitair Instituut voor de Lerarenopleiding (UNILO). Samenwerkingsverband Katholieke Universiteit Nijmegen en Katholieke Universiteit Brabant.

De lerarenopleiding onder de loep, 1996, Universitair Instituut voor de Lerarenopleiding (UNILO).

DERKSEN N.J.M., 1989, *Eigenlijk wisten we het wel, maar we waren het vergeten. Een onderzoek naar parochie- ontwikkeling en geloofscommunicatie in de parochies van het aartsbisdom Utrecht*. Diss. Heerlen University. Kampen.

DERRICKSON P., 1990, "Instruments Used to Measure Change in Students. Preparing for Ministry: A Summary or Research on Clinical Pastoral Education Students," *Journal of Pastoral Care* 44 4:343- 356.

——, 1995, "What Does CPE Contribute to Pastoral Competence?" *Journal of Supervision and Training in Ministry* 16:137-143.

DE SWAAN A., 1982, *De mens is de mens een zorg*. Amsterdam.

DE VRIES B., 1984, *Overeenkomsten bij stages*. ITS. Nijmegen.

DEWEY J., 1933, *How We Think*. Boston.

—, 1962, *A Common Faith*. New Haven.

—, 1986, *Logic: The Theory of Inquiry. The Later Works*. Vol. 12. Chicago

—, 1994, *The Moral Writings of John Dewey*. Edited by James Gouinlock. Revised Editon. New York.

DINGEMANS G., 1991, *Als hoorder onder de hoorders*. Kampen.

—, 1996, *Manieren van doen. Inleiding tot de studie van de praktische theologie*. Kampen.

DREHSEN V., 1988, *Neuzeitliche Konstitutionsbedingungen der Praktischen Theologie. Aspekte der theologischen Wende zur sozialkulturellen Lebenswelt christlicher Religion*. Gütersloh.

—, 1991, "Praktische Theologie als Kunstlehre im Zeitalter bürgerlicher Kultur," *Praktische Theolo gie und Kultur der Gegenwart. Ein internationaler Dialog*, eds. K.E. Nipkow, D. Rössler, and F. Schweitzer, 103-118. Gütersloh.

DREYER J.S., 1993, "Die moderne gemeente en haar funksionering: die belang, aard en benutting van praktijk kennis," *The Dynamics of the Modern Church*, eds. J.S. Dreyer, and H. Pieterse, 221- 247. Lynnwoodrif. South Africa.

DUDLEY C., 1983, *Building Effective Ministry*. San Francisco.

DUDLEY C., and J. CARROLL, 1991, "Congregational Self-Images for Social Ministry," *Carrier of Faith: Lessons from Congregational Studies*, eds. C. Dudley, J. Carroll, and J. Wind. Westminster.

DUNN W., 1981, *Public Policy Analysis. An Introduction*. Englewood Cliffs.

DURKHEIM E., 1957, *Professional Ethics and Civil Morals*. London.

1984, *The Division of Labour in Society*. New York.

DYKSTRA C., 1991, "Reconceiving Practice," *Shifting Boundaries. Contextual Aproaches to the Structure of Theological Education*, eds. B. Wheeler, and E. Farley, 35-66. Westminster.

EISINGA R., A. FELLING, and J. LAMMERS, 1994, "Religious Affiliation, Income Stratification, and Political Preference in the Netherlands," *The Netherlands' Journal of Social Sciences* 30 2:107-127.

EISINGA R., A. FELLING, J. PETERS, P. SCHEEPERS, E. JACOBS, and R. KONIG, 1992, *Social and Cultural Trends in the Netherlands 1979-1990. Documentation of National Surveys on Religious and Secular Attitudes in 1979, 1985 and 1990*. Steinmetz Archive. Amsterdam.

EISINGA R., and P. SCHEEPERS, 1989, *Etnocentrisme in Nederland*. Diss. Nijmegen. ITS. Nijmegen.

ESTER P., L. HALMAN, and R. DE MOOR, 1993, *The Individualizing Society. Value Change in Europe and North America*. Tilburg.

FABER H., 1961, *Pastoral Care and Clinical Training in America*. Arnhem.

FABERY DE JONGE J., W. BERGER, C. BOEKESTIJN, and J. VAN DER LANS, 1968, *Zielzorger in Nederland. Een onderzoek naar positie, taak en ambt van de pastor*. Meppel.

FARLEY E., 1983, *Theologia: The Fragmentation and Unity of Theological Education.* Philadelphia.

DUDLEY C., 1988, *The Fragility of Knowledge: Theological Education in the Chruch and the University.* Philadelphia.

FELLING A., J. PETERS, and O. SCHREUDER, 1986, *Geloven en leven. Een nationaal onderzoek naar de invloed van religieuze overtuigingen.* Zeist.

DUDLEY C., 1988, "Religion and Politics in the Netherlands," *Journal of Empirical Theology* 1 1:55-72.

FICHTER J., 1988, *A Sociologist Looks at Religion. Michael Glazier.* Wilmington. Delaware.

FIELDING C., 1966, *Education for Ministry.* Dayton. Ohio.

FIRET J., 1988, *Het agogisch moment in het pastoraal optreden.* Kampen. English Translation: *Dynamics in Pastoring.* Grand Rapids. 1987.

FISHBEIN M., 1967, *Readings in Attitude Theory and Measurement.* New York.

FISHBEIN M., and I. AZJEN, 1975, *Belief, Attitude, Intention and Behavior.* New York.

FITCHETT G., and G. GRAY, 1994, "Evaluating the Outcome of Clinical Pastoral Education: A Test of the Clinical Ministry Assessment Profile," *Journal of Supervision and Training in Ministry* 15:3-22.

FODOR J., 1995, *Christian Hermeneutics. Paul Ricoeur and the Refiguring of Theology.* Oxford.

FOWLER J.W., 1981, *Stages of Faith.* San Francisco.

—, 1987, *Faith Development and Pastoral Care.* Philadelphia.

—, 1991, *Weaving the New Creation. Stages of Faith and the Public Church.* San Francisco.

FOX, D.J., 1969. *The Research Process in Education.* New York.

FRIEBE J., 1973, *Pilgerndes Gottesvolk. Eine pastoraltheologische Untersuchung in der kritischen Gemeinde IJmond.* Diss. Nijmegen University. Münster.

FRIEDMAN E.H., 1985, *Generation to Generation. Family Process in Church and Synagoge.* New York.

FUCHS O., 1984, *Theologie und Handeln. Beiträge zur Fundierung der Praktischen Theologie als Handlung stheorie.* Düsseldorf.,

—, 1990, *Zwischen Wahrhaftigkeit und Macht. Pluralismus in der kirche?* Frankfurt.

GABRIEL K., and F.-X. KAUFMANN, 1980, *Zur Soziologie des Katholizismus.* Mainz.

GADAMER H.-G., 1960, *Wahrheit und Methode.* Tübingen.

GEERTZ C., 1969, "Religion as a Cultural System," In *The World Yearbook of Religion. The Religious Situation.* Vol. I, 639-688. London.

—, 1973, "Religion as a Cultural System," *The Interpretation of Cultures.* New York.

GELPI D., 1987, *The Devine Mother. A Trinitarian Theology of the Holy Spirit.* Lanham.

242   J.A. VAN DER VEN

—, 1994, *The Turn to Experience in Contemporary Theology*. New York.
GERKIN, Ch., 1984, *The Living Human Document: Revisioning Pastoral Counseling in A Hermeneutical Mode*. Nashville.
—, 1986, *Widening the Horizons: Pastoral Responses to a Fragmented Society*. Philadelphia.
GIDDENS A., 1978, *Durkheim*. *Harvester. Hassocks*.
—, 1991, *Modernity and Self-Identity. Self and Society in the Late Modern Age*. Stanford.
Gids afrondingsfase opleiding godgeleerdheid. 1996, Predikantsopleiding 1995-1996. Faculteit der Godgeleerdheid. Vrije Universiteit van Amsterdam.
GILLIGAN C., 1982, *In a Different Voice*. Cambridge.
GLICKMAN C., and Th. BEY, 1990, "Supervision," *Handbook of Research on Teacher Education*, eds. R. Houston, M. Haberman, and J. Sikula, 549-566. New York.
GLOCK Ch., and R. STARK, 1965, *Religion and Society in Tension*. Chicago.
GOLDHAMMER R., 1966, *Clinical Supervision. Special Methods for the Supervision of Teachers*. New York.
GRAHAM L.K., 1992, *Care of Persons, Care of Worlds. A Psychosystems Approach to Pastoral Care and Counse ling*. Abingdon. Nashville.
GREELEY A., 1995, *Religion as Poetry*. New Brunswick.
GREINACHER N., 1990, "Demokratisierung in der Kirche," *Theologische Quartalschrift* 170, 253-260.
—, 1992, "Das Heil der Menschen. Oberstes Gesetz in der Kirche," *Theologische Quartalschrift* 172, 2-15.
GRIMES R., 1982, *Beginnings in Ritual Studies*. Washington.
—, 1990, *Ritual Criticism*. Columbia.
GROOME Th., 1991, *Sharing Faith. A Comprehensive Approach to Religious Education and Pastoral Ministry*. San Francisco.
Guidebook of Information particular to the Graduate School of religion and Religious Education. Annex Pastoral Counseling Practicum. *Fordham University*. New York.
GUTIERREZ G., 1977, "De armen in de kerk," *Concilium* 13 4: 82-88.
HAAN P., 1975, "Supervisie als coöperatief leerproces. Achtergronden van Amerikaanse supervisieliteratuur," *Supervisie 1. Theorie en begrippen*, eds. F. Siegers, P. Haan, and A. Knoers, 115-137. Alphen aan de Rijn.
—, 1985, "Pastorale supervisie van buiten getoetst," *Ontginningswerk. Klinisch Pastorale Vorming. Een overzicht. Bijdragen aan Dr. Wybe Zijlstra*, 194-200. Kampen.
—, 1994, "Veranderingen in de maatschappelijke context: hebben deze de opleiding voor pastorale supervisie iets te zeggen?" *Jaarverslag 1994 van de Raad voor Klinische Pastorale Vorming in Nederland*, 36-39.
HAARSMA F., 1967, *Geest en kerk*. Diss. Nijmegen University. Utrecht.

—, 1974, "Supervision: Ein Modell von Reflexion kirchlicher Praxis," *Praktische Theologie heute,* eds. F. Klostermann, and R. Zerfass, 609-623. Grünewald.

—, 1991, *Kandelaar en korenmaat. Pastoraaltheologische studies over kerk en pastoraat.* Kampen.

HABERMAS J., 1975, *Erkenntnis und Interesse. Mit einem neuen Nachwort.* Frankfurt.

—, 1982, *Theorie des kommunikativen Handelns.* Band I-II. Frankfurt.

HAIGHT E., 1994, "Paravision: A Model for Pastoral Supervision," *Journal of Supervision and Training in Ministry,* 15, 86-95.

HALL C.E., 1992, *Head and Heart. The Story of the Clinical Pastoral Education Movement.* Journal of Pastoral Care Publications.

HALL R.H., J.E. HAAS, and N.J. JOHNSON, 1967, "An Examination of the Blau-Scott and Etzioni Typologies," *Administrative Science Quarterly* 12:118-129.

HALMAN L., F. HEUNKS, R. DE MOOR, and H. ZANDERS, 1987, *Traditie, secularisatie en individualisering. Een studie naar de waarden van de Nederlanders in een Europese context.* Tilburg.

HASLINGER H., 1996, *Diakonie zwischen Mensch, Kirche und Gesellschaft. Eine praktisch-theologische Untersuchung der diakonischen Praxis unter dem Kriterium des Subjektseins des Menschen.* Studien zur Theologie und Praxis der Seelsorge, no. 18. Würzburg.

HAWKINS P., and R. SHOHET, 1990, *Supervision in the Helping Professions.* Buckingham.

HÄRING H., 1996, "Religieuze integratie en desintegratie," *Botsende culturen in Nederland?,* ed. J.A. van der Ven, 58-90. Kampen.

HEITINK G., 1977, *Pastoraat als hulpverlening.* Kampen.

—, 1986, "Pastoraat in Nederland. Een overzicht," *Praktische Theologie* 13 5:535-550.

—, 1993, *Praktische theologie. Geschiedenis, theorie, handelingsvelden.* Kampen.

HENAU E., 1989, *De kerk: instrument en teken van heil.* Leuven/Amersfoort

—, 1996, *Pastorale vorming in een postmoderne context. Lezing gehouden op het symposium 'Pastorale vorming van de toekomst — Toekomst van de pastorale vorming te Heerlen', 31 Mei 1996.* Nijmegen University.

HENDRIKS. J., 1990, *Een vitale en aantrekkelijke gemeente. Model en methode van gemeenteopbouw.* Kampen.

—, 1993a, "De stille revolutie in de Gereformeerde kerken?" *Ouderlingenblad* 70:815.

—, 1993b, "Veranderingen in de Gereformeerde Kerken sinds 1960. Wat steekt daarachter?" *Ouderlingeblad* 70:817.

HERMANS C., 1993, *Vorming in perspectief.* Den Haag/Baarn.

HERMANS C., M. SCHERER-RATH, and J. A. VAN DER VEN, 1996, *Ouders en de identiteit van katholieke basisscholen.* NISET. Nijmegen.

HERMANS H., 1996, "Voicing the Self: From Information to Dialogical Interchange," *Psychological Bulletin* 119 1:31-50.
HERMANS H., and E. HERMANS-JANSEN, 1995, *Self-Narratives. The Construction of Meaning in Psychotherapy.* New York.
HERMANS H., and E. HERMANS-JANSEN, and H. KEMPEN, 1993, *The Dialogical Self. Meaning as Movement.* New York.
HEYNS L., and H. PIETERSE, 1990, *A Primer in Practical Theology.* Pretoria.
HICK J., and E. MELTZER, 1989, *Three Faith One God.* New York.
HIJMANS. E., 1994, *Je moet er het beste van maken. Een empirisch onderzoek naar hedendaagse zingevingssyste men.* ITS. Nijmegen.
HILGARD E., R. ATKINSON, and R. ATKINSON, 1953, *Introduction to Psychology.* Fifth Edition 1971. New York.
HILTNER S., 1949, *Pastoral Counseling.* New York.
—, 1958, *Preface to Pastoral Theology.* New York.
—, 1965, "The Heritage of Anton T. Boisen," *Pastoral Psychology* 1 6:5-10.
—, 1972, *Theological Dynamics.* New York.
HILTNER S., and L. COLSTON, 1961, *The Context of Pastoral Counseling.* Abingdon, Nashville.
HOFFMAN M., 1993, "Empathy, Social Cognition, and Moral Education," *Approaches to Moral Development,* ed. A. Garrod, 157-179. New York.
HOLLAND J., and P. HENRIOT, 1983, *Social Analysis: Linking Faith and Justice.* New York.
HOPEWELL, J., 1987, *Congregation: Stories and Structures.* Ed. B. Wheeler. Minneapolis.
HOULE C., 1980, *Continuing Learning in the Professions.* San Francisco.
HOUGH J.C., and J.B. COBB, eds., 1985, *Christian Identity and Theological Education.* Chico, California.
HÖFTE B., 1990, *Bekering en bevrijding.* Diss. Utrecht University. Utrecht.
HUNTER R., 1995, "The Therapeutic Tradition of Pastoral Care and Counseling," *Pastoral Care and Social Conflict,* eds. P. Couture, and R. Hunter, 17-31. Nashville.
HUNTER R., and J. PATTON, 1995, "The Therapeutic Tradition's Theological and Ethical Commitments Viewed Through Its Pedagogical Practices: A Tradition in Transition," *Pastoral Care and Social Conflict,* eds. P. Couture, and R. Hunter, 32-43. Nashville.
IANNACCONE I., 1991, "The Consequences of Religious Market Structures," In *Rationality & Society* 3 2:156-177.
JAGT N., and N. LEUFKENS, 1990, *Supervisie: praktisch gezien, kritisch bekeken.* Deventer.
JAMES W., 1961, *Varieties of Religious Experience.* New York.
JANSSEN H., et al., 1996, *Zeichen der Zeit. Pastoraler Zirkel, Gesellschaftsanalyse, Bibel-Teilen.* Missio-Reihe 13. Aachen.
JANSSEN J., 1994, *Jeugdcultuur. Een actuele geschiedenis.* Utrecht.

JÄGER A., 1986, *Diakonie als christliches Unternehmen*, Gütersloh.

JEHU D., 1973, *Learning Theory and Social Work*. Dutch Translation: *Leertheorie en maatschappelijk werk*. Deventer.

JOHNSON E., 1995, *She Who Is. The Mystery of God in Feminist Theological Discourse*. New York.

JOHNSON M., 1987, *The Body in the Mind*. Chicago.

—, 1993, *Moral Imagination. Implications of Cognitive Science for Ethics*. Chicago.

JOYCE B., and B. SHOWERS, 1980, "Improving Inservice Training. The Messages of Research," *Educational Leadership*. February 1980, 379-385.

KAEMPF B., 1993, "La théologie pratique selon D.F. Schleiermacher," *La théologie pratique*, eds. B. Reymond, and J.-M. Sordet, 7-19. Paris.

KALINAUCKAS P., 1995, "Coaching for CPD," *Continuing Professional Development*, ed. S. Clyne, 133-144. London.

KASKI, 1995, "Kerncijfers 1994/1995. Uit de kerkelijke statistiek van het R.-K. Genootschap in Nederland," *Kerkelijke documentatie 121*. 23 no. 23. Utrecht.

KEGAN R., 1982, *The Evolving Self*. Cambridge.

—, 1995, *In Over Our Heads. The Mental Demands of Modern Life*. Cambridge.

KEIZER J.A., 1988, *Aan tijd gebonden. Over motivatie en arbeidsvreugde van predikanten*. Den Haag.

KELSEY, D.H. 1992, *To Understand God. Truly What's Theological about A Theological School*. Westminster.

Kerkhofs J., 1995, *Waardenonderzoek. Een bijdrage tot pastoraal realisme*,159-170. Leuven/Amersfoort.

KESSELS J., F. KORTHAGEN, Th. SOMERS, and Th. WUBBELS, 1996, *The Relationship between Theory and Practice: Back to the Classics. Paper presented at the Annual Meeting of the American Educational Research Association*. New York.

KINAST R., 1996, "Theological Reflection: Fad or Foundation?" *Seminary Journal* 2 1:11-15.

KLEIN GOLDWIJK B., 1991, *Praktijk of principe. Basisgemeenschappen en de ecclesiologie van Leonardo Boff*. Diss. Nijmegen University. Kampen.

KLINK Th., 1966, "Supervision," *Education for Ministry*, ed. C. Fielding, 196-217. Dayton. Ohio.

KLOSTERMAN F., and R. ZERFASS, eds., 1974, *Praktische Theologie heute*. München-Mainz.

KNITTER P., 1988, *No Other Name? A Critical Survey of Christian Attitudes Towards the World Religions*. New York.

—, 1990, "Wohin der Dialog führt," *Evangelische Kommentare* 10, 606-610.

KNOERS A., 1975, "Supervisie en leertheorie," *Supervisie 1. Theorie en begrippen*, eds. F. Siegers, P. Haan, and A. Knoers, 138-153. Tweede druk. Alphen aan de Rijn.

—, 1987, *Leraarschap: Amb(ach)t of professie*. Afscheidscollege. Nijmegen University. Assen/Maastircht.

KOHLBERG L., 1981, *The Philosophy of Moral Development*. San Francisco.

KOHUT H., 1971, *The Analysis of the Self*. New York.

—, 1977, *The Restoration of the Self*. Madison. Connecticut.

KOLB D., 1984, *Experiential Learning*. Englewood Cliffs.

KOMPF M., and R. BOND, 1995, *Through the Looking Glass: Some Criticims of Reflection*. Paper presented to the American Educational Research Association Annual Meeting. San Francisco.

KORSTEN H., H. MEERTENS, and A. REIJNEN, 1973, *Werken aan de basis*. Opbouwwerk en Pastoraat. Nijmegen.

KORTHAGEN F., 1988, "The Influence of Learning Orientations on the Development of Reflective Teaching," *Teachers' Professional Learning*, ed. J. Calderhead, 35-50. London.

—, 1992, "Reflectie en de professionele ontwikkeling van leraren," *Pedagogische Studien* 69, 112- 123.

KRATHWOHL D., B. BLOOM, and B. MASIA, 1964, *Taxonomy of Eduactional Objectives. Handbook II. Affective Domain*. New York.

KRÜGER J., 1989, *Metatheism*. Pretoria.

KUHN T., 1970, *The Structure of Scientific Revolutions*. Second enlarged Edition. Chicago.

KUNNEMAN H., 1996, *Van theemutscultuur naar walkman-ego*. Contouren van postmoderne individualiteit. Amsterdam/Meppel.

KÜNG H., 1967, *Die Kirche*. München.

—, 1978, *Existiert Gott?* Dutch translation. *Bestaat God? Antwoord op de vraag naar God in deze tijd*. Hilversum.

KWAKMAN F., and J. VAN OERS, 1993, *Het geloof in de katholieke basisschool. Over legitimaties voor de katholieke basisschool in een multi-etnische en geseculariseerde samenleving*. Serie Theologie & Empirie 19. Kampen/Weinheim.

Landelijke Huisartsenvereniging, 1987, *Basistakenpakket van de huisarts*. Vademecum Juni 1987.

LASSALLE R., 1995, *The Jesuit Martyrs of the University of Central America. An American University and the Historical Reality of the Reign of God*. Diss. Graduate Theological Union. Berkeley. Califor nia.

—, 1996, *Making Sense of the UCA Model for Christian Education. Thoughts on Practical Foundations for Theology in the Americas. Internal Paper*. Jesuit School of Theology at Berkeley. California.

LAWSON E., and R. MCCAULEY, 1993, *Rethinking Religion. Connecting Cognition and Culture*. Cambridge.

LAZARUS R., 1991, *Emotion and Adaptation*. New York.

LEE C., 1988, "Toward a Social Ecology of the Minister's Family," *Pastoral Psychology* 36, 249-259.

LOUW D., 1993, *Pastoraat als ontmoeting*. Pretoria.

LUCKMANN Th., 1967, *The Invisible Religion*. London.

LUHMANN N., 1992, *Funktion der Religion*. Frankfurt.

LUTHER H., 1992, *Religion und Alltag. Bausteine zu einer Praktischen Theologie des Subjekts*. Stuttgart.

MACINTYRE A., 1981, *After Virtue*. Notre Dame.

MARION J.-l., 1991, *Dieu sans l'être*. Paris.

MASAMBAMA MPOLO J., and D. NWACHUKU, 1991, *Pastoral Care and Counselling in Africa Today*. New York.

MAY R., 1969, *Love and Will*. Norton. New York.

MCGAGHIE W., 1993, "Evaluating Competence for Professional Practice," *Educating Professionals. Responding to New Expectations for Competence and Accountability*, eds. L. Curry, J. Wergin, et al, 229-261 San Francisco.

MCLAREN P., 1993, *Schooling as a Ritual Performance. Towards a Political Economy of Educational Symbols and Gestures*. London/New York.

MENOZZI D., 1989, "Het belang van de katholieke reactie op de revolutie," *Concilium* 1, 59-67.

MERTON R., 1968, *Social Theory and Social Structure*. New York.

METTE N., 1978, *Theorie der Praxis. Wissenschaftliche und methodologische Untersuchungen zur Theorie- Praxis-Problematik innerhalb der praktischen Theologie*. Düsseldorf.

METTE N., and BLASBERG-KUHNKE, 1986, *Kirche auf dem Weg ins Jahr 2000. Zur Situation und Zukunft der Pastoral*. Düsseldorf.

METZ J.-B., 1977, *Glaube in Geschichte und Gesellschaft*. Mainz.

MILES M., 1992, *Practicing Christianity. Critical Perspectives for an Embodied Spirituality*. New York.

MILIS L., 1991, *De Heidense Middeleeuwen. Belgisch historisch instituut te Rome bibliotheek 32*. Brussel/Rome.

—, 1995, *De heidense middeleeuwen. Wetenschappelijke nascholing*. Universiteit Gent.

MILL J.S., 1973, *A System of Logic Ratiocinative and Inductive. Collected Works*. Vol. VII. Toronto.

MILLER J., 1986, "Practice: Learning and Supervision," *The foundations of Pastoral studies and Practical Theology*, ed. P. Ballard, no. 4. Cardiff.

Ministry Experience Report of Incoming D.Min.Students, 1995, *D.Min.Program*. Catholic Theological Union. Chicago.

MINTZBERG H., 1979, *The Structuring of Organizations. A Synthesis of the Research*. Englewood Cliffs.

—, 1989, *Mintzberg on Management*. Dutch Translation (1991).

Mintzberg over management. De wereld van onze organisaties. Amsterdam/Antwerpen.

MOLTMANN J., 1975, *Kirche in der Kraft des Geistes*. München.

MORIARTY P., 1988, *Field Education Program*. Franciscan School of Theology. Berkeley.

MORRIS M.L., and D. BLANTON WHITE, 1994, "Denominational Perception of Stress and the Provision of Support Services for Clergy Families," *Pastoral Psychology* 42, 345-364

MUDGE L., and J. POLLING, 1987, *Formation and Reflection*. Philadelphia.

MUSKENS M., 1995, "Toekomst van de kerkgebouwen," *Analecta Bisdom Breda* 9 9:238-250.

NADEAU J.-G., 1987, La prostitution, une affaire de sens. Étude de pratiques sociales et pastorales. *Héritage et projet*, no. 34. Montreal.

NAUTA R., 1995, "Het kairologisch misverstand. Pastoraat in een individualistische cultuur," *Praktische Theologie* 22 2:6-20.

NIPKOW. K.E., 1990, *Bildung als Lebensbegleitung und Erneuerung. Kirchliche Bildungsverantwortung in Gemein de, Schule und Gesellschaft.* Gütersloh.

—, 1991, "Praktische Theologie und gegenwärtige Kultur. Auf der Suche nach einem neuen Paradig ma," *Praktische Theologie und Kultur der Gegenwart. Ein internationaler Dialog*, eds. K.E. Nipkow, D. Rössler, and F. Schweitzer, 132-154. Gütersloh.

NOUWEN H., 1979, *The Wounded Healer*. New York.

O'CONNELL KILLEN P., and J. DE BEER, 1994, *The Art of Theological Reflection*. New York.

ODEN T., 1966, *Kerygma and Counseling*. Philadelphia.

O'GORMAN R., and B. TUCKER, 1995, *The Field Education Manual. A Study of Some 27 Field Education Manuals According to Nine Categories.* Loyola University. Institute of Pastoral Studies. Chicago.

OSMER R.R., 1990, *A Teachable Spirit. Recovering the Teaching Office in the Church.* Westminster.

PASCAL Bl., 1976, *Pensées. Chronologie, Introduction etc. par D. Descotes.* Paris.

Pastoraaltheologische studierichting Nijmegen, 1970, Nota sectie pastoraaltheologie. Faculteit der Godgeleerdheid. Nijmegen University.

PATTON J., 1990, "Self-Evaluation Through Relational Experience," *Clergy Assessment and Career Develop ment*, eds. R. Hunt, J. Hinkle, and H. Maloney, 123-128. Nashville.

PEETERS H., 1984, *Burgers en modernisering*. Deventer.

PETERS J., and J. GERRIS, 1995, "Familialims: sociaal-culturele verschuivingen in de jaren tachtig en de samenhang met gezin en opvoeding," *Gezin: onderzoek en diagnostiek*, ed. J. Gerris. Assen.

PIAGET J., 1975, *Introduction à l'epistémologie Génétique. Tome III. German Translation. Die Entwicklung des Erkennens III. Das biologische Denken. Das psychologische Denken. Das soziologische Denken.* Stuttgart.

PIETERSE H., 1987, *Communicative Preaching*. Pretoria.

—, 1993, *Praktiese teologie as kommunikatiewe handelingsteorie.* Pretoria.

—, 1995, *Desmond Tutu's Message. A Qualitative Analysis.* Kampen/ Weinheim.

PITTMAN D., R. HABITO, and T. MUCK, eds., 1996, *Ministry and Theology in Global Perspective. Contemporary Challenges for the Church*. Grand Rapids.

PIXLEY G., 1984, "Het volk Gods in de bijbelse traditie," *Concilium* 17 6: 23-30.

PLOEGER A., 1989, *Diskurs*. Groningen.

POHIER J., 1985, *Dieu fractures*. Paris.

POLING J., 1991, *The Abuse of Power*. Nashville, Tennessee.

POWELL R.C., 1975, *Fifty Years of Learning. Through Supervised Encounter With Living Human Documents*. New York.

PRUYSER P., 1976, *The Minister as Diagnostician*. Philadelphia.

RAEDTS P., 1990, "De christelijke Middeleeuwen als mythe," *Tijdschrift voor Theologie* 30 2:146-158.

—, 1995, *Toerisme in de tijd? Over het nut van Middeleeuwse geschiedenis*. Inaugurele rede, Nijmegen University.

RAHNER K., 1964, "Die Grundfunktionen der Kirche. Theologische und pastoraltheologische Vorüberlegug," *Handbuch der Pastoraltheologie*. Band I, eds. F.X Arnold, K. Rahner, V. Schurr, and L. Weber, 216-219. Freiburg.

—, 1966, "De zonde in de kerk," *De kerk van Vaticanum II*, ed. G. Barauna, 431-447. Baarn.

—, 1975, "Anonymer und expliziter Glaube," *Schriften zur Theologie* 12, 76-84. Einsiedeln.

RANEY R., and J. RIVERS J., 1989, "Professional Growth and Support Through Coaching," *Educational Leadership*. May 1989, 35-38.

Rapportage minderheden, 1995, Concentratie en segregatie. Sociaal en cultureel planbureau. Rijswijk.

REIJNEN A.
1996, *Terugblik met het oog op de toekomst. Lezing gehouden op het symposium 'Pastorale vorming van de toekomst — Toekomst van de pastorale vorming' te Heerlen 31 Mei 1996*. UTP. Heerlen.

Revue des sciences religieuses., Théologie pratique et/ou pastorale. 69, no. 3.

REYMOND B., and J.-M., eds., 1993, "La Théologie pratique. Statut-Méthodes Perspectives D'avenir," *Le Point Théologique*, no. 57. Paris.

RHOADS D., 1976, *Israel in Revolution*, 6-74. Philadelphia.

RICE R.E., and L. RICHLIN, 1993, "Broadening the Concept of the Scholarship in the Professions," *Educating Professionals*, eds. L. Curry, J.F. Wergin, et. al., 279-315). San Francisco.

RICOEUR P., 1968, *Politiek en geloof*. Utrecht.

—, 1978, "Naming God," *Union Seminary Quarterly* 34, 215-227.

—, 1987, *Hermeneutics and the Human Sciences*. Cambridge.

—, 1991, *From Text to Action. Essays in Hermeneutics II*. Evanston.

—, 1992, *Soi-même comme un autre*. English Translation: *Oneself as Another*. University of Chicago Press. Chicago.

RIP A., and P. GROENEWEGEN, 1980, *Macht over kennis. Mogelijkheden van wetenschapsbeleid.* Alphen aan de Rijn.

ROELOFS E., S. VEENMAN, and J. RAEMAEKERS, 1993, "Teamgerichte nascholing en coaching: Effecten op het didactisch handelen van leerkrachten in combinatieklassen," *Pedagogische Studien* 70, 352-367.

ROGERS C., 1942, *Counseling and Psychotherapy.* Boston.

—, 1951, *Clientcentered Therapy.* Boston.

—, 1961, *On Becoming a Person.* Boston.

RÖSSLER D., 1986, *Grundriss der Praktischen Theologie.* Berlin.

—, 1991, "Die Einheit der Praktischen Theologie," *Praktische Theologie und Kultur der Gegenwart. Ein internationaler Dialog,* eds. K.E. Nipkow, D. Rössler, and F. Schweitzer, 43-54. Gütersloh.

ROEMER J., G. SCHIPPERS, and J.A. VAN DER VEN, 1994, "Kun je evenwichtigheid leren?" *Niet bij gebruik alleen. Voorlichting aan alcohol en drugs in het perspectief van zingeving,* eds. G. Schippers, and J.A. van der Ven, 92-112. Kampen.

ROOF W., and W. MCKINNEY, 1987, *American Mainline Religion.* New Brunswick. New York.

ROSSI P., and H. FREEMAN, 1989, *Evaluation. A Systematic Approach.* London.

ROWATT G., 1982, "What does ACPE expect of ministry," *Journal of Pastoral Care* 36 3:147-159.

SADMEL S., 1969, *The First Christian Century in Judaism and Christianity.* New York.

SAVAGE J., 1996, *Listening and Caring Skills in Ministry.* Nashville.

SCHEEPERS P., 1995, *Maatschappelijke vooroordelen in perspectief.* Inaugurele rede. ITS. Nijmegen.

—, 1996, "Botsende culturen in Nederland: Longitudinale trends in etnocentrische reacties onder kerkelijke mensen," *Botsende culturen in Nederland,* ed. J.A. van der Ven, 16-43. Kampen.

SCHEER A., 1985, "De beleving van liturgische riten en symbolen," *Pastoraal tussen ideaal en werkelijkheid,* ed. J.A. van der Ven. Kampen.

SCHILDERMAN J.B.A.M., C.A.M. VISSCHER, J.A. VAN DER VEN, and A.J.A. FELLING, 1993, *Professionalisering van het pastorale ambt.* NISET. Nijmegen.

SCHILLEBEECKX E., 1974, *Jezus, Het verhaal van een levende.* Bloemendaal.

—, 1977, *Gerechtigheid en liefde, genade en bevrijding.* Bloemendaal.

—, 1983, *Theologisch geloofsverstaan anno 1983.* Nijmegen.

—, 1985, *Pleidooi voor mensen in de kerk.* Baarn.

—, 1989, *Mensen als verhaal van God.* Baarn.

—, 1990, "Identiteit, eigenheid en universaliteit van Gods heil in Jezus," *Tijdschrift voor Theologie* 30, 259-275.

—, 1996, "Auf der Suche nach einer Kultur der Gerechtigkeit und liebe Marginalismus und Humanis mus," *Vom Rande Her? Zur Idee des Marginalismus,* ed. K.-P. Pfeiffer.Würzburg.

SCHIPPERS K.A., et. al., 1990, *Kerkelijke presentie in een oude stadswijk. Onderzoek naar buurtpastoraat vanuit behoeften en belangen van bewoners.* Kampen.

SCHLEIERMACHER Fr., 1966, *Brief Outline on the Study of Theology* (orinally published 1830). Richmond.

SCHÖN D., 1983, *The Reflective Practicioner. How Professionals Think in Action.* New York.

—, 1991, *Educating the Reflective Practicioner. Toward a New Design for Teaching and Learnig in the Professions.* San Francisco.

SCHOONENBERG P., 1991, *De Geest, het Woord en de Zoon.* Kampen.

SCHREITER R., 1984, *Constructing Local Theologies.* New York.

SCHREUDER O., 1994, "Culturele individualisering," *Individualisering en religie,* ed. J.A. van der Ven, 37-59. Baarn.

SCHULLER D., M. BREKKE, and M. STROMMEN, 1975, *Readiness for Ministry. Volume 1. Criteria. The Association of Theological Schools in the United States and Canada.* Vandalia. Ohio.

SCHWEITZER F., 1987, *Lebensgeschichte und Religion. Religiöse Entwicklung und Erziehung im Kindes- und Jugendalter.* München.

—, 1991, "Praktische Theologie, Kultur der Gegenwart und die Sozialwissenschaften. Interdisziplinär Beziehungen und die Einheit der Disciplin," *Praktische Theologie und Kultur der Gegenwart. Ein internationaler Dialog,* eds. K.E. Nipkow, D. Rössler, and F. Schweitzer, 170-184. Gütersloh.

SCHWEITZER F., K.E. NIPKOW, G. FAUST-SIEHL, and B. KRUPKA eds., 1995, *Religionsunterricht und Entwicklungspsychologie. Elementarisierung in der Praxis.* Gütersloh.

SELMAN R., 1980, *The Growth of Interpersonal Understanding.* New York.

SEMMELROTH O., 1966, "De kerk, het nieuwe Godsvolk," *De kerk van Vaticanum II,* ed. G. Barauna, 451-465. Bilthoven.

SHAWCHUCK N., and R. HENSER, 1996, *Managing the Congregation. Building Effective Systems to Serve People.* Nashville.

SHORE B., 1996, *Culture in Mind. Cognition, Culture, and the Problem of Meaning.* New York.

SIEGERS F., 1995, *Instellingssupervisie. Leren over werk in de context van leiden — begeleiden — (samen)werken.* Houten/Diegem.

SIEGERS F., and D. HAAN, *Handboek supervisie.* Tweede druk. Alphen aan de Rijn.

SIMONS P., 1992, *Leren denken, denkend leren. Referaat tijdens het symposium "Een goede raad, de leraar tussen onderwijs en arbeidsmarkt" ter gelegenheid van het afscheid van Prof. Dr. A. Knoers als voorzitter van de Onderwijsraad,* 13-27. Den Haag.

SKINNER B., 1974, *About Behaviorism.* New York.

SOBRINO J., 1989, *The True Church and the Poor.* New York.

Sociaal en cultureel rapport, 1992, Sociaal en Cultureel Planbureau. Rijswijk.

252 J.A. VAN DER VEN

SONESON J., 1993, *Pragmatism and Pluralism. John Dewey's Significance for Theology*. Minneapolis.
SONNBERGER Kl., 1995, *Die Leitung der Pfarrgemeinde. Eine empirisch-theologische Studie unter niederländischen und deutschen Katholiken*. Serie Theologie & Empirie 25. Weinheim/Kampen.
SONNBERGER Kl., and A. POLSPOEL, 1995, "Identiteitsontwikkeling en pastorale competentie," *Praktische Theologie* 22 2:264-275.
SONNBERGER Kl., and J.A. VAN DER VEN, 1995, The Structure of the Church. *Journal of Empirical Theology* 8 1:24-45.
SPRUIT L., 1991, *Religie en abortus. Interactiemodellen ter verklaring van de houding tegenover abortus*. Diss. Nijmegen. ITS. Nijmegen.
STARK R., and W.S. BAINBRIDGE, 1985, *The Future of Religion. Secularization, Revival and Cult Formation*. Berkeley.
—, 1987, *A Theory of Religion*. New York.
Startbekwaamheden leraar primair onderwijs, 1995, Concept-rapport in opdracht van het Ministerie van Onderwijs, Cultuur en Wetenschappen. Vereniging Samenwerkende Landelijke Pedagogische Centra.
STEGGINK O., and K. WAAYMAN K., 1985, *Spiritualiteit en mystiek*. Nijmegen.
STEINKAMP H., 1988, "Selbst 'wenn die Betreuten sich ändern,'" *Diakonia*, 78-89.
—, 1991, *Sozialpastoral*. Freiburg.
STOLLBERG D., 1969, *Therapeutische Seelsorge. Die Amerikanische Seelsorgebewegung. Darstellug und Kritik. Mit einer Dokumentation*. München.
STONE H.W., 1994, "Religious Beliefs in Pastoral Caregiving," *Journal of Supervision and Training in Ministry* 15, 63-69.
—, 1994a, *Brief Pastoral Counseling. Short-term Approaches and Strategies*. Minneapolis.
STROMMEN P., 1980, "Models of Ministry," *Ministry in America. A Report and Analysis, based on an In-Depth Survey of 47 Denominations in the United States and Canada, with Interpretation by 18 Experts*, eds. D. Schuller, P. Strommen and, M. Brekke, 54-89. San Francisco.
TAYLOR C., 1991, *The Skilled Pastor. Counseling as the Practice of Theology*. Minneapolis.
TEISMAN G., 1992, *Complexe besluitvorming. Een pluricentrisch perspectief op besluitvorming over ruimtelijke investeringen*. Den Haag.
TER BORG M., 1990, "Publieke religie in Nederland," *Religie in de Nederlandse samenleving*, eds. O. Schreuder, and L. van Snippenbeurg, 165-184. Baarn.
TERPSTRA M., 1991, "Zo spreken de schuldigen". *Hoofdstukken uit een genealogie van de schuld*, 98-135 Baarn.
TER VOERT M., 1994, *Religie en het burgerlijk-kapitalistisch ethos*. Diss. Nijmegen University. ITS. Nijmegen.
THEISSEN G., 1977, *Soziologie der Jesusbewegung*. München.
—, 1979, *Studien zur Soziologie des Urchristentums*. Tübingen.

—, 1983, *Psychologische Aspekte paulinischer Theologie*. Göttingen.

THORNTON E.E., 1970, *Professional Education for Ministry*. New York.

TILLICH P., 1966, *Systematic Theology*. Chicago.

TOULMIN S., 1990, *Cosmopolis. The Hidden Agenda of Modernity*. New York.

TRACY D., 1981, *The Analogical Imagination*. New York.

ULEYN A., 1969, *The Recognition of Guilt. A Study in Pastoral Psychology*. Dublin.

UTP Stagegids. 1995, Heerlen. Juni 1995.

VAN BEUGEN M., 1971, *Sociale technologie en het instrumentele aspect van agogische actie*. Assen.

VAN DAM B., 1993, *Een generatie met verschillende gezichten. Culturele diversiteit onder de jonge volwassenen van de jaren tachtig*. Diss. Nijmegen University. ITS. Nijmegen.

VANDECREEK L., and GLOCKNER, 1993, "Do Gender Issues Affect Clinical Pastoral Education Supervision?" *Journal of Pastoral Care* 47 3:253-262.

VANDECREEK L., and J. VALENTINO, 1991a, "Affective and Cognitive Changes in First-Unit Clinical Pastoral Education Students," *Journal of Pastoral Care* 45 4:382-394.

—, 1991b, "Symptoms of Depression Among Clinical Pastoral Education Students and Their Impact on Learning," *Journal of Supervision and Training Ministry* 13, 3-19.

VAN DEN AKKER P., 1995, "Modernisering en gezinswaarden in Europees perspectief. Enige resultaten van de European Values Study 1981-1990," *Gezin: onderzoek en diagnostiek*, ed. J. Gerris. Assen.

VAN DEN HOOGEN T., and P. VAN GERVEN, 1991, "Gemeenteopbouw in de spiegel van de diakonie," *Praktische Theologie* 18 4:414-435.

VAN DER VEN J.A., 1985a, "Evaluatie van de pastoraal tussen ideaal en werkelijkheid," *Pastoraal tussen ideaal en werkelijkheid*, ed. J.A. van der Ven, 9-34. Kampen.

—, 1985b, "Wat is pastoraaltheologie? Een analyse van het werk van Frans Haarsma," *Toekomst voor de kerk? Studies voor Frans Haarsma*, ed. J.A. van der Ven, 11-44. Kampen.

—, 1991, "De identiteit van pastorale counseling," *Praktische Theologie* 18 2:230-256.

—, 1993a, "Katholieke kerk en katholicisme in historisch en empirisch perspectief," *Kerk op de helling*, eds. J. Peters, J.A. van der Ven, and L. Spruit, 62-92. Kampen.

—, 1993b, "Die qualitative Inhaltsanalyse," *Paradigmenentwicklung in der Praktischen Theologie*. Serie Theorie & Empirie, eds. J.A. van der Ven, and H.-G. Ziebertz,113-164. Kampen.

—, 1993c, "Pastorale protocolanalyse I. Pastoraat in vernieuwing," *Praktische Theologie* 20 5:475- 495.

—, 1993d, *Practical Theology: An Empirical Approach*. Kampen.

—, 1994a, "Religious Values in the Interreligious Dialogue," *Religion and Theology*. Vol. 1/3.

—, 1994b, "Religieuze individualisering," *Individualisering en religie*, ed. J.A. van der Ven, 60-97. Baarn.

—, 1994c, "The Communicative Identity of the Local Church," *Concilium* 5,26-37.

—, 1994d, "Kontingenz und Religion in einer säkularisierten und multikulturellen Gesellschaft," *Religiöser Pluralismus und interreligiöses Lernen*, eds. J.A. Van der Ven, and H.G. Zie bertz, 15-38. Kampen/ Weinheim.

—, 1995a, "Het religieus bewustzijn van jongeren en de crisis van het jongerenpastoraat," *Praktische Theologie* 22 3:342-364.

—, 1996a, *Ecclesiology in Context*. Grand Rapids. Michigan.

—, 1996b, "De structuur van het religieuze bewustzijn. Verkenning van de spannig tussen religiositeit en kerkelijkheid," *Tijdschrift voor Theologie* 36 1:39-60.

—, 1996c, "Human Well-being and the Cult of the Individual," *Happiness, Well-Being and the Meaning of Life*, eds. V. Brümmer, and M. Sarot M, 99-121. Kampen.

—, 1997, *Formation of the Moral Self*. Grand Rapids.

VAN DER VEN J.A., and B. BIEMANS, 1994, *Religie in fragmenten. Een onderzoek onder studenten*. Serie Theologie & Empirie 20. Kampen/Weinheim.

VAN DER VEN J.A., and E. VOSSEN, 1995, *Suffering: Why for God's Sake? Pastoral Research in Theodicy*. Serie Theologie & Empirie 23. Kampen/ Weinheim.

VAN DER VEN J.A., and H.-G. ZIEBERTZ, 1995, "Relgionspädagogische Perspektiven zur interreligiösen Bildung," *Bilanz der Religionspädagogik*, eds. H.-G. Ziebertz, and W. Simon, 259-273). Düsseldorf.

VAN DE SPIJKER A., 1984, *Pastorale competentie*. Heerlen.

VAN HARSKAMP A., 1986, *Theologie: tekst in context*. diss. Nijmegen University. Nijmegen.

VAN HEMERT M., 1991, *Achtergronden van kerkelijk gedrag. Een onderzoek in zeven rooms-katholieke parochies*. KASKI. Den Haag.

VAN KNIPPENBERG M., 1987, *Dood en religie*. Diss. Nijmegen University. Kampen.

VAN NIEUWENHOVE J., 1991, *Bronnen van bevrijding. Varianten in de theologie van Gustavo Gutierrez*. Kampen.

VAN ROODEN P., 1996, *Religieuze regimes. Over godsdienst en maatschappij in Nederland, 1570-1990*. Amsterdam.

VAN ROSSUM R., 1988, "Jezus' uniciteit in missionair perspectief," *Tijdschrift voor Theologie* 28 3: 272-288.

VAN STRIEN P., 1986, *Praktijk als wetenschap. Methodologie van het sociaal-wetenschappelijk handelen*. Assen/Maastricht.

VAN UDEN M., 1988, *Rouw, religie en ritueel*. Baarn.

VERLOOP N., and Th. WUBBELS, 1994, "Recente ontwikkelingen in het onderzoek naar leraren en lerarenopleiding," *Pedagogische Studien* 71, 168-186.

VIAU M., 1987, *Introduction aux études pastorales*. Montreal.

1993, *La Nouvelle théologie pratique*. Montreal.

VISSER J., 1989, "Kirchenstruktur und Glaubensvermittlung," *Internationale Kirchliche Zeitschrift* 79 3:174- 191.

Vitaal leraarschap, 1993, *Beleidreactie naar aanleiding van het rapport 'Een beroep met perspectief' van de Commissie Toekomst Leraarschap.* Ministerie van Onderwijs en Wetenschappen. Den Haag.

VOGELS W., 1986, *God's Universal Covenant*. Ottawa.

VOLP R., 1974, "Praktische Theologie als Theoriebildung und Kompetenzgewinnung bei F.D. Schleiermacher," *Praktische Theologie heute*, eds. F. Klostermann, and R. Zerfass, 52-64. München.

VON BRACHEL H.-U., and N. METTE, 1985, *Kommunikation und Solidaritat. Beitrage zur Diskussion des handlunstheoretischen Ansatzes von Helmut Peukert in Theologie und Sozialwissenschaften.*

VON WRIGHT, 1968, *An Essay in Deontic Logic and the General Theory of Action*. Helsinki.

VOSSEN H., 1985, *Vrijwilligerseducatie en pastoraat aan rouwenden*. Diss. Nijmegen University. Kampen.

—, 1991, "Klinische Pastorale Vorming als religieus-commuicatief leerproces," *Praktische Theolo gie* 18 2:176-196.

VROOM H.M., 1988, *Religies en de waarheid*. Kampen.

WAITE D., 1995, *Rethinking Instructional Supervision. Notes on Its Language and Culture*. London/Washington.

WALES C., A. NARDI, and R. STAGER, 1993, "Emphasizing Critical Thinking and Problem Solving," *Educating Professionals. Responding to New Expectations for Competence and Accountability*, eds. L. Curry, and J. Wergin, et al., 178-211. San Francisco.

WALGRAVE J., 1961, "Standpunten en stromingen in de huidige moraaltheologie," *Tijdschrift voor Theologie* 1 1:48-70.

WALSCH J., 1996, "Dialogue: Summary of Discussion on Theological Reflection Among East Coast Deans and Rev. Robert Kinast," *Seminary Journal* 2 1:16-18.

WARNER R.S., 1993, "Work in Progress toward a New Paradigm for the Sociological Study of Religion in the United States," *American Journal of Sociology* 98 5:1044-1093.

WEBER M., 1969, "Die Protestantische Ethik und der Geist des Kapitalismus," *Die Protestantische Ethik I*. München/Hamburg.

—, 1978, *Gesammelte Aufsätze zur Religionssoziologie*. Tübingen.

WESS. P., 1989, *Gemeindekirche — Ort des Glaubens. Die Praxis als Fundament und als Konsequenz der Theologie*. Graz/Wien/Köln.

WEST C., 1989, *The American Evasion of Philosophy. A Genealogy of Pragmatism*. Wisconsin.

—, 1993a, *Prophetic Thought in Postmodern Times. Beyond Eurocentrism and Multiculturalism*. Volume I. Monroe. Maine.

—, 993b, *Prophetic Reflections. Notes on Race And Power in America. Beyond Eurocentrism and Multiculturalism*. Volume I. Monroe. Maine.

WHEELER B., and E. FARLEY E., 1991, *Shifting Boundaries. Contextual Approaches to the Structure of Theological Education*. Westminster.

WHITEHEAD J., and E. WHITEHEAD, 1995, *Method in Ministry. Theological Reflection and Christian Ministry*. First Edition 1980. Revised and Updated Edition 1995. Kansas City.

WICKS R., 1995, *Handbook of Spirituality for Ministers*. New York.

WICKS R., R. PARSONS, and D. CAPPS, 1985, *Clinical Handbook of Pastoral Counseling*. Volume 1. New York.

WICKS R., and R. PARSONS, 1993, *Clinical Handbook of Pastoral Counseling*. Volume 2. New York.

WIJSEN F., 1994, *There Is Only One God. A Social-Scientific and Theological Study of Popular Religion and Evagelization in Sukumaland, Northwest Tanzania*. Kampen.

WIJSEN F., 1996, "Der pastorale Zirkel in der Ausbildung im kirchlichen Dienst," *Zeichen der Zeit. Pastoraler Zirkel, Gesellschaftsanalyse*, Bibel-Teilen. Missio-Reihe 13, eds. H. Janssen, et al., 45- 56. Aachen.

WILHELM Th., 1969, *Theorie der Schule*. Stuttgart.

WILLIAMS B., 1993, *Shame and Necessity*. Berkeley.

WILSON-ROBINSON P., 1995, "Something Within Reaches Out: Multicultural Dialogues," *Journal of Supervision and Training in Ministry*, 16, 170-195.

WUTHNOW R., 1993, *Christianity in the Twenty-first Century. Reflections on the Challlenges Ahead*. New York.

ZERFASS R., 1986, *Menschliche Seelsorge. Für eine Spiritualität von Priestern und Laien im Gemeindedienst*. Freiburg im Breisgau.

ZIEBERTZ H.-G., 1990, *Moralerziehung im Wertpluralismus*. Kampen/Weinheim.

—, 1991, *Sexualität im Wertpluralismus*. Mainz.

—, 1994, *Empirische Religionspädagogik*. Weinheim.

ZIJLSTRA W., 1969, *Klinisch pastorale vorming. Een voorlopige analyse van het leer- en groepsproces van zeven cursussen*. Assen.

—, 1989, *Op zoek naar een nieuwe horizon. Handboek voor klinische pastorale vorming*. Nijkerk.

ZULEHNER P., 1988, "Ecclesiastical Atheism," *Journal of Empirical Theology* 1 2:5-20.

—, 1989, *Praktische Theologie*. Band I-IV. Düsseldorf.

PRINTED ON PERMANENT PAPER • IMPRIME SUR PAPIER PERMANENT • GEDRUKT OP DUURZAAM PAPIER - ISO 9706

ORIENTALISTE, KLEIN DALENSTRAAT 42, B-3020 HERENT